JOANNE GREENBERG

The King's Persons

Holt, Rinehart and Winston · *New York* / *Chicago* / *San Francisco*

Published simultaneously in Canada by Holt, Rinehart
and Winston of Canada, Limited.

Library of Congress Catalog Card Number: 63-7271

Published, February, 1963
Second Printing, April, 1963

Designer: Ernst Reichl
83274-0113
Printed in the United States of America

To Julius L. Goldenberg

"Gute Ruhe, gute Ruhe."

"SCIENDUM QUOQUE QUOD OMNES JUDEI UBICUMQUE IN REGNO SUNT, SUB TUTELA ET DEFENSIONE REGIS LIGEA DEBENT ESSE, NEC QUILIBET EORUM ALICUI DIVITI SE POTEST SUBDERE SINE REGIS LICENTIA. QUOD SI QUISPIAM DETINUERIT EOS VEL PECUNIAM EORUM PERQUIRAT REX SI VULT TAMQUAM SUUM PROPRIUM."

"Know you also that all Jews wherever they might be in the kingdom are under the protection and defense of the liege king nor may anyone subjoin their wealth without the king's permission. And if anyone should detain them or their monies, the king will prosecute if he wishes according to his custom."

—EARLY LAW ATTRIBUTED TO
EDWARD THE CONFESSOR

The King's Persons

WHEN Philip II ascended the throne of France, he imprisoned all of his male subjects who were Jews. The Jews of England, whose territory included Brittany and Anjou on the Continent, looked on in horror as letters for ransom poured from Philip's prisons. For some the ransom came, sent by families and friends throughout France and Christendom. For some there was nothing. When the money ceased, Philip exiled the ransomed ones, ordering them from France before the end of June of the year 1182. The remnants of a once powerful and wealthy community scattered to the arms of their deliverers in Germany, Spain and England. They came to London and Norwich like ragged ghosts, walking through the foggy, still chilly streets with neither purpose nor pride. Far to the north, York's Jewish community waited for its share of wanderers with curiosity, with pity, with apprehension, with bitter cynicism and with great sorrow. The Jewish families in York had lived for generations in peace with their Christian neighbors, but their brothers in French prisons had cried to them that it is the business of men to suffer.

"We have been given a chance to live great history," the Rabbi Elias had said.

"We are feeding from our mouths men already dead," the Slaughterer said. They sat in the Rabbi's house, winding away the night in their discussion. The room was filled with men and with the smell of men and the Rabbi's wife, who poured out their thin wine, had trouble reaching over the shoulders of the many crowded about the small wooden trestle table.

"Let us greet them with dignity!" the Rabbi said. "Let us welcome them with open hearts."

"When they have reached York, we should be celebrating," a man said. "Let us sing our greetings to them; their bitterness should end in joy and their lamentation close with laughter."

"Ah!"—and a hand went up in the ancient gesture of argumentation—"but is it not true that there will be many newly widowed, newly orphaned, who are in mourning as well as in exile? Would it be fitting, then, to greet them with feasts and with gaiety?"

Rabbi Elias looked at Baruch, who sat with his son at a place of honor. Baruch was one of the wealthiest men in England, and his decisions, although neither would admit it, carried more weight than the Rabbi's. The financier swept a few crumbs from beneath his splendidly embroidered sleeve. His gestures were quick and decisive as if he were impatient of a world which measured its time in such long minutes. "The point is not how we greet them," he said; "the point is what we will do with them once they get here. These are my relatives, too," he added, as if to excuse himself to the Rabbi's astonished look, "but they are sick and wretched. They have nothing. We will have to pay their tax for the first few years; are we to set them up in business as well?"

"My God!" Rabbi Elias raised both his arms. "Are there not few enough? We will surely find places for them. Let us greet them as honored guests, not as burdens!"

Abram, Baruch's son, made the gesture custom demanded when speaking before his father, but his face was troubled. When he began to speak, Baruch sighed with impatience. "Men of York . . ." Abram began. Baruch coughed behind his hand. "If we weep at weddings, why not feast at funerals? Let us put a little joy into this cup of shame from which these people have been drinking for so long. The trip to London has been long enough for early wounds to heal somewhat. A little lightness——"

"It is not fitting!" another man interrupted.

And so it went round and round. It is written: If each of a Jew's words were a blade of grass, who wouldn't be in Eden? And the grass—not Eden's but England's—grew while they asked back and forth what was to be done.

The cocks crowed, the day opened, and God had decided how it would come to the Jews of York and to the Jews of France. Thick fog shredded in the trees and drops of water gathered at the leaf's edge. A cold that seemed to be a last vengeful flick of the whip of winter stung the cheeks and reddened the hands of the Watches who cried the morning hours, and the maids stirred the water in their pails to see if it was frozen. When what light there was proclaimed full day, the Jews of York went out to await their brethren. With so many of the exiles going to Spain and so many staying in London, none knew how many would be bringing their few, sad belongings of other times down the York Road, now a thick, brown mire. Most certainly they would not come by horse. They would have had to spend all of their hidden money for food and bribes for protection during their travel—money sewed into garments, money stealthily ripped from the seam-edges and the linings of coats, money palmed into palms for favors. It would not be regal, this entrance.

The clouds whipped their grey horses over the moors, and the little blue flowers that grew by the fair grounds were lost at the very feet in the fog. Even the birds, crying through the greyness, sounded plaintive and hollow. Out the Mickle Gate went the Jews of York to meet their brothers, pushing with their feet in the thick mud beyond where the stone markers declared that York began by the Grace of Jesus Christ. The men went first—Rabbi Elias, with that evenly threadbare look of his; Baruch, magnificent in fur, walking as if he were in a race; Abram barely keeping up with his father and wretched in his new red shirt; Josce, Baruch's sometime partner, in his marten cape, laughing at the ludicrous struggle he was having in the mud; friends and relatives of the exiles eager for news and not knowing whether to be joyous or sad; ready for both and, with their eyes, trying to pierce the fog ahead of them as if it were history.

After the men the women followed, and their sound went up before them. They were consumed with curiosity to see what the French ladies would bring—even the rags of it—and what ideas and what nice ways, and what tales they would have to tell. For some there was to be only heavy news. Many had been killed in Philip's prisons, but the hunger to know was greater than sorrow. The men of York went often to France on business, and letters by messenger came weekly from Troyes and Montpellier, but the women stayed home and apart, and felt as if they were far from the great world. London was days away, and in their isolation the souls of York hungered for glimpses of great cities. Here was some of the world to come to them down this thick road. The wind was cold and full of rain, and it blew against the robes of the women, almost tangling them in each other. Rana, Baruch's wife, walked without turning her head. She was a plumpish, young-looking woman, but when she caught glimpses of her son and husband in their magnificent clothes, walking ahead with the men, little lines of worry and confusion appeared about her eyes. They were so different from each other. Baruch had Abram dress as if he were a prince, and the son hated the gaudy splendor and the position that seemed to demand it. Even in this sorry meeting, Rana knew that there would be a big show, and that they would take the most prominent of the refugees into their home and Baruch would discourse on the quality of his wine and the richness of his possessions. Why even Bett, our kitchen servant, he would say, has a crimson cape. Rana's thoughts turned to her house. She hoped that the girl was seeing to all that was to be done. She held her fine linen neckpiece tighter against the unseasonable chill.

It was midmorning now, and from the churches and monasteries the bells sounded, to which all York gave ear, Christian and Jew alike, to the measuring of the day. Not many were walking the York Road at this time except the deputation. A few farmers, a traveling beggar or so, and two monks from Welbeck monastery with some sheep. The monks turned their faces aside when they saw the Jews, and uttered the old prayer, "*pro judeis . . .*" that besought God to show the light to these lost souls and to lead them into the True Way.

Abram felt a leaden chill as he watched them signing themselves with the cross and praying for him. He looked at his father, but he was not able to understand the expression he saw in Baruch's face.

The voice of Josce came to them from among the men, in Hebrew so as not to be understood by the passing brothers: "If I had that one's muscle, I, too, would pray for the Jews."

"You are not fair," Elias answered him; "there has been nothing for us here in York but peace and kindness."

"Hypocrite!" muttered Baruch.

Over the rise the welcomers went and, in a break in the fog, they saw, only twenty yards away, the whipping of cloaks. The pilgrims had arrived.

"Shalom Aleichem, brothers. Peace be with you," Josce yelled ahead into the fog.

"Unto you, be peace," came from the nowhere ahead.

They began to run toward the voices. They grappled with the fog until the forms of the men they sought suddenly became clear to them. They were almost face to face with their guests and they stopped, shocked. Then there was a frantic searching among the figures for the sister, the friend, the daughter-in-law. People were laughing and crying, and over the gestures of relief or loss, names flew and other names answered. "Who knows aught of Moses the Lean?" "Who has heard of my little sister, sent into France a bride?"

The Rabbi Elias went forward into the press of excited people and he did not call out a name. He was suddenly struck with the kind of despair that would not let him speak, although he, too, had dear ones for whom he longed to ask. There was something horrifying to him about the tattered people holding out disembodied hands for help through the tatters of the fog, the crying, the laughter that was too close to screaming, as men did in the worst kind of pain. Mutely, he stumbled out of the thick of the meeting. The fog was beginning to lift a little from the hollow where they were, and as he went off to the side, he saw another man, a tall, elderly man standing stock-still away from the others.

Elias went toward him and stood before him. The man turned slightly, so that Elias saw who he was. With a gasp for breath, the Rabbi put his hands out before him, touching the other man's rabbinical robes almost as if to test whether his eyes had deceived him. Standing in exile, making of exile a kind of ritual, stood Yomtob of Joigny, one of the greatest of living rabbis; a saint, some said, a brilliant Biblical scholar, a poet, a wit, a shining soul among Jews, and he was standing before Elias in the very same mud of the York Road. The two Rabbis stood so for a moment and then they embraced each other in greeting, but it seemed to Elias as if Yomtob fell into his arms. Suddenly the noise of the others enveloped them as if the wanderers had remembered once more the celebrity that they had brought with them to open the doors for them. They crowded around and Baruch greeted the famous Rabbi as his guest and took him by the hand. Seeing that gesture, Elias realized all at once that he was no longer the leader of the Jewish Congregation at York. When the sun shines, even the day star is no longer seen; and Elias was rueful that he had thought of this at all. He followed the almost triumphal party of Baruch and Rana and the officers of the Synagogue, who were leading the exhausted Yomtob to the comfort of Baruch's splendid house.

From the rear of the crowd, Abram, the son of Baruch, looked about at the stragglers. He saw men with the marks of bitterness and suffering on every feature, in every least lift of breathing. In his sickness to see his people so, in his questioning of a God who could watch men tear at one another for sole possession of His Name, Abram cursed. He cursed evil men and God who was silent and he cursed himself because he was alive, hating life and yet holding to it with all the strength he had. How could a man be named one name when he changed so many times? No wonder his father's house was always filled with guests and food and wine and loud celebrations. Better to stop the mouth before the scream escapes. These seekers of asylum, if they were celebrated enough, would be waiting for him in his father's house. The others would have to stay for a while at the huts of relatives or at the Community Hall which every good-sized Jewish community supported for travelers. Or victims, Abram thought, or victims.

They entered the city again by the Mickle Gate, past gardens carefully tended by the nuns of St. Trinity, past mud and thatch huts from which the wisps of smoke of midday cooking fires hung heavily. Few of the streets were cobbled and the sewage lay in the ruts and troughs at the sides of the mud roads and stank in the thick air. Still, York was a prosperous city and its Jews were wealthy. At the head of Northstreet, the party turned down past the tavern owned by Will the Owl. Northstreet was cobbled and its houses were well kept. The bottom of the street ended in a close and there two great houses of stone stood opposite one another like guardians. The houses belonged to Josce and Baruch, and stood as signs for all to see that they were among the wealthiest Jews in England. At the windows, glass gleamed, and Baruch felt a surge of pride as the wanderers drew in their breaths with the wonder of finding, at the end of the world in their imagining, such luxury. With a slow wave of his ringed hand, Baruch motioned everyone to the splendid house. When all were inside and had been welcomed, he noticed that Yomtob and Elias were not in the group. As he opened his mouth to inquire, cursing to himself for having lost them, his son, Abram, as if relishing his father's defeat said with that scornful half-smile of his, "Alas, honored father, the Rabbis are meditating in Elias's thatched hut." Baruch slapped his hands together with impatience and called to Rana more loudly than he would have: "Cups, woman! And the French wine!"

French wine was costly in the north of England. How often had the French Jews laughed with tolerant superiority as they watched the heavy barrels set on ships for the cold islands whose inhabitants they thought somewhat beneath themselves. Now their own vintage, memory of a lost land and of lost vineyards, was being offered back to them. For a moment, the thought of this as some kind of devilish charity made them cringe from the heavy goblets, but looking at the weeping Rana and the gaunt Abram, they remembered that here at last were friends whose hands were open only to welcome, whose joy to give them refuge made French wine flow only because it was the best. Weeping, the ragged travelers drank.

NORTHSTREET enfolded its weary guests with the ancient mixture of pity, curiosity, scorn and love. Some of the ragged, poor wanderers had been impoverished to the very bones and were strange and bitter with their hosts as if they blamed them for being prosperous and alive. Some sat by the walls gazing through eyes that were rigid in their heads as if they had been watching a great spectacle which had galloped by and left them staring, their eyes not quick enough to catch all of the event. But most of them wept a little in their strange night beds, rose to the sunny morning, and finding themselves alive, went on living, and after a while, laughed, because it was habit with them. At tables rich with food, men would tell the stories of their lives in France and their experiences of prison and exile. It soon became almost an etiquette to have some guest discuss his trials. Baruch kept a continual banquet at his great stone house, sitting at ease at the tables loaded with poultry and fish and baked goods and French wine. He always invited Yomtob the Scholar to the place of honor, but most of the time the sage sent only polite apologies and stayed with Reb Elias in his smoky mud-and-wattle house. When these excuses came, Baruch would raise his hands in wonderment and say he did not understand, but he lied and he knew that he lied. When he sat down again, his face would be strained even in the softening light and he would look the length of his great table and see in the face of Abram, his son, what was perhaps some kind of mocking and his own face would go harder still.

And then Yomtob sent to say that he would come. He had been

silent for these long weeks, mentioning nothing of the past, savoring no experiences, shocked with exile, people said. Now that he was to be at Baruch's table, Northstreet buzzed with excitement. Perhaps this was to be the evening that the great poet and scholar would set his seal upon the time with his own words. Somehow, his voice in the event was what would translate it into History for all ages. As the afternoon wore on, the house filled with eager people, so that those seated at the table had standing men crowded at their backs, and Baruch's wife, Rana, and her maids had to push through the press to serve the food. They ran back and forth in a kind of rage of work. Baruch, dressed for History, sat at the host's place with Yomtob like a grey shadow at his right hand. The financier had agonized over his mantle, his rings, his house and table, for hours, wondering whether to let this great page of the chronicle show him with his best clothes and his beard combed, or casually, as if such things came to him unasked, every day. A man who drops a gold mark in the street must pick it up as if he could also choose not to.

The talk went here and there while Baruch pressed meat and wine upon the scholar, urging him to eat and be satisfied. Rana caught her husband's eye for a moment as she took a trencher from the table and she tried to judge his spirit quickly without seeming to mark it. Baruch of York was not an easy man. She wondered if he would interrupt the meal with a lecture or a scolding. For all the years of her marriage to the mercurial man, she had inserted herself like a sheath of smoke between him and the world, shielding them from one another.

At the far end of the table sat the restless Abram. Baruch looked at him, and Yomtob, following the look, saw a young man richly but carelessly dressed, whose face was a barrier. Behind that face the spirit seemed to be in a world far away from the noise and activity in which his body was only an unwilling presence. Yomtob wished to call that spirit from its dream and so he addressed a gentle play of wit in Abram's direction. The startled, sad eyes came back from the other world suddenly, and the young man fumbled in his reply. Baruch's face darkened and he coughed into his sleeve. As he did so, Rana felt a familiar hot rise at the back of her skull, which was her message of caution where her family was concerned. The intuition was harder for her than actual rage when it came, for she often found herself, in panic, saying anything to mollify and calm; and always she made things worse and herself ridiculous and Baruch would speak sternly to her. The little anxious voice threaded itself through her mind, yet she could not tell how or why.

"Yes, Rabbi," Abram was saying, "the French we speak must sound barbarous to you who were raised in France."

"To some Jews," Baruch's partner, Josce said, "nothing but Hebrew is important, but it makes me proud to see how many languages others of us speak."

"Yes," laughed Reb Elias, "but all of them with our stolid Saxon accent." They laughed and Yomtob said, "Not so," gesturing toward Abram. "I heard him as he spoke the blessing over the bread, and his Hebrew is good enough for a scholar." Rana stiffened, and beneath the holiday finery worn for the guests, her heart began to beat as if it would break through her bones and the restraints of her good breeding and her long wifehood. Not that —of all subjects—not that! It was the old wound opened afresh. Baruch looked a long look, a great table's length of it, and though he spoke to Yomtob he kept his eyes fastened on his son.

"Think you so, Rabbi? I agree with you. I had set aside that he should go to the best schools, East and West, to become a scholar." His voice rose. "He has a keen mind, but two years at our own school and he begged me to take him from study. When I brought up the subject of other rabbinical studies, he urged time; when I told him that he should study with the Great Rabbis in Spain, he shrugged. When I reasoned with him, he hardened his heart against me!"

The whole table was stilled, Abram in his place burning with shame. His face had the look of one who had died thus a hundred thousand times and Rabbi Yomtob was moved with sympathy for him. He looked at the young man's hand, nervously picking with a meat knife at the crumbs of his bread. He had been tracing something on the tablecloth, some little picture, unawares, and now Yomtob's eyes made Abram look himself and he grew dizzy and pale at the uncaught lapse of his hand and will. He brushed the place clean hurriedly and looked back at Yomtob with his hurt, defiant face, and Yomtob felt his thoughts say: I shall not speak tonight. So the sage turned to his host and said, "I also have a son and he is dearly loved. The sons of celebrated men must sometimes feel that the love of their fathers is part of a reputation and no more."

"Where is your son, Rabbi?" another said.

"In London," answered Yomtob quietly, "beginning again."

Baruch could not be stopped. "He was my pride—my only

son. . . . He will not even marry! He thinks he does not need what my power can buy. He could be anything in the world and yet he is satisfied only to be a scribe—to sit in the upper room of the synagogue all day or at the market place writing letters for pig-eating Christians!"

The men at the table turned to one another in embarrassment. Yomtob changed the subject by turning to Elias with a question, but Baruch burned through the rest of the meal and Abram's eyes were veiled again. Yomtob had heard many rumors and the witty bits of gossip that wile away time, but he understood in that exchange between father and son what had been meant in the talk about Baruch: a powerful man who is scornful of his Christian neighbors, yet envies them; speaks bitterly to his son, yet loves him; insults his friends and lies to his enemies because of money. Elias had said of Baruch: "If he were not a rich man, he would be a madman."

The food kept coming on as if there was to be no end to it, and Rana scurried in and out, bustling and calling to her maids and giving signs for the putting on of dishes. Red-faced and coif askew, she looked like an older echo of the dancing maids of Syria, who dance themselves into insensibility in their religious ceremonies, and perhaps it was so, for Rana wrought peace by giving the comfort of food. She said her prayers between the kitchen and the table and thanked God with a hurried half-look at her flying maids; for Rana's God was a God of clean cups and tidy straw, and her thanks were the thanks of a careful wife. She would bank Baruch's fires with capons and wine, and would give the guests enough to occupy them to keep their minds from her strange son. Rana would consume the world in a million fires of cooking lest son or husband go a moment hungry.

Elias and Yomtob were walking off their meal before the curfew. Crowds of people were also enjoying the pleasure and ease of wandering by the bridges and the riversides; the orchards and cathedral grounds were full of beggars and lovers. For the first time in what seemed like years, Yomtob felt that the warm air of the summer evening carried the scent of peace. He listened a long moment to the sounds of the day's end: students at the Cathedral School were singing a ribald song set in parts. They had probably written the scandalous words themselves to a liturgical tune. Men and women were playing ball on the green and a group of apprentices, frog-jumping and laughing, flirted outrageously with every ugly woman past the age of thirty. Elias smiled at the old man. "Yes," he said, "it is good."

"I have been away from peace so long that I forget how common a thing it is in some lives. I want to die in a peace like this."

"Oh, why mention death, my friend?" said Elias a little ruefully. "This is your home now—live in it first."

"I will need a business then, or a craft at which to work. I wish I could be a doctor, as good as Reb Moses is, whom the Christians call Maimonides. His fame as a sage has all but obscured his glory as a doctor. Unfortunately, I was a vintner. The wines are mine no longer, so I must look for something else to do."

"Money-lending is a road to great riches here, as you can tell by the two stone houses," Elias said.

Yomtob could see that he was being careful to be scrupulously fair. "Honorably pursued"—he smiled at Elias—"it is an honorable business."

"For myself," Elias said, laughing, "I purvey the wind, but only as it blows from east to west." They both laughed. "Oh, a few sheepskins I make into parchment; perhaps a pair of slippers; sometimes I sell leather. I had, last year, enough gum to temper all the colors of all the painters in England if only I had sold it all, and also I dealt in fish oil."

"Maybe you could use a partner."

They walked on, past the gardens and the sea wall; past Clifford's Tower that had once been part of an earl's stronghold; past the Castle, where the King and his relatives stayed when they were in the shire; past the fish markets closed for the night. The sky was slowly deepening; in these latitudes further north than France, the twilight stayed for a long time, bringing to a kind of mellowness all the colors of the city and the land about them. Yomtob experienced a quiet joy in all of it and this surprised him, for yesterday he had still been dead. "Was it always this way?" he said, looking out across the river.

"Yes," Elias said. "Norwich had an uprising against the Jews when I was a boy, and hatred has flared briefly here and there over the years, but never at York. It is not only the King's promise of protection which we have; it is something more. Our people and the Christians——" Elias broke off suddenly, aware that the Rabbi was not listening. He turned where Yomtob was looking. Two men were standing on the riverbank where the Foss narrowed. They were tradesmen whose faces Elias knew and they were fishing. Simple men, an ordinary occupation; Elias could see nothing notable about them that would cause the celebrated Yomtob to give them his attention, but he was looking hard at them. "What is it, Rabbi?" Elias said.

"I caught their words as we went by," Yomtob answered slowly. "The one in blue said, 'There's one of them now. Where can all these Jews be coming from?' and the other shrugged and answered, 'Roaches in the fall and Jews in the spring, and yet methought there were heathens enough at York.'" He looked at his friend pleadingly and his voice sounded as old as sorrow. "Suddenly the air smells heavy and full of danger. The wind has changed. Let us go inside."

How ready he is to die, Elias thought sadly as he took the old Rabbi by the arm. It was time to go anyway; soon the curfew would sound and the Watches would mass before the jail to march to their posts.

As they went through the streets, Elias found himself peering through the slowly moving dusk at the faces of his Christian neighbors. He looked hard at them, trying to discern, by some quiver or some half-glance, what was in their minds. Was there not a new impatience as they went past him, or a new anxiety waking in their eyes? Or perhaps it was the light or the shadow or the worry to get home before the town slept for the night. . . . They reached Northstreet and paused before the door to Baruch's great house. "I will sleep here tonight," Yomtob said.

"Of course," Elias agreed; "for courtesy." But he knew that Yomtob needed, on this night, the foot-thick stone walls of Baruch's fort.

"I am a sword rusting with disuse," Baruch said. "I am waiting for a hundred shipments, my money is all lent out and taxes are due soon enough."

Josce could only nod. He knew that Baruch complained as a kind of protection from the leveling of God. Josce knew that the business of lending money had seldom been better. Ways were changing as surely as the years. As wars and commerce became more complex, more money was needed to employ the skilled men who supplied the armies and machines. Slowly, the old land-wealth was dwindling and the noblemen were made to supply the money for a war as well as the men. To raise this money and to pay the taxes which seemed to grow and proliferate on every hand, ancestral lands were given over to Jews and others as pledge for the necessary coin. Lands were mortgaged and jewels and even the holy goods of churches, but the laws of landed men and the laws of landed churches did not comprehend a system of silver and gold. The law forbade the lending of money at interest and thus the Jews, conveniently kept as money-lenders and necessary outcasts, traded in money at whatever rates they chose. The King taxed them in a dozen different ways and the rates of interest rose. Since lending for interest was illegal, some of the noble borrowers defaulted and the rates went higher still. Money was in demand despite the outworn laws, despite the railings of the Church, despite the ancient prejudices of the people, and since the loss from taxes had to be absorbed, and since the loss of the defaulting barons had to be made up, why not fur sleeves also, and the jewels for ten fingers? Josce glanced at the proud Baruch who sat across the table, and then somewhat ruefully at his own clothes, which were almost as sumptuous.

Baruch saw the look and raised his eyebrows. "What are you looking at?"

Josce laughed quietly. "I am looking at how we revenge ourselves, since the Christians have made us outcasts and men without titles. Behold, you angels, what Christian man will wear such opulence? Does it not shame you sometimes, Baruch, that we go too splendidly, in a land where splendor means a fief, and where lack of land proclaims us liars in our fur and rubies?"

"What else is there?" Baruch muttered. "There is no inheritance that does not shake with taxes like a tree with nuts—no lands that we can own, no estates or titles or portion of the world that can be ours. Kings rise and fall and their reigns are ruins, but the barons sit secure and tell us, 'Be faithful and you will live.' To the codes which they give us, the occupations which they leave us, we are faithful, and yet we have nothing to assure us that we will live."

"We are not faithful," Josce said. "We steal and overcharge, we clip coins and load our scales with false weights—you know it as well as I do." Josce looked at Baruch and wondered if behind those shrewd eyes there was a real belief in what the lips uttered. He himself was bitter at times about the facts of living as a Jew; his bitterness edged his wit, so that when dealing sometimes with a nobleman or some seneschal who was known to hate the Jews, Josce became as one in an ordeal of red-hot ploughshares, walking on the burning words with deliberate steps. Jews were not allowed to carry swords; words had to be the instruments of re-

23

venge and honor. It suddenly occurred to Josce that only the four or five wealthiest men in their Jewish community needed such honor, such revenge. The modest craftsman or shop-keeper was far from a landed estate, a title and a family shield, and he did not hunger for these things. A wealthy money-lender with a stone house and glass windows was forever waiting at the entryway of nobility and was continually seeing the gate shut in his face. How golden seemed the honors on the other side, and how paltry and meager his own.

He brought his gaze back to his hands that were fiddling with a half-empty goblet. "Well," he said, "at any rate, while there is still business to be transacted, we will be here to transact it. My youngest son is burning with eagerness to accompany you on your trip to Acaster to see the Baron Malabestia and get your loan repaid."

"He is a good lad," said Baruch, a little angry that this boy should honor and admire him more than his own son.

"He will be ready in good time," Josce said, "and hopes to learn much."

"Would that my son had such hopes——" But the Rabbis came to the door outside and Baruch heard them through the sudden tightening of sorrow inside him, and stopped speaking and cov-ered the long-suffered wound with the foliage of daily cares and courtesies.

Rana went to the door, stepping around one of the guests who had fallen asleep on a joint stool and was snoring like the death-rattle of an old horse. As she opened it to the two Rabbis, they heard the Watches calling from the gateposts of the city. They seemed plaintive, those voices crying to one another in the gather-ing darkness, and yet the sound reminded them all of safety and of sleep.

"It is late—too late to go back," she said. "Stay the night!"

"Don't you think Denicosa will miss me?" Elias said, smiling.

"Let her starve herself." Rana laughed. "Come, let us have a little wine." She led them toward the fire. Bett, the servant girl, sleepy-eyed, came with the wine and some glasses, of which it was easy to see that Rana was inordinately proud.

"Madam," said Yomtob, "these are Persian, are they not?"

"Oh," she said vaguely, trying to hide her pride, "I have them in the house."

Baruch guffawed. "What a masterpiece of logic!"

From the corner of the room came the sound of saws scraping

metal. The sleeping guest had changed his position and was breathing in great gulps through his mouth.

"Now there is a man wiser than Rambam," said Josce, "and if he is not wiser, at least he is louder."

"Come, Rabbi," said Baruch, "bring us a gift from France. Tell us a French riddle to tax our English minds."

"Very well . . . I will give you a riddle: What rides not on horse, yet cannot be caught; goes not by boat, yet overtakes the boatman; is greater in famines and more meager at feasts?" They savored it along with their wine for a few moments.

"The wind?" Josce volunteered.

"Destitution?" mused Baruch.

"Both very good," said Yomtob, "but my masters in riddles tell me that it is an hour of time."

"A gentle hint, good Rabbi. Come." Baruch led them into the other room, where a huge pallet had been rolled out on the fresh straw. Removing their outer clothes, they gave their souls into God's keeping in that sweet and graceful evening prayer. Rana first, then Baruch, was as fitting, Yomtob and then Rabbi Elias. They left a space also for the slumbering guest, if he should come to the bed. Abram lay rolled up in a fur cover spread out on the straw.

In the attached servant's quarters, another Name was invoked for holy protection, but similar bones took ease on similar floors and the night, one blanket, overspread them all.

Elias thought before sleep came: Now they are here at last, and we begin to live greatly. He thought of the ancient and endless train of exiles—Persia, Babylon, Rome—and slowly his thoughts went into dreams, and he knew not where the one ended and the other began.

THE witnesses stood uneasily in the great hall, waiting. Outside the breezes of late July bent the grasses of the moors and carried the scent of the youth of the world. It was a day for hunting or for siege or for tournament, not one to be wasted witnessing the payment of the tenth part of a debt to some Jew! Richard de Kuckney, the Baron's new squire, shifted from one foot to another and wondered what he was to do. He thought of the game that his uncle had used to play with him when he was small. As the barley was milled, the uncle would take him to see the flour as it was turned off the great stone wheel. The uncle would sift a handful of it, letting only the finest, whitest powder dust to the sunny floor. "These are the kings and the great archbishops," the uncle would say. Then a second sifting: "And these are the barons of high estate—the Percies and the Malabestias." And then yet another, coarser sifting: "And here we are." What Richard remembered was not the almost full hand of hard, darker grains still in his uncle's palm—the poor, the commons, the clay on which his nobility rested; his memory was of the third sifting —his sifting. Now he was squire to the great Baron Malabestia, and the young lad felt wide-eyed and frightened. Malabestia was a violent man; many said an evil man, and they joked about his name, which had descended with his temper and his strange cruelty from his father. The lad looked at the others who were waiting for the Baron to come, and for the Jew. They were older squires, longer in the Baron's service, harder, hungrier, and they stood like nervous steeds harnessed to this irksome duty and fretting in their harnesses for the sweet wind that lifted the stalks in the summer fields.

Baron Malabestia strode into the hall. He had the look of the second sifting, Richard thought. For over one hundred years, his family had known nothing but complete rule in the villages and lands of their fief. To their men at arms they were as kings; and those lands, where whim and will were as one, were wider by twice or more than those of Richard de Kuckney's father and grandfather. That look, that second-sifting look, which was so easy to perceive in the Baron, was there also in the faces of the others, and Richard hoped in his face also. Honor was not the right to rule, for rule was ordained by God for them from the beginning of history; honor was defense of House and Name, increase in power, increase in homage, increase in lands, increase in the bended knees of vassals; and they would, every man of them here, lay siege, endure to the rind of torture, die, gladly, for honor.

"Bring us something to drink!" Malabestia ordered.

The Jew had followed the Baron into the hall. He was a medium-sized man. Richard would guess him to be a little past middle-age, and there was a hardness about him, a kind of willful look that was seen only on the faces of noblemen. The eyes were quick and observant; they never rested very long on any one thing, but as they passed over him, Richard felt as if his wit, wealth and strength had all been measured and calculated. This man, if he had been a Christian, would have surely been of the noble class, yet he had no title, and it was difficult to know how to treat him. One addressed Jews as if they were commoners and of no account, and yet, many, like this one, were wealthy and powerful. The Jew raised a hand; the fingers gleamed with rings. Richard had stayed too long looking at this stranger. He left the hall quickly.

"And wine, not mead, you cake of dung!" Malabestia called after him.

As they waited, Malabestia sat and motioned his squires also to be seated. The Jew remained where he was. The nobles began to speak of common affairs together—planning for a hunt, the planting after harvest—as if the Jew were invisible to them. When Squire Richard returned with the wine, Malabestia waved the Jew to a bench that stood by. "Sit down!"

The Jew acted as if he had heard only the words and not the insult that was in the way they were spoken. He sat quietly. One of the squires giggled. Malabestia was peering at the Jew at whom he had not really looked until now. "You are not the Jew of Lincoln!"

"No, my Lord, I am not," and the stranger smiled faintly. "That man sold your debt to me—I bought it from him. The sum owed, however, will remain the same."

Malabestia's face suddenly went pale with rage. The witnesses were only his squires, but the insult of the Lincoln Jew, in sending this—this servant was not to be endured. "Who are you then, you dog?"

"I am called Baruch of York. . . . You call that name Benedict, I believe," the Jew answered mildly.

"Are you the master or the servant of the Lincoln money-lender? Are you his liegeman or is he yours?"

Malabestia understood no other relationships between men not of the same line of blood. It was the manner of his whole life and the lives of all of his fathers' fathers, and he could conceive of no other. It was the lack of these laws of relationship and duty, in part, that made him wonder if Jews were of the same stuff of humanity as himself.

"I am neither," Baruch answered in a voice so mild that it belied the quick eyes and the willful hand of rings.

"My debt is to the Jew of Lincoln," Malabestia continued. "If I decide not to give the money to you, how can Lincoln hurt me?"

"Your debt, my Lord, is like the coin that passes between men."

Squire Richard, for a reason which he did not know, was astonished by these things. This less-than-commoner, this Jew's Jew, was explaining money and finance to one of the greatest barons in Yorkshire! The look on Malabestia's face blended rage and surprise, for the speech had nothing in it of either sarcasm or flattery, and yet he suspected a subtle little smoke of disdain in the tone of the money man.

"A baron has responsibilities . . ." Malabestia said. "He must support many churches and pay many taxes. To get money for these things, I borrow from Jews, which is a crime. Being illegal, both King and Church can by willing it, nullify at any time the debt which I contracted. What if I decide not to pay?"

"We have no force of our own to compel you, my Lord, and this you know, but need is with us, and so are time, custom, tax and desire. If your debt to me is not paid, no lender, Jew or otherwise, will lend you so much as a broken penny. You will, in short, be moneyless forever."

It occurred to Richard suddenly that it was to the best interest of Church and King to have the money lent and the tithes and taxes paid. He was ashamed of the subtlety of his thinking. . . . Jews' minds worked in such a way, but he suddenly understood why it was that the Jews were called The King's Persons and were protected by the King. Malabestia growled with displeasure and brought the sack of coins from his belt.

The Jew rose and went to the great door. Opening it a crack, he called out to someone in the court. The door opened wider and

28

from the brilliant stab of sunlight, a boy walked. The door was shut and the two of them came back to the table. He must be some sort of apprentice, the squire thought. The boy was very decorous and grave in his young way. He had a roll of parchment and a pouch of writing things.

"The son of my friend . . ." Baruch said, by way of explanation.

The boy gave Baruch the parchment and made ready the instruments of writing which he had in a little bag about his waist, where any noble lad of his age would have carried a dagger. With a little undue ceremony, the boy produced a block of ink which Baruch spat upon and which the boy then rubbed up until it was ready. The pens, the parchment, and quickly the whole transaction was tracked out before them in letters.

"I will go to York Cathedral tomorrow," said Baruch, "and put this roll in the Vault of Contracts that all men may know, Christian and Jew, what part of this debt has been paid."

Here was another horror then! These heathens, whom it was Richard's Christian duty to despise, were allowed into cathedrals with the evil contracts of their usury. If this necessity were to be tolerated, why on holy ground? Was a man to come straight from a whore to the Eucharist? He had heard so many sermons against the Jews and their evil snares that he believed implicitly the assumption that men of God did no business with them, abhorred them. . . . In the cathedral . . . ?"

"What if I should need more?" the Baron was saying. The room was very quiet.

Baruch smiled a kind of slow, twisting smile, and it was plain to all of them then that the Malabestia was tied to this kind of eternal borrowing and repaying for as long as the order of their English life prevailed. The King wanted it, the Church wanted it, the Jews wanted it, and the Baron would need more, and more, and always more of the coin that the new form of life demanded. Every silver mark was a little death to rule by noblemen. Every gold mark was a fire of life to the landless, nameless merchantman and artisan who pledged his faith to the whole nation under a single King.

Baruch spoke for a while, slowly and a little wryly of the dangers of lending money, of interest rates, the honesty of borrowers, which was all, he said, that could lower them.

As he was beginning to warm to his subject, Malabestia cut in: "Teach that to your servants, not to us!"

Baruch laughed quietly. "I did forget myself. Come on, Samuel—let us to our business." The boy spread the parchment wide again.

"Baron, your name here, please, to show that you are the borrower." Malabestia gripped the pen in his fist. "I can sign my name," and he drew the rude characters below the carefully formed letters which described him in Latin and in the tongue of the Jews. The two older squires came forward and signed, and then Richard came and bent and took the strange, light tool in his hand, and bore down on the parchment with it so that the ink splattered widely and the pen splayed out and cracked apart. The grave lad could stand it no longer. With a guffaw that sounded out in the hall, he hid his face behind a hand.

"Samuel!" thundered the Jew in remonstrance, but it was too late. In his own eyes the twinkle played, which was too much of a luxury in a world of angry men. "Complete the work," he said sharply to the boy.

Another pen and Richard again approached the parchment. As he bent to sign his mark, Baruch looked at him, a quick, devouring look and said, "Are you not the grandson of Thomas de Kuckney?"

The young squire trembled at the backs of his legs as he spelled out crudely his sign. Old Thomas de Kuckney had been one of the murderers of Thomas Becket, now Saint. The murder had been done by retainers faithful to their King and eager to rid him of an enemy who plagued him. By the time thought came to the murderers that they had killed a priest of Christ before His altar, both England and Rome were afire. By the time repentance came, the barons of Yorkshire had to repent not only the murder of an archbishop, but the martyring of a saint. The shame that had cleft the pride of the House and stripped the Kuckneys of half of their wealth in fines and offerings, lay buried in the young squire also.

Richard de Kuckney lifted his head from his labors and answered with the excessive pride of the guilty, "Yes, I am the grandson of Thomas de Kuckney."

"An honest man," Baruch conceded. He picked up the finished parchment, rolled it up briskly, put it in a hard leather case which he had for the purpose and signaled to the boy to gather up the pens and the ink.

Malabestia had been quiet for a time, but suddenly and sharply, he raised his head and asked, "How many Jews are there in York at this moment?"

"Well," said Baruch, "the names of the families listed are thirteen, but to those are to be added the number of souls who have just come to York and their exile from France. I should say about three hundred. Some will leave, I imagine, for Spain or Africa. I assure you, my Lords, England will prosper for their presence. We do what is needed. We are like earthworms of the soil; we tunnel through it and leave the earth richer for our passing. This your King knows as France does not. Philip expelled our people for piety. He will someday call them back for commerce and for wealth," and picking up their tools, the dark, splendidly dressed strangers left Malabestia's hall.

Because his father had killed a saint, Lord Robert de Kuckney had sent his son to the hardest school of knighthood, the despotism of Malabestia. Because of the allusion to the shamed grandfather, Richard de Kuckney would make an enemy of Benedict of York, and through him, of all of his strange people, so foreign to the standards of the baronial codes and the life which he was going to redeem at any cost.

To the young squire, it seemed impossible that the country was to be filled with these people. They were beautiful enough in their dark way, but he was to come to believe that it was the beauty of the Devil. They dressed like princes and yet destroyed the fabric of the life of prince and baron.

"Will not our King protect his barons from the hands of mad Jews?" Richard had asked.

Malabestia had answered him shortly: "The King would take your title and my title and throw them both into his coffers. The Jews are his cows. We feed them at one end and he milks them at the other, but enough is lost between. . . . I should like very much to carve, one day, some of what is lost between."

So did Richard de Kuckney, squire, learn more and more of the tides of hatred that were running against the animals who called themselves Jews. For his family and their shame, and for his lord's family and their pride, he also hated them; but in his simple squire's sleep, he saw the letters, the thick lines and the thin, flowing across the creamy sheet of a mysterious roll, and when he woke, it was with the memory of the Jewish boy's youthful hand creating what was a word in the mind, a word on the tongue and now a word forever.

31

IT was a bright, clear day; a day to make the stones sing. Rushing water would pour from them in joy if God (blessed be He) willed it again as he had done in times of old. Abram remembered the phrases and they ran together in his mind and made him smile to himself. His people were like children. Even Yomtob seemed to have too easy a faith, and he, Abram, was all alone with his doubting, which he defended to himself in the fold-on-fold of logic, the uses of which he had learned from the pious teachers of the Law. Abram had many secrets—his disbelief, his talent, his desire. How could a God be good who was so easily called into battle by every man with an enemy? Who is the one righteous people? He remembered the bitterest of all jests he had ever heard: it had been uttered by an old Jew full of trouble who, having heard of a massacre and of his only son's death, had lifted his weeping eyes to heaven and said, "O God, O God, choose another people!" Of their being sent from France, Yomtob had said, "We have sinned mightily. God's will be done."

Abram had been sent on an errand to Southwell, and he bore in his saddle packets food which the anxious Rana had made him take over Baruch's objections. Everyone knew that all the Jewish houses between York and Southwell would be shamed if they did not provide from their tables, and yet there it all was to be thrown out along the way or given to a beggar. To the left of the road stood an old, weather-beaten rock which Abram had known in many games of his childhood; it had been chair, throne, vantage point, game-base and fort, and he knew every hollow of it in his knees and fingers. He looked at it and laughed and said aloud, "As well as I know you, if I touched you with a stick there would come no water." Then the voice of Yomtob, or of his mind's Yomtob answered him, saying, "But then, you are no Moses."

He traveled at a good pace. Past the fork and on to the Selby Road, past Selby, Goole and Doncaster and across the Barnby moor. The summer beauty of the hills, the bright blue sky, the lightness of summer clothes made him forget restrictions and the many admonitions of his parents, and he rode singing or reciting verses, or conversing in loud rhymes with his horse. Before he was aware of being hungry and a bit tired, he was well on his way to Southwell and passing the Welbeck Abbey. The road was muddy as usual, and churned with the footprints of laden beasts. He looked out over the abbey's lands and marked with admiration the signs of labor in the care of the land and houses. These monks were not singing to the stars while the earth crumbled under them. He knew that Jews owned much of this land and that, silently, from monasteries where the Brothers were no more than renters, Jewish money-lenders forced them to exchange their products for the interest due on their loans. But here the monks said their prayers under their own, not Jewish, auspices. They had taken land which no one else thought worth the using and had poured their prayers and labor into it until it woke to their hands.

The Brothers called themselves Praemonstratensians—a French order, one of the few foreign orders in England, and they were hard workers who supported themselves and their great abbey with their own exertions. Who had told him of this? he wondered. . . . Oh, yes, Bett, their Christian servant girl with the fierce sort of pride that she had. According to her, these Brothers had drained the swamps and brought the Yorkshire marshes to life and had given glory to the earth even as to God with their work. Now, as he neared the great sheepfolds, he realized the wisdom of these men as well as the difficulty of their task. They did not, as Bett had said, reclaim the marshland, but they had utilized to the very fullest every arable inch and had filled in many spots which could be saved the death of stagnant waters and decaying vegetation. On the wold marsh-clumps they grazed great healthy sheep, and he could see spaces marked off where the land was to lie fallow and rest for a time. The abbey itself looked very new; everything reflected the pride of these men in their accomplishment. The House was simple and austere; no art or prettiness relieved the great shiplike lines. Around the House were gathered many smaller buildings: storehouses, tool sheds, sheeppens and a small fishpond, weaving sheds and washing sheds. Abram got down from his horse, took some of the food from his packet and walked toward the sheeppens near which there were some trees and a little patch of soft grass.

On one of the stiles of the sheeppen, a young Brother was sitting and gazing with great intensity at the sky. Abram had seen Christians making the Sign of the Cross, but he had never seen them praying, really, and he thought for a moment that this might be some kind of rite or other. He wondered if he were intruding on something sacred in this strange faith, but suddenly the Brother clapped his hands above his head and began to laugh, swaying on the stile like a magpie on a limb, his dark apron flying around the white undergarment. He saw Abram then, and stopped laughing at once and got as red as a girl.

"The old man has been chasing the five-legged cow for so long, and now, just as he has caught up with her, they have both been transformed into three hunting horns."

Abram looked up into the sky where the thick clouds of mid-July formed and re-formed against the rise of the hills to the north.

"Nonsense," he said. "Any fool can see that those are not horns at all, but a rabbit with a beard lighting a table lamp. See where his paws stick out?" and he pointed. They both looked at the clouds then, and after a while, down at each other. They were of the same age; long, thin and bumpy, with clumsy, bony hands and open faces. Each one felt as if he were looking into a mirror, which for one person gave two images, returning monk for Jew and Jew for monk. The Brother eased himself on the stile. His feet hung down nearly touching the rich mud in which the baby sheep waited with their funny, only half-sheeplike sounds.

"My children," the Brother said, "still in their little baby fleeces. One of the good Brothers is coming down to see them and count them and name them and enter the names in the book for this year. They were born in May, early, and since God has granted them life up to now, we may recognize them as ours."

"Why don't you count them yourself?" Abram asked.

"Well, I am newly born also—newly in our Order, and for a while my duties must be checked by my Brothers, even the smallest things. Yet a while, and I will be as responsible as the rest."

"I wish I could sit at that ease," Abram said. "Usually, I am in a dark booth at the market, writing letters and reading them for those who cannot. Other days I am in the dark house, writing my father's accounts." Strangely enough, he did not mention his other work: the copying of the Torah into rich, thick black characters beautiful with sound, on his even, perfectly prepared parchment page. The Brother looked at him for a long while, drinking in the sight of one so conversant with written signs.

"I write but little," he said (lying, for he wrote not at all).

34

"Our Brothers are not the ones who give glory to God by inscribing books or by much reading or by study."

The same thing happened to both of them at once. Even while they looked at each other, they became wildly curious. They stopped speaking and were very silent. Each wanted to ask; yet each also wanted to wait until the other had made the first move. Finally Abram broke the pause, saying, "How does one come into the Order? I mean—how did you?"

"Well," said the boy, "until recently, many were brought in as infants and children by parents who believed it to be the chosen life for them; or as a pledge made in sickness, or as a prayer for better times, counting it a Grace. Some, like myself, have always been wishing for this life, it seems, and I have begged my parents' leave to go to God for as long as I can remember."

"Why?" blurted Abram, and then was ashamed and wished he had not asked. He turned his head away.

Poor Jew! the Brother thought, and his heart softened in him. "Ah," he said, "have you not had old memories—your first in the world, which you hold to yourself tighter than any others? Mine are of a line of Brothers who came once a year to our little parish church to sing of the joy of Christ's Nativity. They would file into the dark church with their long cassocks swinging in unison, and the Abbot would go before and a boy holding a censer; it was a heavenly aroma. They would sing: the sound of them filled every corner, and one was glad all of a sudden to be alive, even if only enough to be cold and hungry and afraid of the dark —it was no matter; God was there watching and loving His poor frail ones. Well, I was not very clever at my father's smithy, and there were too many other children to feed and settle, so finally the family went to our lord, the Baron Robert de Kuckney and asked him to sponsor me in the Order with a dowry as his own act of piety. Lord Robert is a great patron of this House, and so here I am. We do not do the best singing in England, but then, I have found out that I do not either."

"Welbeck is near your home, then?"

"My people still serve at Castle Kuckney, and it is a great pride to them to have me here. I pray for the souls of all the Barons of Kuckney. The English Brothers among us come of some of the best families in Yorkshire." He caught himself on one of the newly learned nails—the sin of pride. "*Mea culpa*," he said, and that too was newly learned. "I am an undeserving Brother of these Brothers. You have no Religious, have you?"

"Well, we have religious men," Abram said, trying not to smile, "but they are at home. Sometimes our men go away to study under a great teacher." (His heart caught between his teeth as he remembered the latest argument and his father's face.)

"Of course you take vows, though." The monk was very earnest.

"Our love for God is a foregone conclusion. It is understood."

"But what of your vows of obedience, which includes that of chastity?"

Abram laughed aloud. "Our neighbors' gossip and censure insure our chastity before we marry." He laughed again. "Then, of course, is not chastity a sin?"

The young monk knew that the Jew was mocking him ever so slightly, and he wanted to be angry, but the day forbade it with brightness and the young Jew was being honest, and after all, need not one have pity, Christian pity for a heathen's sufferings? "I am Brother Simon," he said.

Abram smiled quietly at his own foolishness. "I am Abram, son of Benedict of York."

"Aha!" said Brother Simon, "then you know my cousin. I have a cousin, Bett, who teaches the women in the home of Benedict of York. She teaches them housekeeping."

Abram wanted to cry with laughter and control was difficult. He could imagine the look on his mother's face if he should tell her about the "teachings" of Bett their servant girl, but he knew that he would never speak of it. Rana was a woman too committed to her own world and her own family; the Christians were no part of either, and she would never see herself as the point of a Christian's joke.

"Don't the Jewish women know how to do the work of a home?" Abram asked wryly.

"Well," the boy answered, stretching a bit on the stile, "Bett says that they cook well enough, but she has also told me some of the things concerning food and the holidays of the heathen calendar, and these things sound strange and unnatural."

"Why does a chicken on a Jew's plate look any different?" Abram was suddenly tired of the distance that seemed to stretch between himself and Christendom. "What is strange about any of our customs? Christians think that they see, but they do not see any more than the shapes in the clouds that we see and do not see." He suddenly became aware of his standing: "May I sit with you on that rail?" he asked.

Brother Simon looked frightened, but said, "Certainly."

As Abram jumped up to sit beside the Brother, he caught the monk's lips moving in quick prayer.

"I am not an incarnation of the Devil. It seems to me as if I am always crying to someone across a great barrier—being misunderstood, echoing not as I had meant to. Are you warding off my evil? I wish I had strength enough to be really evil, but I am only as you are—an unquiet sleeper, turning over and over with questions."

"Can you not try to dissuade your leaders," the young monk said earnestly, "from their taste for blood of Christians in their rituals?"

Indignation and laughter seemed to stand side by side in Abram as he spoke with Brother Simon, yet he felt somehow that this Brother was not closed against his words, not frightened of him or of his honesty.

He told Simon of the wine, not blood, which blessed all holy meals and feasts, and he spoke of the abhorrence of Jews for the unclean. As he did, he felt the monk drinking in his words. He grew expansive and large of gesture, enjoying the proofs as they came to him, amplifying the points of his explanation almost joyfully. He felt wonderfully free.

When he was finished, Brother Simon looked for a long time at him, his eyes opened very wide with seeing all that was new to him. Then he said slowly, "I never knew such things. Have we been alive together in the same world? Tell me then what you know of my faith."

"Your faith . . ." said Abram, and suddenly all of the years of whisperings of hatred among his own people opened in him and he looked into it, the hated one, and saw that his own people also hated. "To me . . . it is a religion of death, whose symbol is a cross, an engine of death, and whose God died. Christian men make celibates of themselves and waste God's gracious gift of life. I know that this is cruel to say to you, but it is what I think . . . so you see that we Jews can at least be fearlessly honest."

"What makes you think that your people are better than we at honesty and the rights of explanation?" Simon shouted. "I had always thought your people stupidly vain. Now I find them only misguided."

"And which is harder to cure?" asked Abram with a slow smile. "Better that we were fools and knaves, but the sad truth is that we—that is, most of us—are as deeply committed as you, investing as much love and warmth in our faith as you do in yours; and when your hands turn against us, God pities us for that as much as He glories in it with us."

The young monk reached his hand out toward Abram and said quietly, "Let me learn then, and so may you also."

And Abram thought as he smiled at the Brother: I must not shake his little tree of faith, tell what I will. Few enough sleep securely in salvation and have never cried, "Choose another people!" He said, "I will do what I can, and to learn with you."

There was a drawing back after this; both felt that they had said too much, and yet there it was; in their youth, their brotherhood, their need was pulling them toward one another. Abram had never been in a position to tell or to teach. He might like to hear his own voice, sonorous with the weight of dignity of great words, each one of which bore two thousand years of speaking. This young monk was to Abram as he himself had once been to Baruch, and the father had made it all a matter of ceremonies and comfortable lines of piety said to a God unused to the English tongue. Brother Simon on his part had seldom been accorded credit for the intelligence to question or to learn at all, and when teaching is given across, and not poured from a height, it falls more gently on the head and more deeply into the heart. Brother Simon was pleased.

As they sat musing in the quiet-seeming drone of summer insects, a voice broke on them, a nasal, sharp voice, and they turned to see a great, tall monk looming there. He seemed taller than they, although they were sitting on the stile above him.

"*Ave, pastor bonus,*" he said with the sting in his voice that somehow frightened them beyond being surprised. "Does the good shepherd tend his sheep?"

His voice had softened until it was almost a whisper, but there was something in it that was of the same quality as his face, a quality of harnessed madness. Abram could imagine that same whisper saying: Kill him!

The monk's hair was short and the color of rust. A sparse, nondescript beard straggled along the ridge of his gaunt face and his eyes were watery and somehow vague; but his smile—for he was smiling now—was a wild, horrifying thing, a smile without mirth or even a sense of life, switching on and suddenly off to leave the mask of a corpse behind.

"The good shepherd." The laugh was dry and cynical. "Ah—

Sir!" He had seen Abram the Jew and the unmistakable cut of his clothes and beard. "Sir!" and again that laughter without mirth, smile without depth and a sudden clearing of those vague eyes as if passion had swept them bare. They were merciless and full of hate.

He laughed again, stopped suddenly, and came into the sheepfold. His voice had been low, but each word was pronounced with great care. He spoke in French, excellent French; he was certainly of the nobility and young Brother Simon became as a small boy before him, rude, clumsy and defensive. He stumbled from the stile and splayed into the mud. The little lambs, frightened, bleated away. The gaunt Brother faced them both, but he turned the cleared, penetrating eyes like lances on Abram, impaling him. Brother Simon had shrunk into nonexistence.

"Sir." (Again that awful smile and the slight barbed edge of the dagger-word.) "We have never met. You are . . . ?"

"I am Abram, son of Benedict of York."

"Son of *whom?*" the Brother said, and the eyes again clouded over as if he had already decided and had stopped listening.

"Son of Benedict of York," said Abram loudly, and it seemed to him as if he spoke too loudly then, but yet as to a wall, unhearing.

The smile opened up slowly and then dropped like a sheet from a dead man. "I am Brother Louis . . ." the monk said slowly. "Fauconbridge." He let the name trail out of his mouth so slowly that it seemed as if minutes had passed between start and end. They were only the flashing by of Abram's spinning thoughts, and a kind of rope of panic spinning in his blood. He said good day and began to walk away. He stopped suddenly by the field's edge and realized that his hands were clammy with fear. He forced himself to go on without turning back to look at the two Brothers who had not moved from their places. The day spread beautifully before him, the sun, the perfumed air, the sounds of birds: glorious, gay July. . . . But why was he so cold?

"I AM gold, pale gold. My hair is like the winter sun and my skin is clear and fine. I ride out on this diamond-hard, diamond-cold day in February on my black palfrey; slim as a weasel he is, and he sniffs the air and tosses his beautiful head. I am gold, pale gold. Scarlet is my cloak, flowing on behind me. It is lined with tawny marten, soft and warm, and its closing is a hook of gold with golden catches. Before me goes loud the call of my announcing horn. My horse's ankles are slender and they strike sparks against the icy road. I am the Duchess of Burgundy, the very most beautiful Duchess of Burgundy riding out for my pleasing. . . ."

"Halloo, Bett; gooin' up tow see yer people up to Kuckney-hill?"

It was Peter the Miller, standing by the road's side with his great round face a-smile and his heavy hands just hanging down. She said she was.

"Ye'er gooin' fine enough," he said, pointing to the gentle grey donkey which Baruch had given her to ride. She said she was. Did she have something to take with her to her parents, showing her master thought well of her? She said she did, and good-bye, and the Very Most Beautiful Duchess of Burgundy moved on down the road. . . . "Four hounds follow me; they are grey and violent. The high-held hawk preens in the sunlight. I am gold, pale gold. . . ."

What she had learned and how she had changed, Bett herself did not know. She had been nine or so when Baruch had seen her standing in the mud yard of Kuckney Castle, where her mother worked as a kitchen wench and her father was a laborer in wood. Baruch had needed a servant for his house in the York Jewry, a young maid who could be trained to the strange customs of his house. He had found her parents and spoken with them; terms were exchanged which she did not understand, and when it was all arranged, she suddenly realized that it meant leaving this place and these people, her whole life's home. All that was familiar would be changed. She was readying the welling tears for their moment, when the rich stranger, foreign-smelling and oddly garbed, lifted her up on to a small pillion behind the saddle of his fine horse. By the time her tremulous wonder had faded, they had moved into the life that was the life of the stone house at York; the life of other ways; the life of Jews. Five years had passed, broken by visits home in which she spent much of her time working at the side of her working parents; now in the castle yard when the supply of candles was short, now in the pig-pens, now in preparation for a feast. She had seen and spoken with her parents, but the children, her brothers and sisters, had forgotten her, and the friends of her young days in the yard's mud seemed to feel that a strangeness was in her and in her new ways. She dressed well—Baruch would have it no other way—and she had got out of touch with the castle and its life, which was the all and only life of her kinsmen. The hay, the millet, the oat harvests, the dairy, the kitchens, the stables—she had long since become unused to them and to each separate living part of all of it, the subtle private jokes and the uproarious private scandals which lit the lives of these now strangers. The arm of the scythe had once been an extension of her own arm, but now it was a strange and dangerous thing, and she ached with the use of it. For Bett, beyond anyone's knowledge, least of all her own, had become a person of cities, and was becoming a Jew.

She had listened as a child listens when he is told not to; she had sucked in every word, every gesture of these foreign stran-gers in whose home she worked. She had heard with great eyes and open ears, the hundred thousand conversations of Baruch, Josce and Abram, of Rana and Anna. She had spent the night in terror beseeching the Holy Virgin (Blessed be the Name) for mercy when she learned of the horrible deaths of the Jews of Arles at the hands of a savage mob. She had prayed to Jesus Christus, who strangely resembled Abram in her mind, for His Holy Grace in maintaining good weather through the High Holydays, and if possible, through Succos as well. She had learned rather more than Rana would have thought, of cere-monial matters in the home, and would have been more shocked than Rana would believe had she seen the familiar basting ladle dipped in the milk. Most of all, she had learned, in the strange half-conscious way of children, names, moneys, usages and tales from the many reports which travelers brought to the house of Baruch of York. Few eleven-year-old girls knew that Philip the second had ascended the throne of France, and that affairs were most unsettled in the Rhine countries. Few Englishmen at all thought of how the price of land in Cologne was rising; few barons knew that there were rumors from Cordova. . . .

She was almost fifteen now, and the names she heard were used to feed her dreams, which were so different from those of her sisters. They wanted to wear buckles such as the ladies at Kuckney wore. Bett had known that these were considered quite, quite provincial. Now, to be really well-dressed, one would have to study the French fashions.

She rode and dreamt, now duchess, now queen, now abbess of a great convent, for Bett was religious. She and Baruch's other servants attended Mass faithfully and were scrupulous, often at his insistence, in their gifts to the poor and to the Church. But lately, and even guarded from herself, was beginning a great wash of loneliness, rising in her as she knelt before her Lord and prayed. The God of whom priests spoke had become for her a servant's God, a priest and nun's God. She wished that the Christ to whom she sent her supplications in the beautiful church could belong also to the tables of Northstreet, and that the Blessed Virgin could wear the strange embroidered shawls that Rana wore for her finery. The top of her mind exulted in the strange Latin— *Benedictus es Domine* . . . ; the bottom ran echoing with *Boruchu es Adoshem.* . . .

De Kuckney's lands began and Bett could see the evidences of his care. Painstakingly tended, the small trees were weathering the hard winter to replenish future generations of Kuckneys with the wealth that this one had taken. Not a loose stick lay on the ground, for the common gift of the moors, peat, was lacking here, and only wood could be burnt against the winter cold— scarce wood, precious wood, for which the children scoured the groves and looted the winter vineyards. Soon the woods gave way to cleared lands measured out in neat handkerchiefs for Tim, Sim and Kim each a swath, and for the Bishop one tenth of the fruit of their raising, and for the Lord one tenth. The Lord's own fields—oat, hay and fallow—lay beyond and then the castle on a little lift in the land, and Bett thought, even after all this time, still quite impressive. As the years went on, she waited to be un-caring about the look of it, bare and grey in the winter, crown-ing the green gardens and fields in the summer, but she never came to it without a little rise in her heart. A boy was leading some pigs along the road, and she felt suddenly sad that she did not know him. She drove the little donkey faster, but the boy

42

and his charges had disappeared around a bend and turned down into a little grove. Boys and girls who would have been her life were now strangers, and the Jews had done this. She kicked the donkey harder than she had done before.

The castle yard was the same as it had always been. She found her mother sitting in a little niche out of the wind and in the weak sunlight, plucking a chicken. Some others were there also, preparing various wild birds and fowl for the evening. The mother was a small woman, and when she looked up and recognized her daughter, the eyes wrinkled almost closed with the sun.

The mother greeted Bett matter-of-factly and asked after her health. Bett returned the greetings and suddenly there was no more to say. About them, the women gossiped and chattered as the feathers flew. The dress she was wearing was too fine to soil with offal and feathers, so Bett stood for a time before the mother as if she were waiting for something.

"You're very fine," the mother said at last, and there was a resentment and a bitterness in her voice. Bett had no reply. At last she said, "Is there something for me to do at the cottage? Perhaps you will be serving the Lord's feast tonight."

"I know where I belong," the mother said pointedly. "I will come when I can, and you, if you be still able, may serve your father. You seem to be his favorite now that you are scarce about the place. I will come with choice food from Kuckney's meal. As good as York's, you may be sure." The other women tittered.

Bett had once been able to make herself belong with these women in the courtyard of this now foreign place. She had only to ease her way among them with laughter and a joke, and soon it seemed as if she had never left, but now it was not only her fine clothes that made the women tighten their wrinkled mouths against her. It would take somewhat more, this time, than the unobtrusive slipping-in that she used to do. She was a woman now; her breasts had developed a little since her last visit, and went before her as if to say: I am a woman, a grown person, and no longer a child to be accepted along with the rain and the influenza. There was also something indefinably citified about her. She gave the women good day and went to seek out her father.

She found him repairing a wall in the mill. Oh, he had aged! The mother was eternal, and had not given any warning of this stooping, this bending, this thickening of the features. He saw her and dropped his hammer and it rang on the mill floor; the big, square man; he was like one of his own beams, rough and rude and full of solidness. Now he was old. The father came toward her and put his big hands on her shoulders where they left great whitened patches of sawdust and flour.

"Aw, it's Bett! An' I'm glad you've a-come," he said. Had she been wearing rubies and gold and the diadem of kings, he would not have noticed, and somehow, this time, it annoyed her. Must she always and still be and be forever Little Bett, Carpenter's Bett? She looked at this thick man, who was not at all like Baruch (whose corner of an eye saw a person back to Adam; his nation, his purse and his habits). "Aw, ye're a grown woman now." She could see that somehow this puzzled him. "If only your older brother ud ha' lived to stand beside of you . . . why you must be fourteen years!"

"Fifteen," she reminded him.

"Yes," he said, "ye were the second 'un. Time is moving by us, Bett; yer mother and I are no longer young."

He picked up his hammer and, having shared all with her of which he was then capable, he began to work again before the wall.

"I will be at the cottage," she cried through the dust of flour that whirled with every stroke of his hammer. He probably did not hear her.

At their fire they sat together and relived De Kuckney's meal by way of its leavings. Bett was used to this, for the same thing was done at Baruch's great home in York, and except for the prominent bits and bones of pork, the leavings looked and tasted much the same. Bett gorged on the rich feast of the pig. It was something she missed greatly at her meals at her master's house.

Her mother laughed. "Those Jews will not eat good meat, and for that you must come to us." There was hurt pride there; the mother was looking at her daughter's red cape and the shoes she wore.

Bett's timing with her parents was no better than Abram's with his. "He sent you some stout cloth—nearly three ells of it, and an ell of good blue linen for a holiday headcloth."

"Rich gifts do not impress me," the mother said shortly. "He can well afford them."

"Jill!" Her husband's reproach was mixed with amazement. The gift was the equal in value of a fine horse. "The Jew of York is a good man, and has treated our Bett good all this time. He do not owe these gifts to us."

The woman pushed the trencher of pork toward the girl.

"I knows cold and hungering that never ends, and work never done. Dragging a plow with my self and stooping in a furrow to drop a child as cows does. I am poor enough for Heaven, but I may never gone there as I give my dauther up to Satan. Look at her! Shoes even, and a dress of colors like a lady! Judas sold our Christ for silver pieces, or so says the priest, and you sold our dauther for ane!"

"Keep your peace, 'oman!" the big man roared. "Ther money kept us some winters well, and our Bett is safe and lives well with as values her. The Jew swore that he would let her gone to Holy Mass and hear the priest and get confession an' the sacraments."

"They are the Devil's promises, who is none Christian man!"

The carpenter's heavy hand was raised and his wife cowered away from it and the children began to moan. Bett saw then that their quarrel was not with her, or really with the Jew, but with their will and their faith and with their Dear Christ, whose vicars denied them a world now because of the one to come; and with the clouds whose rain falls also on the Just; and with the Blessed Virgin, who hears, but does not grant; and with the earth, the terrible and uncaring earth, which had let them increase with child and had cut them back again by starvation, and Bett waited and was silent and soon the anger dropped from them and they ate, wearily.

The children were insatiable for news of their sister's strange life. One never left the land, but she had. No one rose above clay, but she wore things of beauty. No woman held aught of truth or holy wisdom, who was a vessel of filth, but Bett could write her name and was learning, she said, all the figures of writing, and she would read also, she said. The children asked and begged. What did she do all the day, and did the Jews eat children, and did the Jews really have beaks like birds, and how was it to live in York and did she wear red dresses? It was always this way—a mad desire of the children to have a princess, even if it must be only Bett.

"Well," she said finally, "I shall give you a riddle to guess. It is a riddle from France: What is it that does not ride on horse, yet cannot be caught; goes not by boat, yet overtakes the boatman; and is greater in famines and more meager at feasts?"

45

They were all stopped like birds whom the hunter approaches. Their mouths were stopped mid-open, as if they thought through them.

"I have not wits to make head or tail out of this," said the father, muttering.

"What is the answer?" said a sister.

"Well . . . you should guess," Bett said. . . . Silence.

At last she said, "You see, Josce said that it was the wind, and my master Baruch said that it was destitution, but the scholar, Yomtob of Joigny, who is staying with us at the stone house and is from France, says it is an hour of time."

"Silly heathen nonsense," the mother muttered. "Either it be or it be not."

"But do you not see"—and Bett was somehow desperate to prove the point—"they all fit, and it could be any one of those things."

"Well, the Jews be good enough as masters, but they have not the vir——"

"But the riddle——"

"Witch!" shouted the mother. "Evil one!"

"Have we not riddles also?" Bett asked.

"They are not the same at all," said the mother darkly, and she hid her face.

So did Bett learn in the crack-cold month of February, that she was a stranger, un-Jew, un-Christian, not of the city nor yet of the land, not titled nor yet common, nor yet free nor yet bound. There were other such in York city, but none it seemed to her as perplexed as she. The next morning she sorted flax with the other women in the courtyard, but she knew now that to them she was as a foreigner.

"Lord Robert says that there will be a tourney here in autumn-time," a woman was saying, "a big 'un and all of the three counties to it."

"A hard mercy," another answered. "It is well for all of us to go, and food and wine and a spectacle, too, but the fighting and the raping and the drunken looting will be for weeks, and lords that do go lordly in fighting do also in their drinking and swinishness."

"What is it to raise an extra sheep, to have good harvests or marry off a daughter when pillage will come and sweep off every mouthful of meat and grain an' leave starvation's scythe a-

46

gleaming in the sun; my geese to his table and my flax to his whore?"

"You forget then, the honor of the house."

"I eats it then, and belch as richly as I does if I was feasting!"

"Honor can clothe my Lord's bone, but I be common and needs bread."

Toward the middle of the day, Bett looked up from the table and saw De Kuckney himself passing through the yard. He gave her a long, close look and went on toward the stables. Not handsome, she thought; nothing about him is handsome at all. And she found herself imagining Abram.

The stolid laborer stood uncomfortably before his lord. He had seen and spoken with the master many times, but those had been concerned with his wood, or his work or a Christmas blessing. Each in his condition, master and laborer shared a common life: this land, this castle. He half knew what his master wanted to see him about. He waited, painfully awkward, before the table. He had helped to work on that table, but it gave him no help now, in return.

"Was your daughter well?" De Kuckney asked.

"Oh, well enough, thank God," the father blurted out. "She does well in service to her master."

"And does he think well of her and of her service?"

"Aye, that he does, my Lord." He was proud of his Bett, and his heart had lifted with pride as he had seen her away in her fine clothes and riding the little donkey. "The Jew sends her to us well and fine." Something stopped him from mentioning the gift of cloth—not that De Kuckney would have any rights on it, but . . . His mind's finger went softly, persuasively before his lips.

"What does she tell you of her life there? Does she say anything about her service?"

The father knew his rights as well as any man, and his right as a servant was the right to be stupid. "Oh, yes; she says she likes it well. She gave us a riddle too—something about a horse and a boatman and the wind—I did not get the way of it. She is good for work at York. She says she goes often to the Market Fairs."

Lord Robert dismissed his plodding servant. He got up and walked to his window and leaned out over the thick inner side of the ledge. Away to the east lay his lands that would soon have to be mortgaged to those Jews, strangers to his life and his cause. He did not know the purposes of these people, or what changed

47

ways their power symbolized. What he knew was that the old names and the old lands were being ripped apart; barons and knights and almost all of the religious houses owed to the Jews and paid great moneys for the mere privilege of keeping what had always been theirs. Lord Robert thought of the fees he owed to the King, and of his debts to the Church. Half of the wealth and lands of his house had been given up in reparation and penance. Now, these new fees, growing larger all the time, were not to be paid in the old ways: services, usufruct or craftmanship or in time, but in the rare coin. They would accept bezants, marks from Germany, even the heathen coin of the Saracen and the black Moor. It was all money; everyone needed it, sought after it, leased away ancestral lands for it.

"Damn them!" He turned and dug his heels into the floor. Jews and the churches, kings and kin had hedged him about with their laws and wills and he was a prisoner, trapped in a drowning stream of debt and shame. And there was a son, a beloved son, to whom he was to bequeath this shame . . . a son who would never have a proper knighting because the ceremony had now to be bought and a man was taxed for it to the top of his head. "Damn them! Damn them!"

"WHY am I so afraid?" Yomtob asked. "The sun shines down upon me and yet I huddle my garments about me; the moon's face is clear, not a sound ripples the night and yet I do not sleep, lest I should wake too late to run from some unseen evil. Am I so accustomed to dying that I have lost life?"

"I suppose that running from danger can become a habit, so that one does it even against the need," Elias said.

They were sitting in the Community Hall before the great fire that burned against their faces while their backs tingled with the cold. They had come there to discuss the news that was flying all over York, that the young Prince, old King Henry's beloved hope, the heir to England's throne, was dead. Now the brothers are measuring each other over the dropped crown, they said, and they spoke of the heaviness of being a king when sons grow up around the throne feeling their strength and their lives in the June of increase, hungering to try their wills. One place, one throne, and an old man who was already slowing and beginning to be cautious. The sons, can they help but wonder: How much longer can the dry leaf cling?

Rumor abounded of the brothers in league against their father, and the men spoke of it with awe and sorrow. In spite of his heavy taxes, King Henry had been good to the Jews, his Persons. Soon the talk drifted again to the fear that waited closer to their hearts since this unplanned, unlooked-for thing had happened; they spoke of wars and of accusations and of persecutions.

It is not strange that men should take pride in sufferings which exalt their spirits, yet many boast also of sufferings which degrade them, as if suffering itself were good and to suffer were a virtue and to be desired. "Were you in Paris on Good Friday?" and "Why, Paris was Eden compared to Angers!" "These modern woes are but smoke and noise. Who here was at Blois?" and there was a muttering of yes and no among the listeners.

"I was," said a man, "and though it was more than ten years ago, I think that it was the worst, the very worst. . . ." He moved his hand by the side of his face in memory.

"I had had business in Montpellier, and had come back through the green June countryside, and I remember being so happy . . ." and his voice caught at something that he must have remembered also, but would not speak of. "I was going home. Who can fathom the mysteries of the Lord? There was nothing in all that green, nor in the bright sound of my horse's feet, nor in the gay sun that could say to me, a happy man, 'Before the day dies you shall see death and clasp the beloved dead in your arms.' There was no warning for a poor, foolish man come from Montpellier. As I got close to the city, I heard a yell go up and then another. It was not a cheer, and it seemed strange to me, that sound, but I was a happy man and a fool; and my curiosity was happy, saying, 'I wonder what spectacle is come to town today?' The roads were empty. I turned into the Street of Three Saints, and I saw a man running toward me, and he was waving at me frantically. I stared at him. He looked so strange to me that I had to stop my horse to look at him. It was like seeing a frightened animal, and I had to look hard at him before I realized that I knew him. Before I could ask him what had happened, he screamed, 'They are burning the Jewry! Flee for your life!' I felt the shock of his words, and at the same time, some horrible truth, more horrible than the surprise, that I was not surprised, not really disbelieving at all. . . . I remember whispering, 'It is here . . . here at last.' And as I stopped, unable to decide what to do or how to reach my family, I saw a mob coming down the street. I recognized some of them—louts who stood about the smithy, and a halfwit, too, and others. I turned my horse and he began to run, but when we got to the crossing, there seemed to be another crowd, and they were waiting, and I saw some of our people with them."

Someone spoke in an urgent whisper: "Did you see the Rabbis, the great Rabbis?"

The man acted as if he had not heard. "They took me from my horse, that sea of arms and awful faces, and I was tossed like a chip of wood on a millrace down to the square before the cathedral. Such a pack of people, all screaming and shouting. I tried to ask, to hear, to find out what the reason was, for all this madness, but there were only the arms and the thick, mad faces. I had no horse—my clothes were almost ripped from me. Then I smelled . . . that smell which was terrifying above all others, more than the smell of the hot, angry men around me. They had begun to build fires. Then there was a great blow and I fell all dark about the brain and there was nothing else for a time."

"Did you see the Rabbis?" the insistent questioner interrupted.

"Yes . . . I saw them then . . . their bodies . . . just their bodies," and he covered his face with his hand.

It was this one part, this one answer that Abram had been straining to hear for so long. Two great Rabbis had been in Blois on that horrible day, and had died the death of martyrs. It was part of the slowly growing ritual remembrance, that these two sons of the One God had stood their ground before their mad tormentors, and had countered blasphemies with holy prayers, and that they had been bound, singly and then together, and had been thrown into a horrible fire while the mob stood howling around them. Then it was told how they rose, these two, in the fire, and let the flames burn their bonds, and how they embraced in pious exaltation in the heart of the fire, walking together with smiles of graciousness on their faces, from the fire into the crowd, unsinged, unharmed. The rabble had drawn back in awe, and some went on their knees. So much does a crowd resemble a great beast pursued by a gadfly that it can turn in a minute, bringing life or death with one swing of its horrible head. A Templar had stepped forward from the crowd and cried, "Witchcraft!" Fresh from one minute of veneration, the two were stoned, beaten and mauled to death with the sudden wrath of the mob.

The Christians remembered them in that way: horrible in disfigurement. The Jews remembered them in the gracious embrace of the learned, and they begged the survivors of Blois to have seen their vision.

"The miracle!" Abram shouted in despair. "What about the miracle!"

"I—I was struck down—I do not know, but he was there—ask him," and he pointed to another old man sitting quietly at the side.

A hundred times the question had been asked of him, and he said all that he had ever been able to say: "Yes, I was at Blois. There was such a pack of people there, and one looked only to get away."

Abram shook with impatience. If only I had been there—I might have proven or disproven, and once and for all put an end to these ifs and if nots that go on and on in my mind. . . . Were even the participants of miracles themselves unaware? Great men! Who that really knew would speak?

The talk went on—other sacrifices, other deaths. The wine merchant was telling about the English uprisings at Norwich and Lincoln, and the senseless accusations of ignorant men, and it seemed that, as the tales were told, a shadow, an echo of the same savagery was growing in the victims. They were caught in the shadows of the past and the inflections of hatred grew in their voices. They listened to each recollection more and more avidly, almost savoring the degradations which they had suffered, and the evil of the mobs which had tormented them. At the end of each recital a groan of anger would go up. Here, here was the proof that the world of Christians was no more than a herd of animals; examples of the utter evil of their neighbors. Was it not clear, they nodded to one another, that these were not truly men, but half-men only, degenerate and coarse by birth? Suddenly, the slights of acquaintances, the hurried impatience, the careless gesture of every Christian assumed the greatest importance, and hating, the little group, swimming in this sudden sea of treachery, clung close and felt their own grave differences welter away in the push of the current. A man put his arm on the silent Abram's shoulder, and two-year-long enemies, whom even the

51

Bible's adjuration of love could not unite, conjured horrors with their arms linked.

"Your Christian servants," one of the French was saying, "are they not indifferent about the laws of food?"

"Ah, but they never touch the food and they handle the household things only under our eyes. Even the best of them has not the Natural Horror."

"Ah, but what natural loathing could rise in their strange blood if they (Saving the Lord's presence) would pick up a knife for flesh and cut a cheese with it?"

"Animals have no horror at defilement."

"I cannot understand it, really," another said. "Christians have hounded us throughout the world, yet they are tender with their children . . . they even pray, after a fashion."

"You think that they are as we? See your neighbors turn against you, and you will see men who are little more than beasts."

"What do you expect? They are Christians. They have not the moral background of Jewish persons. Their priests are unnatural men. And their women! Forgetting God's Laws, they turn into convents without a care for their own flesh and blood. They are not human, not moral."

"The basic weakness in Christians is not their souls," said Baruch pedantically, "but their brains. Every Jew reads and studies, but they do not, and their brains thus dry up and become stiff, their wits forsake them and they become incapable of thought."

"Observe a child—how he will strike another, even his father unknowing—without real hate and without evil because he knows nothing."

"You observe these murder-mad children with men's weapons and men's imagination. You are wrong to think that they have souls—they are degenerate!"

Yomtob of Joigny stood up, knocking over his comfortable stool. He was tall before them and his back was to the fire. He flung his hands high over his head, and his voice was loud in the astonished house: "Call them children; call them evil and deny them humanity, and for your luxury you will pay with the bodies of your own children. It is easy to forget one's own vanity and evil and cruelty; the rich clothes that beget envy, the rich jests that beget resentment, the rich derisions that beget hatred. These are the luxuries with which you play, lying and stealing and excusing yourselves with easy trips into your pasts of anguish! Play, then; laugh and be comfortable, and forget your pride and your own stupidity and your own cruelty, and you will pay with the dearest blood and the most precious bones, and your children will pay, and your old men will pay double!"

"But, Rabbi, they are not as we are."

"No," said Yomtob, stilling his voice from wrath to sorrow, "they are not as we are. . . . What is it that we are? God has chosen us from among all others to suffer more, to live in greater responsibility to ourselves and others, to keep our brothers, to question ourselves down to our very charity, seeing that it is always clean, always occasioned by the highest motives. We were not chosen for self-justification; we will pay for it. We were not chosen for judging our brothers; we will pay for it. We were not chosen for pride and wrath; we will pay for it. And if we are guilty of two, we will pay seven times that of which we are guilty!"

He lowered his head. There was a heaviness about him now, and he turned again to the fire. He was weeping.

In the streets of the city, the evening was closing. The winter waited at the corners for passers-by, and whipped at their clothes. The sewage ruts were frozen and the wandering beggars, rhymers, cutpurses and madmen huddled against the houses. Soon it would be spring, and the earth would be freed from its numbing thrall, and the streets would be packed with people. Every several months town government and clergy combined against these vagabonds and wandering madmen, and hordes of them were driven out beyond the limits of York to the Galtres Forest, and told to go somewhere else, or if they were dying, at least to die outside of York. Then, for two days or so, Yorkers would breathe a more private and salubrious air, and then back the rabble would drift. Winter drove them to the city, and they were here today with the unerring, inborn instinct of the beggar and the madman for news. They knew that something had happened, or was happening. The young Prince was dead, and those who loved the King, as almost all had reason to, mourned the sorrow to the aging, proud Henry; and those who loved so large a thing as England, as few could do, mourned for that part of the sorrow. A taciturn John; a gay young Richard, perpetual boy to whom court was only tourney, and whose sole excitement was the game of chivalry; a well-married but useless trinity of daughters; and

53

Geoffrey, the bastard whom England loved, being the son of a great love, and whom none could acknowledge. Men who could see beyond the cries of their bellies and the ease of their bones took the measure of this new wind and wondered if it was not treacherous.

At Allhallows Church, prayers were said for the repose of the young Prince's soul. The priest, an old soldier and full of the zeal for the Battle of God, reflected that the glorious Crusade would, indeed, be begun again in his time if Richard were to come to the throne. Christians were growing in grace, it seemed to him, the grace of suffering indignity by knowing that the Lord's land lay in the hands of the infidels. He saw them, in his mind, advancing on the Holy City, and the Armies of God had been transformed by the earth on which they stepped—no pillaging, no murder marred their consciences. Ever since the day when he came limping back from one of the many false starts to recapture the fervor of Christendom for its birthplace, Father Odo had yearned for the day when a new and finally triumphant Crusade would begin. Prince Richard had always been on fire for the holy work. As he limped down the aisle of the church, holding the hip from which his ruined leg swung heavily, it seemed to the Priest as if he heard the trumpets of salvation ringing around him, and he lifted his face in awe at the thundering *Te Deum* of God's glorious marching men.

ABRAM wanted to give his new-found friend gifts and riches. It seemed to him as if he had been dry and closed away all his life. With this new opening at last, there came a pouring out of generosity and love such as he had never known that he possessed. Since gold or food or trinkets could not pass between them, being forbidden by the laws of both, Abram burned long glorious nights gathering and sifting knowledge which he brought to his friend like offerings of honey. Soon the young monk was drinking at the ancient fountain of Jewish wit and law, the gleanings of which Abram himself had gathered over the crumb-speckled

54

tables of his father and the Rabbis. Baruch suddenly found him more than eager to journey to one place or another on his father's business, and there was, indeed, a new brightness and pleasure in Abram which delighted Rana and drew praise even from Baruch's scanty store. Yet the more Abram spoke with Simon, the keener were his own questions of the teaching of his people, and he now spent hours asking the Rabbis for the proofs of their beliefs.

"Is not heresy glamorous?" Yomtob said to him as they watched the birds that were dancing in the newly warm air above the houses. "Is it not glamorous, alluring, to doubt God, to keep the doubts to yourself, waiting for God to burn you with His lightning in a magnificent martyr's fire? Let me take the allurement from you, and tell you that without doubters and questioners, Judaism would be as dead as a stone. The Lord (Holy be the Name) cannot affirm unless we question, and a man who takes a sealed box from his fathers and does not ask, 'What is here and to what use can I put it?' is no better than a simple animal."

"I did put it to the test. I cursed God."

"And tell me: did God recover, or did He die?"

"Rabbi, you are laughing at me!"

"And am I to blame for that? It is funny, you know. A little lad lying in his bed and saying, 'If there is a God, let Him send lightning.' Well, the Lord is endowed (Praised be He) with an infinite sense of humor, but not with an infinite sense of humoring, and He is not at the beck and call of little boys home from seeing the traveling juggler."

"Then let us say that He recovered, but that I did not." He searched in his thoughts for what he could really choose to put forward to the Rabbi. "Everyone walks so loudly on God's floor. The Christians say that they have God with them and my mother and father and their friends are full of pious gossip and malice in His name. Now the crusaders are out beating on God's drum as if they had created Him. Perhaps He is only the baying voices all over the world."

"Perhaps you are not so much a doubter as a deep believer, who, waking in the world and seeing sin, thinks in the half-sleep of his youth that he discovered it; and yes, we do discover sin newly, in each generation."

"Let Him exist, then; and I hate Him because He sees me, as my friend Brother Simon says, bound for Hell and yet He puts forth no hand to save me."

"How do you know he doesn't?" Yomtob looked away, almost speaking to himself. "Sometimes, in these last hard years in France, I almost felt that I could hear Him crying for the bigots to stop—praying for them to remember their precious humanity. Here in York the people are blown up with vanity and cruelty. God must weep that they do not see the precipice toward which they walk with such great haste."

"Rabbi—those who have the means to dress—may they not dress as well as they like?" And Yomtob saw for a moment, a glimpse of the hidden, slumbering love that Abram had for his father, whose taste and vanity he despised.

"Of course they may, but for the privilege of remembering that they are the sons of Solomon, they may also have to pay by remembering that they are the sons of Judah the Maccabee, and the cost may be greater than they want to pay. Believe me, my son, I saw this very thing happen before, and it was not the wearers of silk and scarlet who paid alone, but the whole Jewish people. All of us."

The picture came suddenly to both at once: of Baruch's hands, soft and with many rings; of his face above the furs, looking that look of his when he was pleased with some arrangement; and each knew what the other was seeing and was suddenly embarrassed.

"Well, there he stands," Abram said bluntly, "with the two Rabbis dancing in the fire at Blois and you weeping at the Community Hall, saying, 'We were not chosen for pride and wrath.' Angels! Angels! I wish I could paint that picture!"

As Abram spoke, Yomtob had the strange feeling that it was years ago, and that he was speaking to one of his old students who was studying to be a rabbinical scholar. Something was in both of them, flirting with them, like a pretty woman who lets the hem of her skirt trail from behind a pillar as a reminder that she herself is out of sight. There was a piety in this young Abram which was waiting for him, pulling at him, playing with him—come and look for me.

"You know," said Abram suddenly, "it is against the Law to paint. I want to picture men and gods as Christians do."

"How long have you wished this?"

"For as long as I can remember. And that, too, I kept secret."

"I think I understand. Scribe is closer to the drawing art of the Christians than any other, and so your father——"

"Why is it with my father that when I am starving," Abram interrupted, "and call out for food, or am thirsty and cry for water—why is it that he is away, or it is not his desire, and then as soon as I am sated and no longer in need, he comes wandering in with a pomegranate in his hand?" The anger had gotten away from him and was running over the banks that he had built to contain it. Yomtob sat looking at him as if waiting for rain. When the young man stopped talking, worn out by rage, the Rabbi waited a long, silent moment.

"Are you so far from confidences and openness that everything is secret with you? It is certainly not against our Law to draw pictures—it is just that the Jew finds little place for them in his life. We never want to replace the Mysterious Name in our souls with someone's picturing of Him. We do not permit representations in our synagogues, our holy books, or as house mementoes as the Christians do, yet if you really wish it, some way might be found to give your hunger purpose and your purpose a fulfillment."

"I want to draw the world—I want to draw what life is."

"God is working in you," Yomtob said, "and He will work His will, but do not let your bitterness make your philosophy for you. Do not hate your father so that you fail to honor his love or pity him his mortality, which is nearer than yours." He looked at Baruch's son, suddenly glad that the day was warm and the air light to breathe and that these wranglings in the rebellious soul were not the usual questions of York's Jews: 'Rabbi, can we eat such-and-such a meat?' and 'Rabbi is such-and-such within the Law?' They, alas, skirted the true Law far more than did the anguishes of this hot firebrand. "Abram, you yourself must thrash out the problem of charity, which needs to be so much more than mere form to be virtuous, and so seldom is. As for myself, I am pleased to hear you. Your passion is what renews the world for an old French exile, and for mankind. I delight to forget for a while the two silver marks that so-and-so found in his cloak on the Sabbath. You know—perhaps the Lord God, in his final impatience with you, may pick you up as he did Jonah and hurl you into faith. Meanwhile, if you are to draw, you must first look. The world is beautiful and sometimes—sometimes even man; so let the Lord bless your eyes and go in peace."

Abram left the bench where the Rabbi sat and walked toward the Ouse Bridge. For a gift he would take his friend Simon through the winding of one of the long strands of a logical disputation, that combination of schooling, prayer and entertainment of which his people were so fond. The meanings and the shades of meanings—how brilliant and complex they were! He had tried once before to lay the whole great panoply of some argument before his friend, but Simon had heard and heard to the end and then said, "Well . . . and so?" with his open, simple look of confusion. The glory of one people was the valueless waste of another. But he would teach Simon to see the wonder of these webs of words and thoughts woven for their own beauty alone, and Simon would teach him perhaps, how the single words of clear perception could test through the web and find if it held. Abram looked about him as he mounted the bridge, which groaned with the half-alive and half-dead beggars who fished and loafed along its wooden palings. The day was clear and brilliant; the sky shone and birds flashed through it on their hundred errands with swiftness and with joy. One of the wandering poets by the river's side was singing his half-sweet half-lustful song:

> "*The gay spring*
> *Flowering;*
> *My virgin almond-branch*
> *Blooms in the heat of my heart.*
> *Open, leaf,*
> *Winter's grief*
> *Falls apart.*
> *And in the sun*
> *One by one*
> *The petals pull.*
> *I will tip its cup*
> *Up and up*
> *'Til I am full.*"

The sun was warm. Abram smiled wryly at the song and at Yomtob's words and at the God he questioned. The bride spring would be matron summer and mother autumn in the endless turn and turn of things. The servant girls would stand and gape at the singers on the Ouse Bridge in their own spring cycle. He thought of Bett, as she would listen and weep and go and give her hard-saved coppers to the sweet-rhyming liars. He tried to think of her with scorn, but somehow, as with Simon, his bitterness would not reach that far. They had a love of the world that seemed to sing through their whole souls and Abram sometimes looked at them and thought: Your church renounces, with its prayers, all the world; yet if it has given life to you, I wish I were a Christian. Questions and anguishes. He looked up at the shining sky that feigned innocence and grated his teeth. "Deceiver!" he muttered. "Deceiver!"

THE Brothers at Welbeck were on their summer schedule, but try as they would, siesta hours became more and more difficult to leave, and the Brothers felt themselves forced to race through their devotions like sweating runners, in order to be finished when the final bell bore them heavily to their sleep. Abbot Adam spoke of it to the half-drowsing white lumps of men resting beside him in the shade of the inner court's big tree.

"There is so much to be done, and one can scarcely believe that another August is upon us. Our sheepfolds are full, the crops are good, and Brother Unam Sanctam has somehow managed to get an excellent wine out of the berries in the western wood. We can see the last of those vineyard-marbles that we had last year. Poor wretch that I am and must be—there is always something about which I must worry. . . . There is an unrest here, and something seems to tug at my sleeve, and I wonder if it is with us, or only that we must be more with the world and its confusions than we wish. In all the health of summer, there is some kind of nervous haste that may be the haste of a worm at the heart of a tree which is our Community."

"Mayhap your worry is only the responsibility of parenthood, Father; we seem to sire a new House almost every year, and we ourselves have grown and enlarged all the time."

"I suppose you are right, Brother Simon. How hard it is to realize that we are just thirty years old! With the help of God and our worthy patrons, the barons of this shire, we prosper, but each year our responsibility trebles. I go to report to our Founding House at Peremontre in October, and we have our own Daughter Houses to visit and correct. Oh, my Brothers, the Rule is not all that must be looked to! There is not time to see as deeply as we would wish. Do you know the feeling one has, when, in the granary, out of the corner of the eye, for the tenth part of a breath, one sees a flick, a start, a something move? Immediately, one thinks: Aha! Was it a rat, so quick and ugly among the heaps of millet? Was it a danger, or only a ball of dust, or was it a memory left over in the side of my eye to deceive me? So it is with the visits one makes, hoping that the glances which one sends out are true seeing, and not only the quick glossing-over of an incident." He moved his thick, farmer's body farther into the dark of the shade. Even as he spoke, he wondered if there was not the faintest smell of discord among the Brothers. Perhaps it was only the pressure of the world upon souls which were striving for the perfect life. He had dreamt sometimes, that blunt, practical Abbot, about some secret illness in the Community, that would burst one day into blasphemy or madness. "Well . . ." he said, and stretched his arm, "that is why we beg the help of God. Soon the circaries will come from France to us, to see if the rats in our granary are rats or ghosts at the eye's edge."

"Father Abbot, when the circaries come, will they forbid me to learn anything of the Jew?" Brother Simon's question was quick and earnest. It had been held in his brain for the right time, and then, perverse demon that the tongue is, it had suddenly been picked off and thrown out into the heat before the Abbot in the middle of an afternoon conversation and in the presence of Brother Lewis Fauconbridge, a man he feared.

"I do not know, Brother, what they will do," Abbot Adam said levelly. "I myself have permitted you to see the young man and to speak with him because I feel that he is ripe fruit for the Salvation of Holy Church. Our visitors might ask, as indeed I do, why you are doing this. I ask myself, since I do not know you to be so interested in conversion, why you are moved toward this infidel. Is it that you are bored, Brother?"

The face of the young monk was quite pale.

Brother Lewis Fauconbridge, sitting beside him, broke from his fixed and secretive stare, and turned toward him. The monk of great family, the son of a baron, faced his peasant Brother in Christ with the urbane, closed look which seemed to give onto the world through an escutcheon, and with heraldry marked above the family eyes. The mouth smiled.

"He is ripe for conversion," Simon said quietly, "but if I am to be honest, Abram of York speaks of many things which up to now I have not even conceived of, but I assure you that our talk has been spiritual and not secular at all. We speak together of the festivals of the Jews, which I remember as having been those of Our Lord. I asked him about the Passover, and the way he described the actions of his people at that time made it for me as if Our Lord was sitting before me with his Holy Mother and the wise old Joseph."

Brother Lewis grinned. "Then is the Devil also gifted as a raconteur?"

"Brothers, these are difficult times for the thinking Christian," said Abbot Adam, hoping to stem the perilous flood of Brother Lewis's anger before it made its rush. "Eleven sees vacant in England where there is no bishop to give his strength and position to Holy Church, and to help bring the word of God to the simple folk who need it as much as they need bread and ale. Eleven cathedrals in England now, unblessed with bishops, closed, silent, and more and more the Jews grasp us in their beholden. Prelate and Prince walk the same way. It is we, the monasteries, who now bring the comforts and graces of the sacraments to many of the people for whom not even priests can be found. The priests leave the country parishes too eagerly, looking, always looking for this fat rent and that wealthy congregation, a town with few requirements, a vantage spot for ambition, a jumping-off place to greater things. The canons at least, know that not that way lies their good. They do not take Christ by the mark or the gold penny." He realized suddenly the sin of pride in his speech and that all canons were not so holy nor all priests so venial or so stupid, and he did a *culpa,* tapping his breast in the quick, unobtrusive way that years of finding himself out in sin had taught him, and the thread of speech was not broken by it.

"The canons are too good for parish churches," Brother Lewis was saying. "The parish folk are satisfied with the ignorant and peasant-born priests. What do they know of the texts on which they must preach!" The remark about the peasant-born was not lost on Abbot Adam, and he smiled his farmer's-son smile that such things no longer moved him to anger. "I will never forget one we had at Bury, once," Brother Lewis continued. "It was on a trip we took, my father and I, and we stopped on the Sabbath and heard the sermon. I swear to you by God's Body that not one word did we grasp out of all the thousands he spoke. Those who are not mad are worse yet—they are hideously dull!"

"But some of the simple priests are gifted in holiness," Brother

Simon said. He was looking into his cupped hands through which imaginary water spilled. "In the tiny settlement where I was born, there was an old church and a priest who seemed to have been a boy with Methuselah. You are right, Brother, he was not a learned man, but to us he was always so gentle that none remembered a word said by him in anger or malice. One time, a woman in the village was dying in childbed, and the child was not her husband's. The husband stood outside the door cursing God and his wife, and blaspheming; and he saw the old priest coming down the road toward him, and the old priest was weeping. He walked with his head down and his beard unkempt and his sobs made him shake. That wronged farmer was a rough, hard man of the earth and no nonsense, but when the priest came there, they both went on their knees and the man stopped his ranting. That hard man went in to his wife then, and forgave her and prayed with her until she died, and after her death he mourned her. It was said that that priest forgave all wrong, even that done to someone whom he loved."

"And you call that holy?" said Brother Lewis. "Is that piousness to you? A poor feeble man, too feeble for wrath? I tell you, Brother Simon, that the Church had better begin to arm itself against its enemies and conquer them with righteous wrath. Jerusalem cries to be avenged; heresies planted by the Devil grow like poisoned fruit and kill our Christian brothers. The fruit must be rooted out and the infidels slain! Your farmer-priests will never do that! Plots are being planned against us, and it is time that we rise like Christ's archangels to defend our cause instead of forgiving the devil. Christian forgiveness begins to pardon Satan and excuse our enemies. You say your priest was holy? I say he was a fool, a slobbering, doddering old peasant! I hate these lamb-eared churchmen; they are keeping us from the time when God will give us the victory over the heathen and the sinner; a victory of sword and fire——"

"But, Brother——"

"It is time that small problems of small men be forgotten and the deep and monstrous stains be seen and cleansed. We are looking at fleas in our shirts while winged monsters escape. The church must rise against her enemies . . . must——"

"Brothers!" Abbot Adam's voice rang against the pressing wall of the heat. "Brothers! Sit down!" Both of them found that they were standing and they sat, heavily. "Where is your charity?" Abbot Adam said, as if he were speaking to two small boys.

"With the Grace of God, this is siesta time, and others rest from their activities and the heat of the day. You do increase the noon with your own passion, a passion better cooled in prayer and in pious service."

"Are these phantoms, Father Abbot?" Brother Lewis asked, in a voice softer but still as cutting. "Are they the stirrings of my mind, or do the Jews teach their heresy to little calf-eyed Brothers in our Order? Is it a dangerous game they play, the little calves of our House?" In spite of this allusion, Brother Simon sat mute in the heat. "They step into the milk, and the other Brothers laugh, and Brother Norbert says, 'Thank God for our Little Brother.' The Brothers love and forgive the Brother calf—not for his learning, or his wit, or his good advice! They say, 'Poor Brother Calf' and they say it with the special love that men have for the weak and the clumsy. Well, this Brother Calf consorts with devils and gives prayers with the sons of Satan!"

Brother Simon ventured weakly, "But, Brother, he is a man of York, son of York men and well known by the Priest of Allhallows. . . . He is not Satan, he is as you and I."

"The Devil gives tongues to his defenders now!" Brother Lewis stood up, his shadow pushed beneath him in the bright glare outside the refuge of the tree. "Don't trust the Jews, Brother Calf; fear them. They and their evil are beyond your depth."

His white garment swung away from them, a burning cloth in the heat.

"A proud man from a proud house," Abbot Adam said quietly. "His pride reminds me too painfully of my own in youth, and how many times I took a knotted rope to scourge a pride that would not go down. If I can trust my own memory, rekindled in this man, he will come limping to the table for his evening rations with the blood wet on his back and the nausea of guilt and of the flogging in his stomach; and he will eat because he wishes not to eat. We all wound the body to tame it, but the peasant so often has seen the necessary fixing of the limits of his life that his great virtue lies that way: so yield an acre; so much labor for the Lord's table and so many strokes in penitence. He kneels, humbles himself, and rises and puts his rods away—the necessary number has been given, and he feels that the Lord must know it and be satisfied. These others, so many of them noble, wealthy and learned, have prouder natures. They scourge, they sweat, they tremble, they faint. It is never enough. It is not sufficient to contemplate Our Lord's pain; they must bear it all, even if it means taking Heaven by force; they are insatiable in their hunger, though God himself orders them to be sated. We may find it hard to love these Saints (if God grants their headlong siege into saint-hood), but they are a great force in our Church. . . ." He knew that he was speaking as one peasant to another, the comfortable well-understood implications of common life. French Adam and English Simon were closer to each other in every subtle memory and unvanquished desire than ever the English Lewis and the English Simon were. Because this closeness was forbidden, the Abbot spoke somewhat harshly: "Brother Simon, I do not feel as Brother Lewis does in regard to your patronage of this—er—person, but I will bid you go carefully, to report to me of your spiritual state and his, often and honestly, and to pray for Special Graces through St. Norbert. Let us not fear to convert heathen, for God is infinite in righteousness and He pities the righteous man."

The Abbot smiled and rose a little heavily because the day was hot and their robes were long and heavy with penitential coarse bits of flax, woven, Brother Simon had once sworn, with foresight as to where they would scratch most cruelly.

"Brother, Brother"—he smiled gently—"never be an abbot. In the concerns of wagons and rye, and folded among the prayers that mark our days, the weight of the souls of the world falls upon us . . . and some of us miss . . . the smell of France. . . . Ah! Well!"—and he clapped his heavy hands together—"Go graciously, with God's blessing, Brother Simon. The Lord help you to prosper in your ways."

He watched the shambling young monk, whose feet always seemed to work each for its own advantage and against the other. The lad went toward the chapel where they would meet for prayer. If anyone can win a soul to God, it is he, Abbot Adam thought, smiling. He steadied his smile against the preference he felt for the clumsy, lowborn boy. "There is a saint who conquers Heaven by force, who wakes angels with his anguish and trembles them with triumphant sacrifice, but the other sort of saint," he said aloud to the buzz-drone of August insects in the tree, "is the one who stumbles in at Heaven's doorway, and trips over his own robe, and falls full length before the throne of Glory."

ONE hundred and fifty retainers in brown, and standards of green with the doe's head. Twelve horses, deep-shouldered, so that the earth shook beneath them. Lances of green and brown with silver spears and swords that gleamed like fire in the sun. The Baron Malabestia and his retainers.

One hundred and twenty men and men-at-arms dressed in scarlet. Ten tall horses caparisoned in red and white and the famous pack of hunting dogs renowned in four counties. The Barons Fauconbridge.

One hundred sixty men and men-at-arms in yellow and brown, like bees. Ten paired horses, pitching their wild heads and neighing for the battle. The retinue of the Barons Percy.

The summer had mellowed slowly over the prospering land; now it was October and the air was chilly in the mornings. The first harvest was gathered and put by, and the brisk air, and the feeling of bounty in the bins made men feel fortunate and reckless. It was the season of tourneys.

Tournaments had been declared illegal by King Henry on pain of a sizable fine. Henry, less the warrior than the statesman, realized that their violence opened feuds, their gatherings hatched plots and their very form strengthened the power of local nobles and weakened his own dream, limited as it was, of nation. Although official tourneys had been stopped, good old friends still met, and having met, tried on bits of armor or new headpieces, and having done this, fenced with each other for the practice. The tournament law was greatly honored in the breach and honored not at all in the observance.

The camps of retainers had been set up in a rye field from which the crop had been harvested a few days before; the hot, sweet smell of the cut stalks still hung in the air over the cursing, brawling, drinking, whoring men. Relatives and friends met and wagered; marriages were contracted and news exchanged. It would be a week of singing and fighting, of broken ribs, ruined shoulders and fine memories.

Inside the castle, the meetings and the matchings, fighting and drinking were the same between the members of the reunited noble families. The babies of proud houses howled in their cradles and the rooms of the women twittered as with birds.

Lord Robert de Kuckney had waited with eagerness to see the man that had been made of his young boy, whom he had sent to be the Baron Malabestia's squire and learn from him the codes and prowesses of knighthood. As soon as he could manage it, he left the hall, crowded with other families, and made his way to where the Baron's horses had been gathered. Malabestia was not there, and for this Lord Robert was glad. It was enough that they had years and separate castles between them without the added mazes of protocol and form. The lad was over by the edge of a stream that ran near the horse meadows. Lord Robert called to him and he turned, and for that brief touch of a second, the man did not recognize his son. He had sent a boy with dark, luminous eyes; a gay, questioning, tender boy, and what was in that still boyish face was a new quality that the father could not name or describe. They embraced and greeted one another, and Lord Robert kept groping, in spite of himself, for the ends of those threads of difference which had changed his son so much. Lord Robert de Kuckney hated war, was frightened of violence and disgusted with the hypocrisy that let fornicators and liars call themselves Christians. To be a provincial petty noble and to feel these things was to be a man utterly alone. In the height of this loneliness, the scandal of his father's part in Thomas Beckett's murder, fell like a beheading axe upon Lord Robert, and dying of these things, he submitted to all the rules he hated, and to his wife, and to the laws of his station. He would have been a walking corpse, except that he had a son.

They went together back to the castle, greeting the groups of men and passing the field where the tourney would take place. Ropes had already been mounted to mark the limits of the field and wooden barricades were being built to keep the rushing battle horses from the crowds of spectators. For the occasion also, every whore in the three counties had put a sprig of parsley behind her ear and trotted out to Kuckney. With that aphrodisiac they all hoped to leave the week's affair rich women, although Kuckney had said of a few of them as they passed that they could now bear nothing but great-grandchildren. As they went to the castle to find the boy's mother (Lady Agnes de Kuckney had lived and believed in the Code with all her soul, and would never have gone seeking a warrior even if it was her son), they saw

66

Malabestia moving among his men. The hard, handsome eyes found them and he broke away from his retainers and came toward them. As he did so, the squire seemed to melt away before Lord Robert's very eyes, and a body, a servant's compliant body, was all that remained.

"Ah, so, you see your squire son!" Malabestia said, greeting them. "Are you proud of him?"

"I hope I have cause to be," Lord Robert answered. "He has told me that he rides well, and much surer than he did, and can handle the heaviest of my swords, and is eager to show me his service at table."

"Ask him if he is seasoned in the ways of camps," Malabestia said sardonically, "if he is woman-broken."

"I have not yet found one to please me," the boy said in a pitiful attempt at dignity.

"Pah!" Malabestia spat on the ground before them. "Tell him what happens to a man's privates when he is too proud to let his posterity be given generously away. Tell him how the parts are soured and sickened and of the gathered poisons weakening his whole body."

Lord Robert had never heard the idea expressed so, but he knew that while Holy Church extolled the virtues of virginity in man and woman, some believed a yet more ancient doctrine and were afraid of the rigors of virtue; yet the boy was young and timid, and Lord Robert was angered at the ugliness that Malabestia had shown to so untried a manhood. "Come," he said to his son, "we will meet your mother now and tell her of your progress." He looked at Malabestia coldly, but he knew that he could not violate the hospitality of his house. It was another law to weigh upon him.

As the two turned from the Baron, he caught his squire by the sleeve and, pulling him, struck him hard in the face and sent him sprawling to the ground, his nose streaming blood. As the enraged Lord Robert went hand to knife, instinctively, Malabestia smiled that charming, ingratiating smile of his and said, "Like a loving father, I discipline my squires. When will the boy learn to set a saddle straight? Be well improved," he said pleasantly to the boy, sitting, blood-spattered in the dusty courtyard. It was the Baron's right to discipline a wayward squire. Another justice unjust that hung about Lord Robert's neck and weighed on him.

The affair had, indeed, been well attended and the onlookers turned, snickering behind their hands at the joke. Keeping himself hard in check, Lord Robert permitted his son to get up by himself and they walked, not arm in arm as they had before, into the hall. As they went alone through the corridors to where the mother was, Lord Robert said softly, "What do you do that he shames us so?"

"Nothing," Richard answered. "Perhaps I did not tighten the saddle girth enough this morning. It does not matter at any rate. What I did was nothing, but I knew that his action would be so."

"You knew?"

"Not when it would come, or why, but I knew that he would strike me here, at your house, before you and your guests."

"But why?"

"Because it amuses him."

And Lord Robert knew then that what had changed in his son was everything he had wished to save. He had been saddened by the boy's knowledge of this baron's twisted pleasures, but what made him sick with grief was the tone in which the boy had spoken: as if they could be virtues.

The feasters crowded the hall and they rose and fell like waves, going outside to relieve themselves in the court or greeting old friends while the meal was in progress. The De Kuckneys had impoverished their holdings to provide these wines, meads, pigs, chickens and fish, and they wanted their hospitality to be without stint or limit. Drunk men fell away from the table into the straw, or forward on their arms to sleep. Words flew and challenges to drinking or fighting passed across the trestle tables.

On an evening when it was an insult not to be at least red-faced with drink, one man alone sat staring darkly ahead from his high place at the table. Baron Malabestia, unsmiling and still as wood. He had drunk toasts with long draughts and passed the flagons, but it was known—and people crossed themselves when they spoke of it—that drink did strange things to him. Others were drawn out of themselves, more human in their cups. They fought or swore or made love wildly. Some fell down swinishly and snored in the filthy straw, but Malabestia put by what was human and recognizable in himself and became like the statue of a man. Drunk, he had been known to kill—not lumbering or bearlike, aroused by an insult or in a flash of jealousy, regretted later. He seemed to become ice; his knife quick, his murdering wordless, and no change in his eyes after it had been done.

When the rowdy jokes had all been told again and the old war songs rehearsed, Malabestia rose slowly, almost as if in a dream and stood, waiting, in his place. Some saw him and stopped, brought short by his very difference from themselves, with their rumpled clothes and greasy, red, smiling faces. Some, who did not see, were silenced by Richard, who knew by now when to break the squire's code of courtesy. The Baron's voice was dry as he spoke. His voice was soft and mocking and the tones of it made them all lean forward and strain to listen, sobering them.

"I am tired of strangling. . . . How much more will we have to give in taxes before we will be wrung dry? God's wounds! I would like to give my recompenses with a hard sword!" Recompense to whom? some of them wondered in their drink-hazed way. They were sworn to the King, and they received all of their power and protection from him. The King was Law and Order; he was invested with God's oils of anointing—yet he was a man after all. They shifted on their benches, not wishing to be made to think just now, when the evening had been so merry, yet wondering, too, at the back of their minds, what was to be done, and remembering their old wealth, their old honor, their old uncontested sway over their lands.

"The demands cannot be met," Malabestia continued, "and so we see the Jews—King's Persons—who help the King to rob us blind! If we could act together, we Northmen, and show the King together that we will not be dishonored and impoverished, who knows but that our cause may triumph? William of Scotland and his wild-looking madmen have harassed us with their skirmishes. We must end this harassment so that the King will have no excuse for what his hands are doing in our coffers. After William, the King will have us to deal with!"

"Souls," Lord Robert shouted into the momentary silence of shock and wonder, "you have run dry at that far table! Wine, then, for those men! Drink deeply, good friends!" He had seen the dangerous looks, the beginning of treason, and he had thought: Let them hate whom they will, but not in my hall, even before the rivalries of the field. Then he went to see what more he could put out before them. As he left the hall, he saw Richard coming toward him, feigning another purpose, and he ducked around the corner of the entryway until his son should come.

Richard was very much the squire now. "My Lord, the Malabestia is offended."

"I know it, Squire," the father said formally, "but I will not have this hall bloodied with arguments even before the tourney. There are friends here, and loyal subjects and some will take it amiss if anything be said against the King."

"I know that, Sir, but maybe you can soften the Baron."

"Perhaps . . . perhaps . . . I will tell him——"

"My Lord"—it was his son interrupting him, not the Baron's squire—"not with words. He is a prideful man. I have eaten gravel for speaking anything to him when he was put out."

"You forget, my son, that I am not the man's squire."

"Even so, my Lord." (Again the quiet servant.)

"Well, what would you have me do? I see him sitting there like a bow drawn back for shooting, and those about him look to see if their weapons are handy."

"Play a joke on me, my Lord, a joke with something of cruelty in it. It will turn him away from his dark mood because he enjoys to see pain sometimes on people's faces."

"Let be what must be, in his own strange life," Lord Robert said, shuddering, "but my son in my house . . ." and then he remembered the vanished sweetness of the young boy who stood, almost a man, before him. His son was better off than he; Richard was well woven into the cloth and he did not fight. A wife would not despise him for his cowardice. "Go, then, my son," he said, "and set your joke, and I will help you." He knew that to save the situation from becoming a battleground of treasons, he must sacrifice some bit more of the dignity of his name and house. Others could sacrifice their sons to this end without a qualm, but Lord Robert had been struck by a love which was greater than pride, and so the sacrifices were deep blows to him and the familiar agony of them was old in his bones.

The following day was clear and cold—perfect weather. The lords rose, and finding provision short, rode out to see what their luck and skill could get. It was remembered (not without a few discreet smiles behind the hand) that the Baron Malabestia was in charge of the Royal Pantry, an ancient family privilege that gave a little comfortable yearly rent for the lord or knight who would keep his larder well provisioned if and when the King should be at York. The family had also kept the King's duckpond, and the present Malabestia held also the title of King's Justice, which offered a fine revenue in bribes alone. It was smiled about that the man who had shaken the tree of justice for silver a hundred times would never have thought to shake a duck from the duck-pond for a party of hunters.

It had been a rare battle. The field was littered with bits of clothing, broken shafts, horse trappings, blood-stained bits better not identified and six dead birds.

Richard de Kuckney looked at the wreckage and tried to remember what had become of five of Malabestia's small arms, which he had been left behind to try to find. The riot had started simply, in the usual way, man against man with two chances to unhorse, one going and one back. Someone had felt unfairly treated—it was forgotten who; there were no rules set for what constituted a foul blow, or whether being dragged fairly came under the definition of being unhorsed. Words flew—someone shot an arrow into the young Percy's horse—and the battle had begun in earnest.

Richard had fixed Malabestia's seat, weaponed him, and along with all the rest, the Baron had ridden to the rescue of his honor. Soon everyone had been unhorsed and was fighting like a drunken blacksmith. As the violence of the fight increased and grudges mounted, the few rules of chivalrous combat still remaining were thrown to the winds and men went at each other cursing and clubbing wildly.

After a long time, when the eyes saw colored flashes and the heads rang, the fighting slowed to a heavy, deliberate slamming of weapon against weapon. The young Tampton retired from the fight with an ear off; another was knocked senseless. On and on it went, for the pride of these men was to be able to say that their fight had gone on for a full day.

Finally the sun began to catch its yellowing rays in the trees and the stumbling gentry limped back to the castle and the soothing mead. Richard stayed to seek among the real remains of what would become, with the passage of the night, a thrilling moment of brave and noble men. He found one spear half-buried in the ground, another broken against a rock. Someone had lost a chain mace and it lay evil on the ground, a tool for a wild man, not for a baron, really, not for a Christian gentleman who was only playing at death. He collected the spears and the heads of two others that he found. These would be rehafted and used again for practice. Weapons were hard to come by and had to be saved.

Richard straightened and looked at the darkening sky. Already it was cool and sweet. He tasted the autumn flavor of the world. The evening was lowering with a kind of wistful resignation, and with it was the close quiet of the first star in the sky, for it was still softly light. He tried to harden himself to the beauty gathering like a gift for him in the darkening circle of the fields and trees. He knew that beneath still stars this night, the humble evening prayers would be said together, victor and victim, and they would praise a God of peace, to be forgotten yet again in the hot battle-fury of bright noontime, tomorrow. He shut his mind against the paradox and locked it with a ringing curse into the luminous night and went to his duties.

"THREE times in the herbs and three times in three waters in which gold marks have been boiled, and space it to run three days." Bett was trying to bleach her hair. In the years before it had not mattered somehow that the brown, lanky strands got in her face and were full of sleeping-straw and were greasy; but one day, a week before, she had gone to Abram with a message and he had looked up from his scribe's place at the market booth and had jested, "Ah, the lily-rose of Northstreet; the very rose, well manured and full of thorns!" It had cut her to the heart. Why not before, all the years of his scholarly ridicule, and should she not, by now, be used to it and laugh?

Suddenly she seemed to be two people, one of them always looking at the other and noting the greasy hair and the thin face. Already she had consulted a wise woman and had done what was to be done to make a plain girl beautiful. The woman had told her that she must needs have the proper eyes in which to mirror her beauty, and Abram's were always so cold for her that she knew, even while she rubbed on unguents and chanted spells that it was in vain. And yet he was unmarried, free, a loose thread in the cloth that the housewife in her yearned to set aright.

Time after time, Baruch the Father would come to the table and speak of matches with this and that one: the hundred marks here, the prestige there, the honor-laden name somewhere else;

and every time Abram swung free, away from his father and mother, away from all the phantom parents whose mirages hung over the table with tense faces, tight smiles and unmarried daughters. Many Jews betrothed their children when they were yet infants, hoping to assure something at least for them in time to come. The father would tell his daughter, hardly in shoes, that should he die, her future family would take her for their own and raise her with the love that they would give a daughter. So with the son also, yet Baruch had waited and Abram was grown almost to his teens before his father had sifted the prospects for the most advantageous match. He was always afraid of parents who might lose their money or have a scandal destroy their names, and so Abram grew tired of the wrangling and the guessing and the pulling out of gossip and scandal, and as soon as he was master of himself, declared to his astonished relatives that he would not marry at all. . . . Bett was free to dream, and of late she had dreamt much of him.

When she was finished with her medications and spells, she strolled casually by the side of the house where the windowpanes, pride of the family, would reflect—must reflect—the brilliant, shining aureole of her hair. Passing by them she caught sight, in one, of the top of her head. It was Bett's head and Bett's hair—and no different. She did not know whether to curse or cry and stood dumbly for a minute between the windows and between alternatives. He saw her there, just standing.

"Is it not time for something to do, or are we grand enough to have a servant who can have her servant scrape the trenchers?" Then he saw that her dumbness was not idle, but despairing. Two great, slow tears had moved into her eyes and had overswelled them and spilled out, only touching her cheeks for a moment before they dropped from her face to her stained skirt. "What is the matter?" he said embarrassedly, his discomfort making his voice hard.

She broke from her mold and began to run to the door of the house and then turned, as if she could not decide where to take herself in tears. Abram grabbed her arm. The contact, the hard hold of his hand, seemed to break her and she burst into loud sobs. Now he held a sobbing, boneless creature who swayed and stumbled before him. "Be quiet!" he barked, as red as fire. "They will think I have beaten you!" The sobs grew louder. To silence her he pushed her mouth hard against his shoulder and, quite suddenly, her whole body was close to him and the new-washed hair

73

very soft against his face. To push her away, he knew, would start the sobs again, and so he stood with her in that strange position, one arm supporting her awkwardly by her arm, the other holding her head to his shoulder. Had it not been so stiff and self-conscious, it would have been an embrace. As the moments wore on and her sobbing lessened, he found that his arm was going to sleep. When he moved to ease it, she turned out of his hold and away, miserably, with her head down.

"I was going to tell you something," she said, "something important, and with your silly jesting you have made me forget what it is."

It was the innocence in her which had always touched him, so that he joked with her and was free and happy in her presence. Now it was frightening him. The same purity, the same truth in her, which had gladdened him and made him unafraid to share his reality with her, was now somehow a subtle and potent weapon against him. His mind picked about among the new feelings. "What is it?"

She was gasping, trying to control herself.

"What is it? Something that my mother said, or my father?"

She took a deep breath and her face changed and quietened. He felt a great reprieve.

"No . . . no," she said, thinking again and remembering out of her confusion what it was that she had meant to tell him. It was a grave thing, a thing not to be taken lightly.

She had been at Welbeck on the customary Advent pilgrimage of her family, and had seen Brother Simon, her cousin. "My cousin asked me about you. He asked me who knew of your visits to Welbeck and I said that you have not hidden it, surely— I doubted not that the whole of York knew."

Abram was not sure what this was prelude to. There was nothing in the Law against having a Christian for an acquaintance, but friendship was something not quite countenanced by the people; it was something for gossip, a pursing of lips. Friendship with a monk, too, was something indeed. "What does this mean?" he said, wondering if she was trying to help or being maliceful.

Bett made a gesture with her hands, laughing the old quip she had heard years ago, standing behind Baruch at table: "What misery does a Jew have in the winter?"

Abram was puzzled remembering it: Muteness, for his hands are in his sleeves. "What is this—what are you saying to me?" he said louder, and looking hard at her.

"Be mute then, be the Jew in winter. We are afraid for you, for there are men against you who are more powerful than you know, and who hate you and who are violent and waiting for revenge."

"If you mean that Brother Lewis, I know that he——"

"Listen, Master," she said excitedly, "he is one family with the Malabestia!"

"Girl, we have a long history behind us, and it includes dealings with the kings of many nations, the greatest ever known in the world. We have seen Rome, Tyre and Babylon. We do not quail before some second-rung Yorkshire barons. You know that when my father will, he has the King's ear. Is he going to tremble, or is his son going to tremble at some mad monk at Welbeck? That wild one bothers Simon more than me. Simon has to live with him and his ravings." Now they were apart in his mind, she a Christian and he a Jew, and for some reason, unknown to him, he was defending his might to her.

"Master, Master! Is a candle a conflagration? Is a straw a harvest? No, you say; but when the candle is part of all candles, and has the power to call them to flame for its cause, when the straw is a part of all straws and has the power to gather them in its sheaf, then is the candle to be as feared as the conflagration, then is the straw to be given heed to. So must you now . . ." She stopped, amazed. The thick peasant hands had been wild before her, drawing, illustrating, extending her point, and the flow of the language had been (God forgive me, Christ forgive me) Jewish; rabbinical, even. The hard Anglo-saxon that she spoke, warrior's language, square and absolute and loyal, had been given a changed inflection in her mouth. An older rhythm had entered in and she felt herself possessed. She pulled away from him and in the air between them she drew a cross. "Perhaps I, too, must be afraid," she said.

He had been frightened and embarrassed by her tears, but this sudden look that he had been given inside of her made him even more frightened, and he turned and walked past the side of the house into the street. Bett stood alone where he had left her and her face in the failing light was the face of her father before the baron: a servant's face, blank, thick and stupid, studied in seeing nothing, in having no life of its own. It was the first lesson that a peasant child learned and Bett had not forgotten it. Behind such a face the soul could go where it would, and the terrible shocks of life and death in the soul could be hidden from the eyes of all others. Abram, for all her years of love for him, for all the confidences which she had kept, for all the subtleties by which she had shown him that she understood and loved him, did not know her, did not trust her, did not perceive her. She had as well been a horse or a cow. Cowlike, she bent her head and went toward the house.

The evening began to chill and the first star was hung out coldly, although it was not yet twilight. Abram wondered, as he stood in the street, if there were perhaps enemies in these corners who waited to destroy his people and himself through the friendship that he had with the young Brother. Down the street came Josce, singing, thinking of the betrothal feast of his tiny son just two years old. He laughed as he saw the young man standing before his house, looking at the early star.

"Oh, Abram, Abram," he said, "is not the world beautiful!"

"The world is a trap, a hook, a perverse cloth into which we are woven against our wills!"

"My boy, a philosopher is just a common man with a larger flea in his shirt." He winked at Abram. "And if he is eating a bad nut at the same time, he becomes a theologian."

"Josce, you are positively irreverent."

"Well, it is true. When the soup is cold, then man looks out from his deceiving body to ponder the infinite. It is good to question, but have your mother see to your linen also."

"How I envy the Christians sometimes," Abram said. "The solitude."

"We, of all people," Josce answered him, "we, of all people know what it is to be only a small self against history, the night and the stars. The Singer calls out from the Congregation to the Lord. Was there ever so lonely a voice lifted in petition?"

"Josce"—and Abram was serious—"were you always a financier? Was Elias always a rabbi, confirmed in his habits and with a Denicosa to do his washing? Have you always been just so?"

Josce laughed, long and loud, and it was this that told Abram what he wished.

"Oh, Abram . . . I had thought that you at least saw me behind my disguise, that I am no older than you. My vision of myself is still that of a young man, but it is nature's joke that a few grey hairs can make a self-deceiver of me." Josce thought quickly to himself: How can I convince him? I am grey enough to be

76

wise, but I am not wise. Maybe Yomtob could tell this burning questioner. The stupid and the frightened old forget their pasts, but Yomtob remembers and forgives. How young he is—this Abram; all that strength and eagerness spending out on the wind. . . .

Then he turned his thoughts about and found something, and said, "I have a favor to ask of you this night. You know that our youngest boy is Anna's favorite son. The older ones are something of strangers, being to school and away from her breast so long. This one—well, he came very hard to her; she almost died in bearing him and soon she will be saying good-bye to him in yet another ceremony, but these are things important to women. The bride's family is come up from Norwich to make the party and Anna will have nothing to do. Stay by her, Abram, and bear yourself merrily, and try to win her from wistfulness, for at every ceremony of children, the Time-hunter shoots another arrow and shreds her youth. Anna loves you like a son— she took you from your mother, you know—and when you are jolly, you can charm a stone to laughter and make English wine taste like French. Will you do me this favor?"

"I cannot be jolly to order," said Abram sulkily.

"My God! Hold your gaiety in as high a regard as you do your solemnity, for you are always ready to whip out that uncertain virtue as fast as a mother her first-born babe. You are proud enough of that to hang it like a pearl about your neck. Be a little more the spendthrift with your joy, and a little stingier with your hard mercy."

"I will try, if you wish it," Abram answered glumly.

"I wish it," said Josce, laughing.

And Bett watched by the side of the house as they talked. She was looking at where Abram's steps had fallen so that she might measure her own to fall upon them. It was a foolish thing, but it gave her a strange comfort—at least this act of love could not be taken away from her. Let him laugh, then; she would time her steps to his, her breath to his, and the turning of her head, and the holding of her eyes. All of the young apprentices and journeymen, the servants and messengers in York had looked, and some had looked to marry, but never, with any of them, had walking been so, had breath or eyes been so.

The first wound of love is not the deepest one perhaps, but it falls on a new heart, not scarred over with the realities of other meetings and partings, and its pain is great. The body would be martyred now, and the soul to great mysterious tests, to make all worthy for a great day of recognition, which for Bett would only come in the dream.

IT began to snow. The cold, sharpened on the stone of the walls of Welbeck, drew a keener edge across **11** the cheeks of the Brothers at their work, but in this gracious month, it seemed a blessing, for the time that was coming was a holy time, Christ's time, when the story was tender and secret. His triumph over the grave, His Cavalry, His Agony were great and miraculous things; but that He was born and was a little baby, rocked in innocent happiness in the arms of a radiant Mother, was a shared and human joy to which all men had hold, and the Brothers walked more softly during that wondrous month. Also, there was the purity of the snow.

It fell quietly on the tree limbs and banked in the corners of the court.

The Brothers had cleaned the chapel until it shone, and they brought out the best candles and the finest of their simple cloths. Had their Order been a more flamboyant one, there would have been somewhat of a pageant, or at least a presentation of three of the Brothers costumed as Wise Men, but the Praemonstratensians were austere and new, and their reform was still a proud part of their charter; and besides, as Brother Lewis, standing in the court, caustically remarked, no one at Welbeck was wise enough to take the part of a Wise Man, and certainly there were not three.

"Surely there is one, Brother Lewis," said Brother Unam Sanctam. "You mean to exclude yourself from those unfit, do you not?"

"Shut your mouth, you dog dropping!"

Two of the Brothers standing near started for their knives, but then, remembering what they were trying to become, let their hands fall. Violence was common at Welbeck, as it was everywhere, and many of the Brothers, being French, were a little proud to say, "We are hot-blooded, we French—men of passion!"

Brother Lewis walked away. In spite of everything that was here to remind him of man's humility before God, he could not forget that he had been a knight, and the son of a baron, while Brother Unam Sanctam, that miscast ploughboy, was neither French nor of high breeding.

Brother Lewis looked out from the little covered walkway and watched the snow. The hill seemed to move under it as a man moves with pleasure under his blanket to get the more perfect position for his sleep. Abbot Adam appeared from the portal and came to where he stood.

"He came from Her as white, as perfect and as quietly as the snow from heaven, little Jesus from Our Lady's womb."

"Yes," murmured the Brother, a little hard in the mouth because of the chill, "into a world cold with hate and scorn. Christmas is a day only. The others are all Good Friday."

"You talk like an Englishman," said Abbot Adam, trapped into preference. "Can you not enjoy this little season? Brother Norbert goes about his duties singing and Brother Simon smiles over his penances in this glad time."

"He would smile over anything, that calf, including those devil Jews of his."

They looked for a while, each one through his different-seeing eyes, and between them the white flakes fell. It came to Brother Lewis as he looked at the snow, that his piety had never been like others'. When he loved, he had trembled and fainted with love. When he repented, he had broken the scourges on his body; when he hated, he had gone shod and dressed in hate—he ate it and wore it to the eyes. As a man he knew that he loved the Church, but God was strange and far away. Brother Lewis put repentance in place of love, and laid it hard upon himself almost to death. And the hate also remained. Here now were these Jews, and the preachers cried against them that they were evil and heathen. His breeding cried against them and his hatred, for they had killed the Jesus that he could not love; yet when he had answered them in wrath, righteous wrath, the Church had said, "*Caritas, Humilitas*—try to bring them to conversion!"

"They have killed Our Lord," he said aloud to Abbot Adam, "yet *Caritas* and *Humilitas*. I cannot dance, as most men can, now on one foot, now on the other, nor can I leave off hating at the end of a sermon!"

"Brother, I have no love for the Jews either, but in your willful singleness of hate, you go beyond the Will of God."

79

"We spend all our strength trying to convert these hardened souls!"

"That is not for us here to think of," Abbot Adam said gently. "Leave the crusading to the Orders dedicated to it. We have to find our own nobility, Brother Lewis." The Abbot knew that this monastery, this Order were not the ones which the burning-eyed Brother would have chosen, had he had the choice. His family had been patrons of the Praemonstratensians because they could not afford to found and support Houses which took as much to sustain them as did the Black Brothers, who were the "intellectuals" of Holy Church. These White Monks were good, modest, hard-working farmers with not a roll of parchment in a year, and no gold, no lapis luzuli or Italian-French carvings for their chapels. They had given, that provincial family of petty nobles, their firebrand son, also as a donation, and where he might have been a glory to the Black Brothers, he was a source of anguish to the White. The Abbot touched the shoulder of his misplaced son and said gently, "Do not hate, Brother Lewis—hate dries the soul, hate destroys humility, it destroys Grace and Holy Joy. Let your humblings be joyful ones. I have seen you impatient with some of our less clever, less learned Brothers, but we are intent on Heaven here, not earth, and your earthly knowledge may be barrier, not blessing."

"It is not always to be as it has been," Brother Lewis said with the hard edge of his resentment. "My family wants me someday to be an abbot . . . then I shall choose."

"I call that speech a fault!" Abbot Adam said, angered at the Brother perhaps more than he was wont. "At Chapter meeting I will call upon you to lay bare your prideful soul before your Brothers, and we may all thank God that election of abbots comes from Premontre, not here. I know you to be quite devout, and yet you have moments of such stupendous vanity as this. . . . I wonder what five years in our Order has done for you."

The bell began to ring. Its sound was blanketed in the falling snow, but to Brother Lewis it was like a wound that throbbed with every beat. Abbot Adam folded his arms beneath his cape that was drawn close about him. His face was blank; he had pulled his soul away from behind his eyes, praying. The pain of the bell increased in Brother Lewis's head until it drove out all thought with its beating. He walked blindly into the snow. It seemed to burn into his skin the way the banging bells burned into his brain. The swaying line of Brothers filed before him, bound for the chapel. The line of them comforted him in his snow-bell madness. They were no longer single well-known Brothers, too well known, every inflection of voice, every way of scratching, every noise that whistled breath, every grunt in sleep too maddeningly well known. Now, they were anonymously holy in their walk toward God, like the rhythmic saints on the walls of cathedrals and in the books of the Black Monks. So did he join them, masking his face in unseeing, while the bell beat inside him.

They went into the chapel and to their knees on the simple stone. The chapel was bare; nothing was there that might take the eye from the necessary vision of God. No one stirred. He could almost hear the snow falling outside, so quiet were they in their places. The *conversi*, lay Brothers, entered in their soiled, dark clothes. They knelt heavily, dumbly, like patient animals. They seemed to know neither hope nor regret. The Brothers began to chant, and Brother Lewis could see the back of Simon twitching with pleasure as the notes rose in the cold stone room. He would remember to mention it in Chapter as a sin against the flesh— lustful pleasure . . . serpentlike in its coming, so subtle to the soul; and soon the body and mind were eaten up in lust. Brother Lewis sang, lifting his voice and lowering as the chant rose and fell, but some part of him was not with his devotions, was wandering away in a sickness, a bitter, brown ocean, far from God.

They went to their rest after prayers, for this was a special time when ordinary work and daily pursuits were suspended. They would be awake in their chapel splendid with candles to celebrate the Birthday of the Lord in the secret, mysterious time of midnight. Now they would be given a brief sleep, to lie in Christ before the birth of Christ, and then to rise, fresh as if they, too, were newborn; lace not too tightly this night, their penitential ropes, and go to His birthday full of Holy Joy. With all his Brothers, yet alone, Brother Lewis Fauconbridge lay at rest. . . .

It came to him very slowly, his dream of the long valley. It began when he was falling asleep, thinking of high mountains and a bright wind playing about him, and as he climbed up and up toward the summit, he became a dreaming climber. When he reached the height, he looked out over a long valley, unbelievably green and beautiful. The flowers of this valley gave off a rich fragrance, and the sun was warm on his whole body. Suddenly it came to him that this was his valley, his very own beautiful place of peace and happiness. He ran down the mountain toward it, and as he went closer, the trees became more spreading and inviting and the grass softer, and the scent of the flowers yet more enticing. At the end of the valley stood a beautiful little pavilion, and at the end of the pavilion a white castle. Over the heavy portals hung a shield; it was his own family crest; not fire-soot stained or full of bird-droppings, but fresh and clean, with colors brighter than he had ever seen before.

He ran on in the bright wind and sun, and then, tiring a bit, he slowed, enchanted with all the beauty around him. He stopped, and as he looked—as he looked at his castle, his pavilion, his valley, his sky—the whole scene began to change as if it were false from the beginning, and a trap to delude him. The foliage rolled itself up, the trees collapsed, the green grass in great strips sheared back and left a barren earth beneath. The castle fell to pieces like a stick house and disappeared into a smoky, gaping hole. He was caught in the meshes of this dream like a green fly in the spider's web, and he followed himself in the dream where he had to go, as if almost by habit, on a road destined from the beginning; and he watched himself with an odd, knowing terror. The outward sticks and surfaces of his life were pulling away and leaving bare the horror beneath. Under his name and his house was Death. He was dead; he was in Hell.

For all his eye's reach, only bare brown earth and a great hole and a stinking brown smell from the hole. He was held in his tracks by the monstrousness of the deceit. Then, from the hole, the head emerged; a tremendous spider with tremulous hairy legs. It strained and stretched out of the hole. It came to him. He was revolted and horrified, and he stood staring at it. Closer and closer . . . and he screamed, "Christ! Christ!" The spider laughed, and he saw that it was the Devil. The body of the spider began to work and the web began to spin. He became caught in the sticky threads. It was all around him; he could not breathe or struggle. The spider kept weaving and weaving until only his eyes were free. Then the spider came close, very close, with his own awful eyes, until the two were only a small space apart, eye to eye. The terrible eyes, the age-old eyes, the familiar eyes, and Brother Lewis woke, sweat-soaked and screaming, "Christ! Christ! I am strangled!"

They walked to the chapel singing. The sky was luminous and clear, as it can be on those perfect winter nights of snow and a white moon. The stars were close, and the chant, warm with the voices of men, rose in the clear night with the whitened breaths from their mouths. The door of the chapel was open, the lay Brothers already inside, and the candles not yet lit. All was dark except for the cold moon shining through the middle window of the clerestory. They sang to welcome the Baby Jesus, never forgetting in their glad hearts that the world into which the eternal Spirit perpetually comes is poor and cold, and often evil. At the hour of midnight, a breathless silence, for a long minute, and then, candle by candle, light slowly came to bring the world to Him and Him to the world, and it was possible to see the chapel walls around them once more, and the neighbor's face in the flickering light.

Brother Lewis's hair was still wet from his terror, and his mind still in the coils of the dream. He sang like a sleepwalker, heaving his voice up and down with great effort. He wanted only to be dumb; to rest. His body ached from the strangling, and as his mind groped between the strands of the web, he heard himself whisper, "The Devil was choking my life like a Jew! Deceivers! Deceivers!" and he found himself weeping with rage. Finally the brief service was over. The most faithful stayed to continue a mystical vigil over the cradle until dawn, but this time, Brother Lewis could not bring himself to stay. As he rose from his knees, he became very dizzy, and he steadied himself against a heavy pier. Something brushed by his hand. He jumped away, but the thing was on his hand. Large and soft it was; the light was dim, and in a daze he brought his hand close to his eyes to see. It was a spider. He began to tremble. His eyes sought the familiar things around him, but the spider began to grow in his eye and in his mind. The chapel slid away from him and became the brown earth of his dream. He looked for a weapon to fight with, but the thing had grown larger than he now, larger than the chapel, larger than the night of stars. It was enveloping him. He seemed to be coming apart, whirling around in the darkness without anything solid under his feet. He heard sounds, jumbled and confused. He seemed to be pinned to the ground of Hell, pulsing blood, and above him was the horror, larger than the world. When the wildness passed, he opened his eyes and saw the Brothers looking down upon him as he lay writhing on the cold floor of the chapel. There was worry on their faces, and he heard himself scream, "Christ! Christ! The Devil is a Jew!"

"WHAT does it look like?"

   "What should it look like?"

12 ⟨⟩

   "Does it hurt?"

   "No more than any tender thing."

   "How much is gone?"

   "Not enough so that I lose my charm."

   "You are jesting with me, Abram."

   "I am sorry, Simon; it was a harmless joke."

   "The fact of it makes me shiver, and yet you bear it with great bravery."

   "It is not martyrdom at all, I swear not."

   "Show it to me. . . . By Saint Norbert! It looks undressed, like a skinned rabbit. I would not be circumcised for the world!"

   "The Bible decrees it for us, and the ritual of a son is one of the greatest joys of our faith. If the house in which I keep my seeds seems to you poorly protected, you may take it up with the Lord himself."

They stood on either side of the sheepfold. Abram closed the fold of his garment, suddenly embarrassed. "I wear this decree because I am a Jew," he added, "if only a puzzled Jew."

"Oh!" said Simon, and his face was gleaming. "Have you come, then, to believe in our Blessed Savior and our Church?"

Poor Simon—he spoke as if it were as easy as sneezing, and yet perhaps he was wiser than he knew, Abram thought. A pious man can be pious in any tongue to any God, and the questioners send their doubts to all the gods and rage against the nights of every land and every people. The young Brother was looking at him so sorrowfully now; Abram realized with a little pang that probably his friend had been waiting for him to show interest in becoming a Christian. He said slowly, "I am sorry that I did not make myself clear before—that I am interested in your faith, but only as one who will never come to have it."

The young monk blushed with embarrassment and looked at the ground. After a time he looked back at his friend. "I suppose that I really do not wish you to change—I enjoy you as you are —the worse is my fault. I have become more interested than I should be in the life of your people. But——"

"But?"

"But there is a question. Does the testament, your Testament not say, 'Thou shalt not lend upon interest'?"

Abram wondered who had come to them at the House, what count or baron, who had told them how much he owed beyond the debt itself. "Who told you about this?" he asked a little sardonically.

Simon answered with that very open expression which he had, "Old Percy was here and he spoke of it."

The look of candor faded, and Abram knew that the young Brother was guarding the rest of what had been said and what came then into his mind. Old Percy would have cursed the Jews and their ways and Simon would wish to shield his friend from those words. Somehow that very transparent attempt at protection hurt Abram even more than the cruelties would have. It was Old Percy who was making him so sensitive to slights. Old Percy had contracted his debts from Abram's father, and Baruch had said of the Baron, "Let him sweat, then. Rates rise with humors, and he is desperate. We are not thanked anyway; why not be cursed for double the interest?" Baruch had cheated the Baron Percy; Abram was almost sure of it. A desperate man got short shrift at the stone mansion with the glass windows.

"Listen," he said, "the quotation is in your Testament also. Read Deuteronomy again and see for yourself what it says. If you are really interested in money-lending and why we are encouraged so, even as it is against your laws, I can bring men here who know more of it. My father can come, or Josce. . . ."

"Will he not mock me? So many of your people are mocking."

"To a great man, a question is not an attack. Josce will come if you desire it."

"No . . . no . . . I would be afraid—I mean—can you say nothing of it yourself?"

Abram was afraid to speak. He had criticized the justifications so many times in his father, sitting silently at the table while Baruch excused his exorbitance in usury with the tiresome eternal excuses. That the reasons were true was no comfort to Abram, for he had seen them twisted and used to apologize for every bitter squeezing and excess that his father and others employed. He pushed words out, hoping somehow that they would be different from his father's.

"You know, Simon, that in the same passages we have often read different meanings as our faiths dictated. We consider usury to be excessive interest, interest to stifle life, or to break a man's will, and that we oppose. To lend for interest is commerce; without it there would be no trade at all—no Spanish leather or German metal."

"But the lords are losing their lands, and the churches wait like sand birds where the sea encroaches on their nests."

"Simon . . . Can a man keep his gate open and not expect his horses to run out? These barons owe. If they want their sons to be barons, and their bishops to be friendly, they must pay. The Pope demands of bishops not only kisses, but coins, and it is he, not we, who wills it so."

"But some of your lenders *do* charge exorbitantly . . ." Simon said, wondering how it was that a baron who was born so, had to pay to stay so. "Surely that act will bring a man to anger. Why do your men not stop this if they love honesty?"

"All debts are not the same. Some are held for long, and some only for a short time, and some are great and some are given to men of bad reputation . . ." The words were the same that Baruch had used to defend himself when he had defeated, almost to ruin, one of the proudest families in Yorkshire. They were bitter in Abram's mouth. "Simon"—the same words . . . the same words—"we have no protection from King or Church, and one villain costs all the honest men the money of his defection. It must also have occurred to you that the barons willingly desire these debts, or they would not contract them."

"Oh, Abram!"—and the Brother threw up his arms—"does a man weigh tragedy before it falls upon his shoulders? Here are men who say, 'Next year my rye fields will come full to harvest, and I may slaughter my sheep then and bring them all to market, and such and such a honey that my wife keeps will be ready.' This he says, promising himself he will pay. Then comes the harvest time: the rye is blighted and the honey is scanty. What is to be paid? The man has worked just as hard for famine as he has for plenty, and yet he still has plenty's heavy debt. The year turns, and the weights of the debt turn with it, and the interest doubles the bonds of need. The will sickens. . . . *Pecuniam non dabis. . . .*"

"Very well—the earth is to blame—or God is to blame, vulnerable believer that you are. I say that the man is to blame. If he is to be a baron, he must dance to baron's music, even though the tune be set too fast for his feet. The suffering is his own doing. The barons and King make the laws; they bid and forbid; they

86

come to the Jews and then they curse; they exploit us and then they cry for sympathy. Well, if your Popes are so honorable and so holy, tell them to stop borrowing on the relics!"

"Christ defend us! You leave the Popes out of this! The Pope is holy, not a worldly pagan, intent on the silver in his hand!" Their voices were getting louder.

"He bought his throne, you fool!"

"No! no! That office comes from God!"

"Hah! A few more marks and he could have his bishops say he *was* God!"

"The Pope is our Holy Father! His office is given from Our Lord Himself!"

"The Pope's throne is Jewish money! He buys power, and once on his Jewish throne, he quotes Deuteronomy. It is the Bible, so nobody listens!"

"Blasphemer! Heretic!"

"Fool, blind fool!"

They faced each other half in anger and half in fear, because the tone of their voices had been so much more bitter than the words which they had said. They were going, each of them, into a childhood where they had been told: "Fear the Christians," or "Fear the Jews," and their rational words, the words of young men, had held echoes of older days before reasons had to be given.

"We are not leeches!" Abram shouted. His hand caught Simon on the shoulder, and as if body contact exploded a terrible light in him, he shook with rage. Simon's hand came up to protect himself. He knocked Abram's hand away, stumbling a little forward as he did so, and their rage suddenly erupted in their heads in cascades of lights and darknesses. They fought like wild dogs, growling, cursing and spitting; arms flung up, grunts, hard thudding blows, but neither of them felt anything of pain—they did not even know that they struck or were struck. Deaf, dumb and blind in their senses, they were brilliantly alive with anger. From somewhere blood came, and hitting was wet then, and slippery. They began to weary, and when they were tired, they began to shamble, catching their hands in one another's clothing. On and on they fought, and finally Simon, with a great surge of effort, freed himself and, standing a little back, prepared his body for a great, deadening swing of his big, bony fist. Balanced, he poised himself for a second, and then swung the great circle. Nothing. The weight of his rage turned him around with it, and in his blindness and dizzy loss of balance, he lost his opponent. He turned again to seek, but then sight and mind came again, and there was Abram, streaming with blood. They stood grunting heavily, staring at one another with weighted eyes. Abram reached out a hand; Simon came toward it, but he was not steady, and they fell together on one another and then to the ground. The sight of blood became sickening to them, and they lay unable to speak, and the grass reddened from their faces.

"Oh . . . Simon . . . I am frightened!"

"So am I. It is almost time for Vespers. I must get back to be at the chapel." He wiped his lip and brought a streak of blood along on his hand. He looked at it and then his face stilled. "What shall I tell them—I could be expelled from the Order."

"Before that," Abram said huskily, "I will lay all the fault on myself—say that I attacked you. Can you get up?" A minute later they were helping each other to tie up the laces in clothes, straighten robes and stop the welling blood from their noses and lips.

"Climb over the stile. We will use a bit of the water put out for the sheep. Perhaps there will not even be enough damage to bring questions."

But Simon was too optimistic; the fight had been passionate and both looked bruised and cut. As they finished washing in the warm, thick water, the excitement of their fight suddenly left them completely, and a great weariness came on, and they fell again in the soft, trampled earth of the sheepfold. Abram's purse had been torn from his waist in the fight, and had been kicked away. It lay near them and Simon reached out and dragged it to him and handed it heavily to Abram. From it, Abram took a battered bit of barley cake and a piece of yellow cheese. He threw the cheese to Simon. Under the monk's garment, his own purse still hung. He took a knife from it, and cut the cheese in half. He threw half of it to Abram and caught the bread that was thrown to him, cut and threw half of that back also. They sat, holding the food, and a sense of ceremony hung over it.

"This food has been polluted now, by the lights of my faith," Abram said slowly, "but I do not consider it unclean."

"I, too, am forbidden," Simon said quietly. He kept his head down.

"Come." They moved closer together against the heavy weight which they saw marshaled against them—the worlds of Christians and of Jews, for once with jaws set against the same enemy. They seemed to hear the muttering of patriarchs in a never-ending line that reached to Abraham, shocked, in the imagining. The two boys stood and recited, each in his own dead language, the blessings that the separate Fathers had created to thank God for man and for the food that man ate. When they had finished, and brushed the mud and crumbs from their clothes, and lightning had still not struck, they stood together, ceremonially, in friendship. The bells for Vespers began, slowly, to fill the moors. The world's allotted time was over; now it was God's time, a separate God. Brother Simon saw a small, quick figure coming toward them. Brother Unam Sanctam (so named by having placed his finger, eyes shut, on the Credo by those words) came rapidly toward the sheepfolds.

"Brother!" He sent the word like a thrown knife. "What are you doing there? Holy Jesus defend us!" He had seen the high, reddened cheek, the puffy jaw.

"Brother Unam . . . I fell from the stile while trying to balance upon the rail. This fellow here"—he could not dare to say "friend" nor yet want to say "Jew"—"laughed at my attempt, followed me, and met the same fate." Abram stood back and watched Simon, amused at the lameness of his excuse, yet frightened for him. Who knew what these fearsome men would do to any one of them who goes beyond the lighted rooms of what is acceptable and into the twilight of Will-do and Wish-to-do? Brother Unam Sanctam was anything but convinced by the halting Simon. They spoke a few words more, testing each other with eyes and voices, and then the two monks left and re-entered their day, and Abram began to walk back to his horse and the road to York. In his mind he saw Yomtob's face, reflecting a strange look, part pity, part amusement, and in his mind's ear he heard Yomtob say, "Now your life will become valuable to you, now that you have a friend. You will conserve yourself for his sake. Anyone can be perfectly honest in Hell—there is nothing to lose there, but you have changed worlds and become human. Welcome, conserver."

Abram kicked a stone in the road, and the stone went into his mind and hit the Rabbi. "Keep quiet!" he said to the stone and to the Rabbi. "Stay out of this!" But they did not fade.

IN his confusion at his rebellious son, Baruch
conquered his shame and went to Rabbi Yomtob 13
for advice. The Rabbi was sitting before Elias's
fire, tending it gently, putting in the cut turf bit
by small bit, for his host was poor. Even after all the times that
he had seen the great scholar do such things, Baruch felt the
shock of the unseemliness and then the anger for it. "You could
have stayed with us," he said, turning his hand against his mouth.
"You could have come and been with us and been warm and joyful." He was stuttering with embarrassment. "You—you—we
have maids to do such things!"

Yomtob looked up at him and said shamefacedly, "Alas—I am a
poor host to you. Sit down, good Baruch. May I fetch you a
warming drink?"

Baruch was always shaken off balance with this man, and he
needed his help, so he said quickly, "No, no, Rabbi—but I have
come to ask you for your advice."

"My friend, are you a wise man or a fool?" the Rabbi asked
gently, and to Baruch's look of amazement, "Before you ask, then,
remember that it is written: Only the wise come for advice; others
only to have their opinions confirmed."

"I have come for advice, Rabbi. I am beyond my own answering."

Baruch poured out his troubles with his son, and Yomtob saw
as he spoke that there was love in the man for his boy and suffering because of it. The Rabbi answered, speaking of Abram's gifts
as a person and perhaps also as an artist, and Baruch answered that
Abram was a failure as the son of a wealthy man whose power at
picking a bride would have given him the best and most beautiful. Even now, the unseeing son walked in a sea of woman's whispers as in a forest of trees. He did not fit; he was not usual. Sometimes the father would shout at him, "You are mad!" and Abram
would cry back, "The world is mad—I am sane!" and Baruch
would lift his hands and cry that it did not matter which way the
balance rested as long as Abram and the world were at such a
difference. As he finished, the financier shook his hands, muttering, "Insolent! insolent!"

"Good Baruch—you love your son. I see that this is so more fully than I had thought. I think that you love him in his madness, his feelingness, his truth, his wit that is sometimes about to verge on wisdom. Why will you not, then, let him see this love? He feels he has your power and prestige for enemy and not for friend, and is it not a redoubtable enemy that could be a mighty friend?"

"But he scorns me, he rebuffs my offers."

"Offer for him, not selfishly. Offer purely, not withholding, and you may see that he is not so adamant."

"Simply out of love?"

"Simply out of love."

Baruch was filled with wonder at the easiness of it. His face stilled and his hands relaxed, and Yomtob would have warned him that an easy truth is a fool's paradise, but Josce came in with Elias at that moment and something had to be said for this case and for that, and before there was time for cautions, Baruch was gone, carrying a radiance and eagerness on his face like a bridegroom. Yomtob had not given enough weight to the difference in how he said his words and how Baruch heard them. When Yomtob had spoken of love and of giving, he had wished Baruch to hear something that would echo: companionship, wisdom, compassion, time. But Baruch had listened in another language.

Baruch had taken fire, suddenly, with a ruby. He had seen this jewel, a single great knob of blazing red in the handle of a baron's sword. It was the great treasure of the house and was the most famous single jewel in the three counties. Now the wise Rabbi had told him to show his love to his son, and so Baruch would show it. He would get for Abram the baronial ruby to wear. He would make possible that impossible gift and present it, saying, "By this I show my love." It occurred to Baruch that he had given Abram many splendid clothes, but that he had given them always with a certain drawing back, or with a criticism, "You are a shame to me in that old jacket—take this fine cloak." And once he had said, watching his son flinch as if struck, "Wear this gold ring or men will think that we are losing fortunes instead of making them." He had not meant to say these things—it was only that he could not give gracefully and openly; the words stuck in his throat, and forcing them, they came out so differently from what he had meant to say that sometimes he himself was surprised. This time the words would come right. The ruby would be only for Abram. For himself there would be something to call on his whole skill, like what the Christians called a quest. He would present his victory to his beloved boy with the sweetness that he had always felt and never displayed. Baruch looked up into the clear winter morning and suddenly it seemed to him that the world—the whole world—was beautiful.

As he sat in the small scribe's stall, writing on a bill of sale, Abram suddenly thought of Bett. In the middle of a word almost, by some trick that the mind plays, jumping from thought to thought, he remembered how she had cried, and then how she was avoiding him and how she now could no longer tolerate the friendly ridicule that had been their play for years. Abram laughed often, but it was bitter laughter at a world where pretensions never quite decently covered the vanity or stupidity that his neighbors wanted to hide. Only with Bett had his laughter been hearty and sometimes even honest. First he had thought that this was so because she was a servant and of no account; then because she was young and an innocent like Simon. It came to him now that it was that she, like Simon, was good. As he thought of this goodness, warmed by it until he found his client at the booth smiling back at his little half-smile, it came to him that perhaps she loved him and was anguished because of it. In the middle of the noisy, bustling place, he felt a sort of silence come over him, and everything was stopped there as if it were waiting for him to say something to his own mind. He shook himself and went on with his work, but the silence seemed to deepen in him through the morning and he knew that no work would be able to forestall the meeting between himself and his silence.

In the afternoon he could not go to the synagogue for his usual time of copying. He was halfway there when he knew he could not bear the small, close balcony, so he turned and fled across the Ouse Bridge and over the Foss Bridge and out beyond the gate of the city to where the low hills waited brown and desolate for the end of winter. He wanted not to think, and so he went to the moors where the long broomstraw bent against the wind. He wanted to study its compliance, all the million backs bent without struggle or longing. Abram hungered for obedience, the natural, glad acceptance which he saw being lived all about him, but which seemed to be forever alien to him. He felt himself alone, always the single stalk upthrust against the wind. He looked toward the bridge and saw people hurrying about. Someone was going neither to right nor left, but was following the same path he had taken, and the path led up into the hills. He watched it, angry but fascinated that his freedom and the sovereignty of his loneliness had been challenged.

The figure turned around the clump of bushes at the bottom of the hill and reappeared where the path led upward. He saw that it was a woman, and then that it was Bett. For the self, the almost-woman he was joyful, almost eager, but for the servant of his father's wishes he ground his teeth in annoyance. What message now, from the demanding Baruch, or had the Rabbi not seen that he was ahead in his work and sent out for him to catch him up and bind him on the wheel of hours and days?

"What is it?" he called harshly.

She looked up and saw him and there was surprise on her face. He saw then that she had not expected to meet him there and he became embarrassed. She was coming toward him as if she were living out a punishment, too shy to turn and go back to the city and yet aware that the solitude she sought on the moors was no longer there for her. She came to where he was, climbing the last little way as if working, using the heavy, flat step of the servant.

"I came to gather broomstraw," she said. (Why is it such a sin to be alone? Where else can I dream or weep without being judged?)

"I did not know that they grew well here." (I never knew that she came here to get the solitude that I need also. Why did I never know that before?)

"Yes. . . . Master Baruch said that when my morning's work is done I may spend some time in reading. He seems glad that I should desire to learn my letters."

And Abram suddenly remembered the half-attended discussion a few years ago about Bett's reading. He had not even realized that she had done this. He remembered also Baruch's telling the friends and Synagogue officials how he was now, indeed, the first in all of England who had for servant one who read and wrote. It had been for a show, an aggrandizement of Baruch's fortune, but she had accepted the advantage mutely; servant-wise in the closed face and unresisting eyes.

"And do you read, then?" he asked.

"Only in Hebrew," she said, "but I have just this year begun my Latin. Father Odo at Allhallows is letting me sit outside the door of his classroom."

Abram was surprised that he had never really seen this girl be-

93

fore, the quiet, usual worker in his house. He had loved her as a light in his dark house, but now he was seeing her as an almost-woman, a particular, single, special almost-woman. She had fallen against his body, weeping, with her pale face and her newly washed hair, and there had been something in him more than embarrassment or pity. It was not that familiar lust he felt sometimes, seeing a woman in the street or coming upon the lovers under the Foss Bridge on summer nights, but this lank-haired kitchen girl, with her hard hands and mannish Anglo-Saxon speech, somehow gave forth a spirit from herself that was so fragile and tender that he was afraid he might destroy it even with a touch of his hand. How can a hardwood stick burn in a fire and leave so fine an ash? So Abram, seeing her newly, and in full light, and suddenly beautiful to him, leaned forward and would have kissed her except that a single hair that had been swept into her face by the wind moved as if with his breath. With its trembling, he knew how truly fragile she was—a servant, a Christian in a Jewish house, untitled, not of the manor nor of the city—belonging nowhere. Because he was beginning to open to the knowledge of his love, he turned and left her and went to his work.

Baruch spent the afternoon at York Cathedral, sitting in the damp cellar among the chests of records and bills of debt whose rolls were stored in large locked wooden chests. The Dean and Treasurer had unlocked the chest of debts for the usual fee, but Baruch had given them a liberal extra for his privacy and so they had wandered off and left him with the dusty rolls and familiar signatures and formal, heavy words. Somewhere, on one of these rolls, perhaps even on one which he himself had written, was a word, waiting for his eye. A word is a thought and that thought connects with others which, by its waking, are themselves awakened. Baruch had tried many times to show this to his uncaring son—the thrill of creating almost from one single word or number, the destiny of many men.

With this family of petty northern gentry he had never had many dealings. Who were their neighbors? What was their land? What were their revenues? What was their weakness? It all fitted by indirection, by the eye-wink and the gesture, not written but only guessed at, behind the unrelated doings of other families. After a time the picture began to form for him. Why could Abram not see the thrill of it? . . . A monastery in debt, having lost its largest patron. Suddenly the money is repaid and the pa-

cronage restored. The same happening seven years later. Again
five years later and yet again in four years—not steadily well or
ill then, these patrons, but with a sporadic wealth that drained
down and was suddenly replenished. From where? Horses? No—
the land was too poor. Sheep? Sheep bring a modest income and
steady—not sporadic or great. Seven years, five and four. In 1171
they had sold some land and did not need (or get) their advantage. There was choice here then. In those years, those certain
years the family had said, 'Now we will go and get this wealth.'
They had no rich contacts or King's preferments. Mines? Treasures? What was their land? A rocky, wind-beaten place with a
small, dark river, and another tract, richer and wooded where the
river had become great with tributaries. Why were they gone so
long the first time? They should have come to the wealth in 1178
or so? Well, '78 was a bad year for everyone. The storms had
stopped all the shipping in the . . .! There in the cathedral vault,
sitting among the rolls, Baruch burst into a cascade of laughter.
His word, his picture was all before him. Smuggling! The new
demands of the time for money and taxes that bit hard, the increase of pious commitments to religious Houses; a first small attempt at smuggling, perhaps even by accident; the money becoming a necessity; the fear and guilt; the pledge to do it only in the
direst need; the slowly closing gaps between the years of "direst
need"; the old father needing to make excuses; the son needing
none; the pride of family; the great, dark ruby . . . Baruch saw
the land and the people and the nation and the way a man would
look, rubbing the suspicion from his gold and trying to pull it
from his face. He saw it in a great tapestry, all at once and complete.

What an adventure! Now he had sighted both the hunter and
the hunted, and now he could join the chase and divert it to
his own good fortune. By blackmail or bribe or simply piracy,
Baruch could enter this game, and at the end of it, Abram, his
son, would wear the famous ruby for the whole world to see.
This was the hunt for a landless Jew who could not cry a fox
on his ancestral heath; but this was an adventuring a thousand
times more thrilling than the chase or the tourney, and Baruch
sucked the dank air of the vault into his lungs with all the gusto
of men in brisk November woods when the cry is up.

THE messages of glory for Christ's Crusade
seemed to fall like water on thirsty land. As naturally and hungrily as earth drinks rain, the people were drawn up in its great plan with a wave
of happiness. As the words caught from mouth to mouth, it
seemed as if even the stones in the road heard and rejoiced. There
was a gaiety in York that was more than spring, a sort of love per-
vading the city. In June, a community of lax and dissolute nuns
voluntarily amended themselves and did a public penance with
such dedication and sweetness that the whole city wept and
prayed with them. The hundreds of crimes of violence and anger
slowed to a bare few and the alms flowed into the holy places as
never before. Abram thought he had never heard so much singing in the streets. At the market place it seemed that there was
promptness and courtesy where there had been impatience and
laziness, and he noticed that the dealers were giving true weight
—giving it out of gladness somehow and not through fear of the
constables. Perhaps . . . one could almost think that the world
was getting better. Even Baruch was full of light, and when he
asked Abram about his work it was with interest.

"Of course my work on the Holy Books goes ahead as usual, and
there are the tracts and dissertations also as usual, but the Mayor
has asked about for a new code of the laws of the city and the
shire, and I have put my name up for the scribe. That way I
would have the chance—and maybe an extra page at the end of
a section—to do some drawing."

He had expected anger or at least scorn, but Baruch only smiled
and answered, "Well begun! If you get the work, I myself will
buy an extra page of parchment to give over to your heart's desire."

The words were as new to Abram's ears as if they had been
spoken from some lost tongue. His eyes widened and he gaped,
but Baruch, leaving for a business journey smiled and was gone
with his quick blessing, almost gaily, Abram thought. As he left
Northstreet for the market place, still shaking his head with wonder, he saw a sick beggar fallen at the road's edge. So many wanderers ended their lives thus—a whole group of landless men

which this time could not place in its web of custom and law—that men soon became inured and hardened to the sight of dying beggars in the road and passed them by until their stench forced a shallow and riteless burial outside the walls. To Abram's great amazement, a group of passers-by stopped and knelt down by the fallen man and picked him up, sharing his weight among them and moving off toward St. Mary's Convent where there was a hospital and almshouse. Abram rubbed his chin and murmured, "Will even I someday praise God for man? Something is with us—something good and noble at last is with us!"

Baruch sat his horse's jog with his body lulled and heavy and his mind full of plans and excitement. It would not do to give his noble smugglers up to law. Law would leave them hung up for the ravens and their lands, ruby and all, in escheat to the King. What was needed was a way to close off the stream of their wealth, or to prevent their getting to it and yet not to alert the forces of the King's greed. Henry was a good king; honorable and just, but the need for gold was pressing him close also, and these preachers rattling for Crusade forgot to speak about the thousands of marks of money that a king would need to raise an earthly siege for paradise. What preachers did not utter, Jews and kings and nobles all wondered on. Baruch set himself to think what could be done to dry the stream that fed the tree that held his son's red apple. It came again, suddenly and full of humor, so that he laughed aloud and spoke it wittily into the wind, "Behold, a saying: What is the sinner's curse? . . . A righteous enemy." Somehow, it must come to pass that one who did not love this nobleman would be at his table and in his courtyard watching—someone to whom intrigue was not so strange a thing. The root was growing toward the Baron Malabestia, who might know only enough to know later that he had been used. Baruch picked up his horse's reins and kicked the jog into a purposeful long stride.

"Master Abram," Bett said, "what has come upon the world at last is Christ. Let me take you to the gathering on Foss Isle so that you may see for yourself what is really changing us all."

"I have heard sermons enough," he said a little tartly. "False Christians kill Christ every day and curse us for killing Him once a year. What more is there to know?"

"The new part of it—something splendid and good," she said.

She took his hand to pull him, as she had done for so long a time. She had used to lead him home from his studies so that he would not dawdle on the way, the tiny, grave servant girl tugging at her master's dreaming boy as one might pull a calf. Now she realized yet again with the shock of time that it was a man's hand that she held and she dropped it like a burning thing. She wanted to laugh, but somehow crying was nearer, so she turned her head and began to walk the way to Foss Isle and he followed.

The camp was as motley as any he had ever seen at Thursday Market or the fair. Old men, beggars and children, the wheat of any gathering were in great numbers; but here and there, hungry, eager journeymen-craftsmen moved, and now and then a fur collar was seen, and priests and monks and nuns walked about in groups of good size. A man greeted the two of them happily, seeing that they were strangers, but he made no remark about the presence of a Jew, and Abram realized that this was a different gathering of people from any he had ever seen. They all had a look of happiness, of eager joy, but there were no mimes or tumblers here, performing, as there were at the fairs, and this was not the joy of spectacle or of action, of drinking or of selling or buying or gambling or drabbing. The man saw Abram's studious face alert and his eyes going over the encampment and he told them how many there had been to hear one or another of the angelic preachers, and of those who had come just to meet and to hope and share the joy of their great and common dream—a new world of beauty, purity and sacrifice. Just the day before, three pickpockets had come to the encampment, where they had hoped to steal a fortune from the rapt listeners to the preacher. Much to their surprise, the outcome was that they themselves confessed and were penitent and the crowd, which would normally have beaten them to a flicker of life, cheered itself hoarse and wept with them, sharing a triumph that seemed to be greater than all of the separate sharers in it.

"Is there to be preaching today?" Abram asked.

The man shifted his weight, unnerved perhaps, at Abram's evenness of tone. "No, but before sunset we shall be hearing anecdotes from those who themselves have been—or who have spoken to those who have been—in Our Dear Lord's Holy Land. Each truth will be a morsel to feed us and keep our souls alive until The Day—The Day."

98

Abram wanted to ask what day it was, half thinking of his own people who waited also for "A Day," but Bett's finger made a little flick against his leg and he was silent. The man bid them go and learn among the people and be refreshed with the great new drink of love and piety that was flowing here.

They went together, and in that place, as seemed as natural as Eden to them, hand in hand and then arm in arm. They met Father Odo, who smiled at them, calling them "my beloved" and the three of them stood, enjoying the slow dying of light in the east, and Father Odo, almost weeping with the desire for God's earthly kingdom, said gently to them, "Not by the sword or the rack— not by fire or force shall it be shown, but by Love. The day is dawning . . . at long last. I feel so strongly in myself that the day is dawning when all men will truly be brothers."

Looking out over the calm water, over the bent heads of men and women kneeling for the prayers of the day's end, Abram's eyes turned up to the transparent sky, without a single cloud's argument or paradox; and he almost believed the gentle, skinny old-soldier wreck of a priest, that perhaps this age, this lifetime was to be different from all the others. Unwilling to kneel and too modest to stand, Abram compromised into a kind of clumsy squat at Bett's side, and when the prayers were ended, lifted her from her knees, cracking in his own joints and laughing a little at it, that this human condition was so subtle as to fling its jokes at a man in the midst of the sweetest and deepest moments of his life. She turned to him, aglow with the happening, and hand upon hand, arm through arm and breast to breast they went, strong together in a long embrace, which had not been chosen or decided, but which simply was, like the breath in or the sigh out.

They left Foss Isle hand in hand, like two sleepwalkers whose steps are part of their dreaming. But as a man may hear in his dream the ringing of Lauds in the real world and wake, so they woke as they reached the end of the bridge, dropping their linked hands slowly, stepping past their fallen smiles, outdistancing their light. They came to Baruch's stone mansion singly and silently: master and servant. Nor did they look one glance at one another.

The afternoon moved forward, the Watches came on, the moon rose. Across the street from Baruch's great house, Josce and Anna lay together in their own mansion, watching the cold moon through the glass panes of their windows. The night was clear and cold and they whispered lest they should wake the little ones sleeping in the other room.

"Sometimes I believe that their hunger for this Crusade has really made men better," Josce was saying, reporting to Anna the taking of the beggar from the street, which he also had seen. "And people are also paying their debts."

"Strong cause to say so on just this night," his wife said, moving closer to him in the darkness. "You remember the servant girl we had some four years ago? That one your boy called 'snowflake' because she had a tread like Goliath. She was married the year before the exiles came from France and I had forgotten her these four years. She came back today, and came in and put a silver mark on the table and a small iron pot also and said, 'Mistress, these things I took when I was in your service.' And before I could regain myself enough to question her, she was up and gone away. Even our own people seem to be touched a little by the angels."

"Even so?" Josce said, because he knew she had more to say and he was kind.

She took a breath.

"Look at Baruch. Before he went away on this latest trip of his, he seemed to have lost much of his haughtiness and distance, even with his family. I used to be ashamed for Rana in public, to hear him make his jests and have his rages. Now he seems changed and I am glad for all of us."

Josce looked at the clear moon, like a liquid in the bottles of their windowpanes, and because he loved her, he allowed himself the freedom of his skepticism: "I am glad for York and for the world that they are taken by this love—for they are in love with this Crusade, and for a time it seems to make them good. Yet I have my misgivings, and about the change in our Baruch, many misgivings."

He wanted to tell her what he had told Rabbi Yomtob, that he and Baruch were great dangers to the community. Baruch, perhaps more proudly and resplendently and dishonestly, but her well-loved Josce, because his vital work was seen as an evil thing. He and Baruch and the many others all over Christendom, Christians and Jews, would finance this love's pilgrimage, this Crusade, and would know, even as they did so, that the trade routes, business contacts and arrangements—the nurture of lifetimes—would be destroyed, and that they and their money would be hated almost as much as the Saracen himself. He looked over at her, lying on her back and watching, straight and girlish as she was sometimes, and he became suddenly shy to speak of the deepest of his fears—that the Crusade might be somehow a part of their destruction; and so he said, "Baruch is gay because he is like a knight fighting a well-trained enemy. He is in challenge. He will win and I am afraid of what he will win. I have heard rumors of his inquiries concerning a great family to the south, and although I do not know just how or why, I think that he is planning some course for them that may come against us all."

"Baruch's adventures! Let Rabbi Yomtob handle them. If he goes too far, there are the Community Laws, after all."

"We are Baruch, each one, in the minds of all men about us in the Christian world. We adhere, like bricks in a wall. Lady—my own Anna—a thousand bricks in a wall. Take one from the middle of that wall. Is it weakened only one one-thousandth?"

He shifted beneath the heavy, lined blanket because what he would say had been on his mind for a while, with its knob of worry lying motionless and heavy. "I too must leave again. There is business in London."

Josce went often; Jewish business made the world its market place, but Anna had been afraid since the exiles from France had shaken the tree of York's security, and a feeling of loneliness welled up in her in anticipation. She touched his arm and said, "Of all the trips you have made—even those so far away—I never resented your absences or feared—until now. Call it superstition, but give me no more the Bill of Divorcement."

"You are a strange wife for a financier," he said, but he was humbled a little, knowing how precious he was to her and how unable to make himself immortal for her sake. Jews who traveled gave their wives a document of divorce before they left in case they did not return. The wives would be free to wed again, free from their husbands' debts or the special taxes of the King against their business. "The Jewry knows that we are one flesh, and that it is but a paper, but merely form . . ."

"It is as if we tempt the Angel of Death with that paper," she said. "With the coming of the French I looked about at the world and it frightens me suddenly. I cannot bear to tempt death when we are so happy. Please, husband, if you must, give the thing to someone to hold, but do not give it to me to see again." They quietened for a while, listening to the sound of breathing in the next room. "Are *they* not reason enough to be frightened and careful?" she asked.

"The Rabbi is frightened," he said. "Sorrow has made a terror in his blood for everyone's safety. We have four, and you worry for ten."

She laughed her delicious laugh, and then she quietened and said, "Ah, yes, but they marry."

"Why think of betrothal feasts?" he teased her. "Think of after the betrothal feasts," and they laughed.

"Do you remember Abram there?" She clucked wonderingly. "Was he not like one visited by an antic spirit? He followed me about like a dog after a rabbit, and cracking the most amazing jokes one after another, with the oddest look on his face!"

"Believe me, dear love, that look was what he conceived of as sympathy, the joke's wit, the tracking companionship."

"Good souls!" she swore. "Why should he take more growing up than anyone else's child?"

"Poor Abram—he resents his knowledge that he could be wise and perhaps great, even; and that to be great means to suffer more and to give more—and all the time he wants only to disappear into the wall and be left alone, but Light keeps shining upon him."

"I am glad that our son is not like him."

"There is a little bit of us which are parents to Abram."

"Parents—was it not only yesterday when we were at a betrothal feast of our own and at a wedding of our own? I was so proud . . ." she said quietly, "so proud. You had a grand, sweet look about you, and your father was weeping and my father was weeping exceedingly."

They saw for a moment the passing of themselves from bridegroom and bride to givers of the ceremonies. The old weeping father would this time be Josce; the woman in the balcony weeping would this time be Anna, weeping with the brutality of time.

She felt it even more keenly than he and said, "I am old now, my love, and my own dear sons push me to Jewbury and its graves."

"Behold then, I shall make you young again. I will re-create what God has created." He laughed. "I will re-bless what He has blessed."

"My husband, I am tired."

"I will awaken you, and after you have been awakened, then you shall sleep."

"My husband, I am not ready."

"You will be ready, madam, in youth or out."

"My husband, in this phase of the moon, the time is not right to love carelessly. I shall conceive."

"Madam, your excuses are as grass before my scythe. Do you know why I have glass put to the windows? Is it because I am vain and nothing more? No. The cold moon glides across the rushes of the floor and there you lie asleep. It touches your coiled hair, gleaming; it takes your eyelids and your cheeks, and when I wake at night while you still sleep, I see what the moon does to my world at night, and I am glad to have glass windows."

He put his hand on her smooth black hair, that lay turned under her coif. It was slightly warm and slightly scented. He breathed long and slow, and began then to brush her face over with his lips. " 'Let him kiss me with the kisses of his mouth: for thy love is better than wine.' "

She moved a little away from him and then a little toward him. "Love, there is not time . . ."

" 'The voice of my beloved, knocking. Open to me, my sister, my love, my dove, my undefiled . . .' "

"Tomorrow is to be an early day . . ."

" 'Oh, my dove . . . cleft of the rock . . . covert of the cliff . . .' " And he began to brush her body with his fingers, as a blind man learns, even though he had the moon to make his seeing glorious. The sounds of the sleepers about them faded, while yet the two became more and more alive. Their hearts beat until they seemed to clatter against each other; their lips, eyes, hands, sought one another. They waited, growing closer and closer, growing greater and greater, moving slowly and yet faster until the beauty of ascent was too much to bear and Josce sobbed at her from his body, "My cup! Oh, my cup! Oh, my chalice!"

Then they sank away from each other and they smiled in the darkness, for they could now hear the sleepers stirring in the straw. They smiled also because these sleepers were their fruits, and it seemed to them that, in being in each other's arms in the enchanted night of the moon, they saw both backward and forward, both the creation and the time before the creation, and that in this they were as gods.

WHEN Abram won the commission to collect, bind and inscribe the City Codex, he ran first to the river to where Bett was washing clothes. He told her quickly, stooping among the women and the piled knots of wrung-out cloths. He was as eager as a boy, full of plans for the drawing of his page, for the decorations of the random borders and the style of script. In the midst of describing the latest idea, he saw his mother coming down toward them with some forgotten thing. He went white and began to stammer, and the feet said run and stay at the same time, so that he almost tripped and fell where he stood. About Bett the old hardness gathered, so that where Abram stumbled and stuttered, she stood dumb and rigid. Rana came and gave Bett the garment, reading their faces and their eyes and their feet. She had noticed the strangeness between them, thinking at first that it was merely each one growing into the place in the world which had been fashioned even before birth, but of late she had scented the shift of the wind with them and she did not like it.

As spring caught into summer, Rana's whips of worry had been beating her through day and night. A thousand subtle signs she perceived, and it angered her that a Christian servant should place her loving so high. She began to carp against Bett for little things not properly done; she hoped to make the girl ugly with criticism and unpleasant work. She had all but forgotten, in her haste for her son, the years of her home that she had shared with this peasant. As summer turned to autumn and the Jewish houses hummed with holiday preparations, Rana became more and more frantic at the weight of Abram's silence. She was fighting with shadows, with ghosts. She would tell Baruch some crumb of fear, and he would ask her what she had seen or heard, and she was struck all the more mute for having nothing to give him. With the world saddening toward winter, Rana found her unsubstantial ghosts weighing upon her like a thousand years. Josce's wife, Anna, was with child and there was extra to do. With presaging every sign for confidence and helping to spin and weave new swaddling bands and birthing cloths, Rana had less time than she wished to watch the coming and going of her son.

For Abram, great spaces of days and nights had become the size of a page of the Codex Eboracum, The Code of York. Baruch had promised him his page, and Abram had set it aside already in the parchment sheaf. He had begun transcribing the shreds and shards of laws struck and amended a dozen times, putting small human figures here and there, bending to shape the chapter letters as the Irish did them, but these were fragments of a thing and only practice. On his page there was to be a drawing of a part of life, a little fragment of the world. Over and over again he drew and planned, sketching his plans on the flat rocks by the riverbank, on the table, on the floor, idly, on the wall beside the fireplace; rubbing them out and beginning again. Was it to be what he loved of the world? What he hated? Women at the well, gossiping? The Jewish streets? The Christian streets? The comedy and tragedy of the market place? They rose and fell before him in his dreams until it was all he could do to keep up with his work on the Law of his own people, sit in his stall at the market place and do the routine inscription of the Code. As the weeks passed and the Mayor and Bailiff saw the first sheets of his copy, they spoke with glowing praise of the fidelity of his pen. For the first time in his life, except before Brother Simon, Abram answered with pride in his tradition, explaining that Jewish scribes spent their lives continuing in perfection the copying of the Law and the Prophets, in which the error of a single word or letter was intolerable. He was happy to stand in the honest sun of the Mayor's hall window and listen to himself say so to the highest men of the city, and as the weeks went by, he noticed a new deference being paid him. The common town-men would not know of his work on the Codex, so he concluded that the officials must have let it be known that he was giving their book a copy of the highest art and quality. He began to realize, dimly, what adulation and pomp meant to his father, and this new understanding pleased him also.

Through the summer and into the autumn, Baruch was on many trips through the shire, and Abram heard here and there that he was doing business or making plans with powerful friends of Baron Malabestia. Josce could not bear to tell the young man, so deluded by the joy of seeing himself in a first full light of his own, and not merely as the penumbra of Baruch's substantial shadow, that the deference was not to him but to Baruch because of his seeming friendship with the most powerful men in the shire.

"It should be his," Josce told Yomtob as they sat at the doorstep and watched the autumn evening life of York about them. "If there was a justice in flattery, Abram would be given 'sir' and 'so please you' for his own sake. I have seen the first few pages of that Code and it is a masterpiece of collection and copying and the script is a work of art."

"Christendom's languages equivocate with us," Yomtob said. "Landless men with no estates have no right to 'sir' at all. Indeed, there is no name and no word of true respect for our Abrams. The man who calls a Jew 'sir' in this land is a toady and a hypocrite and I wonder how hard the waking will be for Abram when it comes to him? He already half-knows that the deference is lies; how bitter to learn, alas, that they are not even lies for him, but for Baruch."

The scholar stretched his legs out long before him and raised his arms high, breathing in a long, full breath. Overhead the gulls dipped and soared, and Yomtob stretched as if he would continue upward and upward and fly at last. "How beautiful they are!" he said as he watched them catch the sudden upwind and stretch into it. "How good and glad and beautiful they are!"

As autumn brought fever to the trees, the hunger for crusade came ever more sharply. "Brothers in Christ's True Word—His land has been captured, His tomb desecrated, His name slandered! Shall we crucify Him again?!"

A thousand voices shouted "No" in the churches, and ten thousand at the corners of streets, and a hundred thousand in the brisk cold of autumn fields and woods. To go forth and rescue Christ's land became a pledge for the sinner repentant, a promise for the dying, a vow for the holy, a wish for children and a blinding dream for the defeated in life and for the hands that yearned to sift mysterious gold and capture the prize of spices. Even the royal sons stopped their intrigues over the head of sad King Henry for a moment, to hear Archbishop Baldwin call a seven-year truce in order that the combatants might turn their arms to the aid of Christ. The impatient Prince Richard was in France, planning the downfall of his aging father. To be impatient is the prerogative of youth and Richard was in his late twenties. The mind of the young man became fired with zeal when he heard the preaching. How splendid it would be to ride with the clean air blowing the banners, with songs and swords and the certainty of salvation; to go to war not with a greasy rabble of camp-cursing soldiers, but with souls pledged to purity, chanting the wonderful psalms of victory; to call one's self and one's army The Armies of the Living God. For the commons, following their lords as foot soldiers, it was a call to great glory. For the Jews it was an omen of terror; a great black vulture lowering over their heads. The blood is up; the Christians are flying their banners—God help us! Once more it would be worth a man's life to cross into Egypt or to go by land to Byzantium, and the rare coin would be rarer yet. A wit said, "York is full of the sounds of the grinding of metal, and Northstreet York of the grinding of teeth."

Bett stood in the background and listened to the talk about the table. She had heard often of the Moslems and their dealings from her master and his friends and guests. The Moslems were like Jews in many ways, Bett knew, and in her mind she had a picture of these people, none of whom she had ever seen. They were knowledgeable, witty, vain—a sophisticated but vigorous people, who looked down on the Christians as barbarians with poor science and worse medicine, whose culture produced illiterate peasant-nobles as tied to their lands and little interests as their workers were. This picture had come to her over the years of listening. Now she knew also the picture which was being painted in the churches by the ardent proponents of Crusade. The Saracens in that telling were cunning, bestial and depraved. The Devil gave them their strength in arms while strengthening also their powers of perversion and sin. They were hideous, they were cruel and evil . . . they were fascinating.

While the Jews spoke and wondered, and the traveling priests used all their ardor, fervor and eloquence, the lords and ladies of each earldom, shire, barony and fief, large or small, planned and counted the harvests, men-at-arms, gold and honor for a thrust at new glory. Baron Malabestia looked from his window at children playing Christian-and-paynim in the courtyard and cursed that he would have to miss this greatest of all opportunities. He had never liked being King's Justice and now the tedious hereditary honor was standing in the way of wealth, fame and adventure. He would have to shake his treasure from trees closer to home. Lord Robert de Kuckney was planning to go, partly to regain the family name, partly to still the scorn of his wife, a woman bred to mother wars and married to a coward. He would take his son with him, and he saw in all the things he hated, at least that saving light—a chance to grow and share with his boy the trials and the joys that might bring them back to one another.

A few, only a few remembered the land, and how it was in hard times, without men about. New songs would have to be written, not only about the glory of bright blood and banners, but also of the rapine of unguarded estates, of harvests rotting in the fields while people starved, lacking the hands to gather it in; of debts and famines, of the bleakness of lonely winters, of the never-to-return. . . .

All through the glowing year, dreams haunted the nights of men. Were there not also spiritual benefits to be won from visiting the Holy Land? A holy battle would confer upon a Christian man great merit, and would stand strong to speak for him in his defense when the Awful Day of Wrath and Judgment came—when Heaven and earth were moved.

The whole shire, the whole nation, the whole world was beginning to thrum with the movements of life, but to Anna, the wife of Josce, it was all but a mirror and a background of the life within her. Through the October autumn she moved heavily and sleepily and she prayed often. In December, she bore her child. It began with an awakening in the fore-dawn light to the familiar energy of her first grip of labor, and in spite of fear of the poisonous night air, she threw a shawl about herself and went out into her little herb garden in back of the house. She wanted to be alone, secret with her event for a little time, before the coming-in of all the neighbors, friends and relatives to join in the ritual wailing that would accompany each twist of her body in birthing, for is it not written: In sorrow shalt thou bring forth children? She sighed quietly, "Oh God, only let Thy will be life."

And so it was. When the reachings of the womb became brighter and longer, Anna took fine, deep breaths. The women came. They came with stools and shawls and bits of bread in case they got hungry; gay with gossip they came, because everyone must bear a child, but here is a time to talk together, and let the men wait for their dinners this day; this is our important work and great, the only great event for a woman beside that of dying. Anna lay in the manner prescribed by ancient law and the custom of a distant place and another time. Clean straw had been brought and made into a little bed, which was strewn with sweet herbs and important medicines: mustard to take the heat from the open womb, hyssop for purity, water and oil and salt to anoint the child and bowls in which to bleed the mother afterwards. The women greeted Anna, patted her hands, rubbed her feet and then settled down to their important task: gossip. They plucked the rumors one by one, turned them over in their hands and popped them into their mouths like chestnuts, delicately. As the other neighbors came, the women made place for them on the newly gathered straw until there was a crowd of women and young children eating and laughing. Every so often they would comfort the mother as the womb urged on to birth, and soon the time drew near.

With a rush of memory as the pains came hard, Anna thought of her poor neighbor, Chere, and the hours of screaming as the womb closed upon the body of the child. Then, with the burning urgency of her own body in its spasm of pushing against the life within her, she thought of the others: Alis the Blonde, with the racking fever; Reine, with wash on wash of dark blood; Mira, Sara, Lisa; how many, many of them! The sound in her ears was all condolence, but she drew no comfort from it. They were comforting like the blind beggars at Foss's side as they comforted each other: the way is easy, brother; we shall walk it together. Her ease came only as the spasms eased. The women finished the long, wailing moan and fell to their gossiping again.

"Rana," one of them was saying, "your little serving-maid has blossomed out this year; quite a flowering."

"She had better get herself a husband," another said. "I have seen her looking after Abram as he passes her in the street."

"Aye, and he looking also. I saw them touch hands by accident at the market, and each pulled away as if having touched a hand in fire."

An older woman laughed: "Indeed, my ladies, fire."

Rana was furious and turned upon the women. "How do you dare to say such a thing! My boy and that wench? Never! He could never desire such. Never!"

Looking at Rana in her anger; far too much anger for so little a word, half spoken in jest, Denicosa felt such pity that she could scarcely keep the look of compassion from flooding her face and making matters worse.

"Oh, women! Women!" At last Anna's pains were turning into their fulfilment, and she had their attention. Another moment of wailing, crying, beseeching, and a little female life flowed out with all her womb's comforts into Denicosa's hands. The wailing drew out into a long sigh of joy: whole she was, and nothing in the birth to cause alarm. From the front room where the men sat waiting and drinking, came a bawdy voice in question, and when the men heard that it was a fine daughter born to Josce, they gave a great cry of joy, even though it was not a son.

Josce came in then, as was prescribed, and asked of his family, formally, who had seen the birth, as it is prescribed to ask. The mother-in-law rose heavily and took full time for her appointed task, replying that nothing was amiss, nor were any exchanges made, nor was anything done against the dignity of the house. Josce stood in the ancient way, and in a voice such as his father had used and his and his, in a long line of the fathers of men, declared that the child was his, and announced his fatherhood of it. He gave thanks for his child and to the helpers of his wife. Then he went to join in the toasting and joking in the front room.

Amid the jubilation and thanksgiving, Rana walked like a ghost, and when Bett came to the house to bring her a message, and she saw the women and gave the familiar blessing to the newborn child in Hebrew, Rana blanched as though she had been struck.

"Go from here!" she said sharply to the girl, "lest you touch something for the ritual and defile it!"

There was a whisper among the women. Rana, by her helpless statement, her look, her tone, had given herself away. A single minute of despair had cost her the secret that she would have guarded with her life, and Denicosa, the gentle wife of Rabbi Elias, felt with her own shapeless body, all the sorrow of the beautiful, bejeweled Rana. The pity she felt walked like an army across her homely face, and by this she compounded the matter a thousand times more than Rana's worst enemy would have done.

EVEN in the spring-tide of the glory of God's
Crusade, change was ripping through the cloth **16**
of custom, and there were many for whom Jeru-
salem was a fever of illness and decay and not a sign of bright,
resurgent life. In many monasteries, the hunger for crusade fed
on boredom and on the subtle passions and whispers of the
body, long withheld. The cry for victory in battle could not be
held by scourge or nail or strings of prayers. It burst from the
Brothers' eyes and mouths; it overflowed their senses; it consumed them. As the call became more poignant and the promises
of grace so rich that they extended beyond the grave, old monks
and young, widowed nuns and virgins began to slip from the
cloisters and to put off the albs and tunics of the monasteries for
the coats of pilgrims and the helmets of warriors. Holy Church,
having encouraged these Crusades with all her splendid ardor
and powers of evocation, was soon at pains to keep her own communities. Her laws, washed over by the eloquence of the alluring voices, were forgotten, and the edicts to keep Brothers and
Sisters where they were, disobeyed. Fugitive from House, cut
off from the land, from past and family, and lacking money,
leaders or the final call of the slowly stirring armies, the Religious, wandering and hungry and belonging nowhere, soon fell
upon the villages for food and shelter. Some turned robber and
worse, and some killed, deluding themselves that victories in the
Holy War to come would wipe their souls white again. The root-
less, swelling in numbers every day, added to the stirring, moving, milling numbers of restless others who needed to be gone
from this land and to start anew somewhere else. Suddenly, it
seemed, they had all emerged from a neat, well-landmarked
country, where each man had a place and a destiny, into a wilderness of wills and forces—into a whirlwind. They were used
to being held close by bonds of duty and order and they
searched, with terror in their souls, for some design in the newly
tattered edges of these days. In the meanwhile, one had to stay
alive. There were others. too, breaking more subtly from the ancient wheel, but also unknowing.

By the end of the year, Baruch's plans had been wound about his quarry, and because the force which he had used was not direct, the tightening was long and slow. Much other business crowded his hours: the circulation of money was speeding faster and faster and the demand was forcing even the most scrupulous merchants and financiers into hard practice for the sake of speed. In the Moslem lands the story was the same, and before too long bezants and marks were flying back and forth between the two great worlds where soon the arrows were to fly. But as Baruch did his work, took orders on shipping to Spain, bought silver and gold from mines as far as Egypt and Byzantium for the English mints, his eagerness, his real spirit, was on the single prize in a petty baron's sword.

The year turned its seasons and Baruch the axis of his force tighter and still tighter. The unequal market was in his favor, and to keep the quarry from risking all and turning to their smuggling again, which might catch and hang them, Baruch managed to introduce them into debt slowly and gently, always extending the golden ball of hope before them: the next harvest, the next sale of fish. Armor and equipage prices were soaring so the whole estate became a vast smithy and leatherworks, and because the lords did not know business or the world outside their own small space in it, they were doomed in their attempt.

Two years after Baruch had sat jubilant in the dim cellar of the cathedral, his middlemen received the ruby-set ancestral sword as part payment of an immense debt. When he heard the terms of the noble family's defeat, he had a sudden sense of fear at his own incredible power. He had never set out to ruin a house before—ruin had been a by-product of his business, and for his own sake, when he could, he softened it; but he had set his bow against this house and brought it down and it was destroyed as surely as by fire. In two generations the name would no longer exist. His mind wrangled and struggled with the power of himself. Beware, O man, against whom I set my hand. Almost like God! It was fearsome to him and yet it was the most thrilling adventure he had ever known. Let the nobles content themselves with fox hunts. A man is more of a challenge than a fox. Abram would know, at last would know the glory of his father and the greatness of his love.

On the eve of the Purim festival, Baruch had his family standing before the door of the synagogue until all of Northstreet was assembled. He had dreamed and planned continually, going over and over in his mind how and where he would give his son the ruby, his great gift. At first it had been a private thing, with a walk on the moors alone together. It would have been Abram's way; Baruch knew that even now, but his own need forbade it; and with time, the first part of the dream had been lost. He had meant to say, "It is my love. Take it and keep it close and show it to no one; or else, if you will, wear it; or if you will not, then throw it down or give it to a beggar, for this is yours. Let the gift be a secret bond of love between us." He had thought out each word of it, but it occurred to Baruch that if his Abram did not wear the jewel, or did, indeed, keep it for himself, or give it away, it would anger him and drive him into the very bitterness that he sought to escape with his son. As the chase had quickened and the challenge sharpened, Baruch had given up the idea of a private presentation. He knew that he would never be able to give and forget, and this he excused to himself, saying, "It is my way—it is what I am, and if he takes me as his father, he must have my ways also."

Triumphant and happy, Baruch stood waiting for Yomtob and Elias. The evening was full of holiday and joy. Spring was breaking the bitter reign of cold and snow, the ancient songs of Esther and her story rang in the streets and houses, and Baruch felt that his moment would cap the time. He was sumptuously dressed, and, as a condition of the knighthood which Christendom denied him, he wore what a fighting man would wear, the colors of his defeated enemy wrapped, as in servitude, about his waist. As the Rabbis appeared, Baruch held up his hand. He thought quickly: I will not make a speech! He drew the great ruby like a lump of fire from his cloak, took his son close, holding Abram's arm out to meet his, and said in his strong voice, "Baruch of York shows his love to his son."

A loud murmur went up. "What is it?" "A jewel, a great jewel!" and then "It is the great ruby!", and "Oh! oh!", and "Magnificent! Oh, see!" Baruch had had the stone removed from the weapon and set in gold so that it could be worn as a clasp or brooch.

Abram took it and looked unbelievingly for a long time at it, so that Baruch thought: He is overcome. He is dazzled by my gift. And his heart swelled with pride. Then Abram's face changed— even in the unsteady light of the torches, there was a succession of faces whose meaning Baruch could not fathom. And then Abram did a strange thing—a thing almost not to be believed by

113

the astonished father. He closed his hand over the stone the way men took ordeal in the days before Henry. Abram was not holding a ruby, but a burning coal. He was sweating, his teeth clenched against the cry of pain that would convict him; his body was rigid. He bore the thing in his hand until Yomtob and Elias mounted the step to him. Yomtob held him almost fainting while Rabbi Elias opened the clenched fist and took the ruby. He would not have been surprised to see a palm burned raw by the great jewel, but the skin was whole and clear. Abram's pain remained in the soul, but Elias was grateful to God, and thanked Him with a breath of prayer that there would now be no talk of miracles here, good or evil. Without further word and not so much as a glance in Baruch's direction, the Rabbis continued into the sanctuary and began the holiday service.

Baruch was dumbfounded. He attempted to peer into Yomtob's face during the prayers, but saw nothing there to enlighten him. Several times he turned to Abram who stood beside him, but Abram was in a wound-shock and did not even seem to be conscious of where he was. At the conclusion of the service the young man left the meeting without a word.

On holiday nights it was the custom to wait about the synagogue courtyard, greeting friends and singing while the women hurried home to perfect their tables. Now Baruch went to where Rabbi Elias was standing, waiting for him, it seemed, with a face that held no hint of holidays. He did not want a scene. Something was not right with Abram, and he would see to that later, but now he wanted to get his ruby and go to his home. When he drew near, Elias put up a hand slowly as a signal to wait. "I must go . . ." Baruch said quickly, fearing some public discussion of this that was, and had always been after all, a private matter.

He was relieved when Elias motioned away those who were waiting to hear Baruch and the two Rabbis. The men left, guiding themselves home with their torches, so that when Yomtob came it was almost dark. He was a white shadow beside Baruch.

"Can God protect us from our choices forever?" he said softly. "Baruch—Baruch, what are you doing to us?"

Baruch tried for his easy laughter. "Rabbis—you are too upset. Of course you have been speaking long against vanity and overdressing, and I realized just now that this ruby would . . . seem a fault; but after all, if a man is free to risk his fortune in moneylending, has he not the right to wear his risk upon his back? The fault is one of love—the action is an outcome of the logic that the Christians themselves make us live by." The smoothness and urbanity of the words were unusual for Baruch before his own people.

"Let us forget the whole morality of two thousand years then," said Yomtob, "since you defend yourself so, and what is left is simple prudence—that we stay alive, we who are here on the sufferance of Christians who hate us."

Yomtob's sorrow kindled an obscure anger in Baruch. "Did someone insult a Christian?" he said. "Did someone make an eyesore in the Christian streets? We must make laws by the belch then, or by the lift of an eyebrow. That kind of folly is for the Jews of Cologne to do, not us, not we free ones!" Before the Rabbi could speak, the angry Baruch went on. "What is all this turning about? Why should we give a rotten apple for what they think of us? Let them all grow like onions with their heads in Hell! We are richer than they, smarter, holier; we read, we are handsomer, cleaner, dress better, live better and use our minds. Why, then should we change our feelings? They are not worth our breath to talk of it!"

It seemed that the louder Baruch was, the softer Yomtob was in answer, for now he brushed his arm before his eyes and said, very softly, "Who is great? If we were great, Elias and I, we would say, 'These things we must do for the sake of mankind.' But we are simple people, small men, lost in Christendom, and so we say that we must do them for our own sake, for the simple prudence that keeps a Jew alive in a world that hates him."

"What do we care for their love or hate?"

"Oh, God!" and Yomtob's cry shattered his old silence, so that his voice cracked in its changing.

"I wish that this were Heaven also, Rabbi, and not only York," Baruch said, knowing that he had all the logic on his side. It was the way things were.

"Only York! Only York!" gasped Yomtob. "Is that how you forgive yourself, you peacock! You self-righteous villain! Who pushes up the rates on loans so that a man pays until he is sucked like an empty husk? Oh, yes, I know what you say"—his anger was burning in his voice; his hands shook with it—"danger keeps the rates up; the bribes we must pay, the risks we must take. Oh, yes, I know all the excuses, but the risk was never so great that you are not smothered in jewels and buried in furs—that two men in York have not millions! If you are so true to your own self-righteousness, why do you foreclose on widows? If you are so noble, why do you slander Christians among yourselves and treat the Christian commoners as if they were dirt? If you are so honest, why do you clip coins!?"

Baruch gasped at the Rabbi's breech of custom. It was a sore spot, an issue which the community by unwritten agreement never mentioned. Clipping coins was illegal by Christian law and by the Holy Book of the Jews also, yet so many did it that it had ceased to be an exceptional thing, and the laws against it proliferated like leaves in springtime. A little rind scraped from a silver or gold mark could add a fat sum to a man's store in a year. Since this sum was uncounted, it was not taxed, and had been responsible for many a fortune in these money-scarce times.

The Rabbi was looking at Baruch. The financier felt himself accused and his face reddened. "Who clips coin?" he said. "I do no more clipping than anyone else—everyone has the right to do what he can. If those ignorant goats don't know any better, they deserve to be swindled!"

"Is that what the Law says—the law of God, of man, of survival?"

"All right!" Baruch shouted. "If I take, I give back plenty in my turn. Do you know what my tax is? Do you know what I pay in bribes? Do you know what I pay in the bribes of position—the charity, the 'donations' to the city, the yearly fees to the Christian poor?!" He knew that the defense was impossible, but the words had started to come and he was compelled to go on, almost by rote. "Who gives what I give? Yes, even to the Christian poor!"

Yomtob's voice was a knife in the darkness. "Your charity is dung!" At last, at last he had shocked Baruch as from a blow. "Those who partake of charity hate it and its giver; those who partake of justice love it and its giver. Be a little less the saint of the almshouse and stop clipping coin and stop resmelting silver with a wash of lead. Your word is like lead, not silver—it rings with falseness and with fatness. Have you ever demanded repayment of a loan without mercy, taken the land and turned it over to the debtor's enemy? Did you never go to a foreclosure in your best garments and say with a gesture of rings: 'Ah, but good friend . . . you are not intelligent'?"

"What do they really know, these barnyard nobles and straw-mattress clergy?" Baruch said.

Elias looked about in the silence that was still ringing with their last words. Even the good Yomtob, desperate to have his words and thoughts felt, was beyond himself. Elias said into the silence, quietly, "When I was very young, a neighbor's child died, and I said, 'God's will be done,' and my mother slapped me. When I asked wherefore, she said, 'Never speak of God's will easily, washing your hands of your neighbor's agony or your own.' Now I say 'God's will be done,' and here is your jewel, Baruch, that may be the heart's blood of a thousand men."

The financier took the stone that he could only grope for, since the torches were gone that had lit its fires. He put it in his pouch absently, and left them.

Elias turned to his friend to calm him, gripping Yomtob's arm. Under the sleeve was the knotted muscle of a far stronger arm than he would have guessed. Yomtob turned his head in the darkness and Elias felt a tear fall on his wrist.

"Some amends will be made—at least the ruby will not be worn."

But the older man had been listening into himself, far away, in France, and he said blindly through the still strange night of this exile, "My sisters, my brothers, my wife—could I not really have saved them? Did I not see the danger in time, or work hard enough to save them?" and to Elias's anguished denial, said, "When I came home from my travel and found house and world a shambles, and my dead thrown into hasty graves in my absence, I declared that I would be forever a living bell that warns and awakens our people that they might save themselves—or if to die, then to die cleanly——" He stopped and smiled in the darkness, ruefully, to his friend. "You see; I am not strong and virtuous. I have my own ghosts to lay at rest. If I can only save something or someone in this land—then—then——" He lifted his hands as if they were weighing the futility of describing what could not be measured or given voice and he let them fall again, too weak for their burden. "Outside these walls there is a Jewish graveyard, and in it there are no trenches with unnumbered slain in riots or slaughter, but I have been to lands and cities where the martyrs' graves crowd one another like the seeds in a pomegranate. God—God!" And then he stopped and turned again, smiling again, saying, "Why do I rail at The One of us all who is without fault in this. Man—man, are there not graves enough?"

IT seemed to Abram now as if the world was
breaking his hold on life. Baruch and he barely
spoke to one another, and when they did, rage
waited behind sudden turnings in their tone, so
that they often found themselves glaring at one another in a hard,
white anger over what had begun as a remark about a dropped
spoon or a cloud in the sky. Rana's sharp eyes were set like lances
against her son and the subdued Bett, so that they never spoke to
one another in the house and had to make labored and intricate
explanations of their goings and comings. When they lied or
equivocated to come together, guilt made them mute with one
another, for they were not clever at deceit. When Abram heard
Bett placate Rana with excuses, his face twitched and he
thought: I have made her debase herself and crawl. She was
proud and true and I have drawn this path for both of us.

After the New Year the bailiff called Abram from his place at
the market stall and brought him before the Mayor. It was rain-
ing and a short trail of moisture had begun on the ledge. Abram
noticed it as he began to listen to the members of the city's leadership. By the time they were finished with their compliments
and elaborate beginnings and ready to tell him what they wished,
the trail had darkened to the floor. Abram listened to the numbing phrases and thought: Someday a man might rank his reputation so—Masters, I am six inches wide, window-to-floor. And
then, Baruch of York: a cubit wide, ceiling-to-floor. And then:
How long it will have to rain for poor King Henry! And he
wanted to laugh.

He knew why they had called him. With all the soothing, window-to-floor's worth, he had guessed on the way to the hall
that he had been called to end his commission on the Code. His
joy had been a rushlight, kindled and blown big in a moment—a
moment and gone. A great work of inscription and a chance to
draw the happenings of the world of men after his own fashion.
They were saying, "Of course you must understand that we cannot spend money on such things as laws and books, when every
farthing will have to go toward enriching the young princes in

their conquest of the Holy Land. Levies will have to be raised from every town and city and we are short of money as it is. But do not throw your work or your hopes to the winds. After Jerusalem is ours . . ."

For a while he harbored thoughts of continuing the Codex on his own, but with the little that he made at the market stall, he knew that he could never afford the expense of so much parchment. And the spirit was gone. He could not even justify to himself the months of time, years perhaps, pulling his time and mind from the duty of his own work in the synagogue for which the community was supporting him. No; it was finished; of the same cloth as his future with his father, the confidence of his mother, the love of his kind and loving Bett. When Rana heard the outcome of his visit to the City Hall, she sniffed, "Pig-eaters!" When he told Baruch that he was going to donate the finished pages to the courts, the financier muttered and turned away. Abram thought: If he still loves me, that is irritation and anger. If he despises me, perhaps it is only impatience and self-pity.

But Abram noticed that the world did not die. In the city, city changes took their course: a new Dean for York's cathedral, a new Treasurer. Some rose and some fell as the wheel turned, but the usual intrigues had lost their old savor. Overshadowing all the land was the promise of the great adventure. For the noblemen of England and their arming men, the year had been measured only by the clanking of their smiths, who were beating plowshares into swords for the great Crusade. Germany was arming also, so was France, so were Flanders and the Rhenish lands. With their feeble and squeaking mints, England was not able to make a tenth of the necessary money, and she was afraid of symbol-riches. Coin lied; it could be clipped, lost, falsely weighed, counterfeited. It was easily stolen and, worse still, varied in value as more or less was mined and minted in any one year and as a country became richer or poorer.

The Jews worked hard to get coins to use. They borrowed coin everywhere. They used even their own private counters, and so hard were they working that they failed to see the questioning looks of their neighbors.

Were heathens and infidels becoming rich with this war to redeem the land of Christ for His anointed? The warnings which had sounded in France years before the expulsion were sounding again. Eyes were beginning to narrow against them.

119

On a quiet Wednesday afternoon, a common Wednesday, and earlier than the month for taxes, a King's messenger rode into York and posted a notice on the door of the Jews' Community Hall on Northstreet. A passer-by read it and ran, calling among the houses for the people to come. They came and stood looking at and whispering to it: What will it mean? Is it true? Is it for me also?

Abram came and pushed close and read aloud:

"All silver and gold, metal in the form of ornaments, jewels, money, household possessions and movable goods to the extent of one-quarter of all such movable goods shall be collected from the Jewish Population of this city in order that the cause of Christ may be advanced in the Holy Land. These donations will be collected by the high Sheriff of the shire, who will be assisted by the King's Justices who are: [and there was a space for the names of the local judges to be inserted, and a crabbed hand had written:]

> Robert Mantel
> Rannulf Glanville
> Hubert Walter
> William fitz Robert
> Richard Malabestia

Those who attempt to withhold their proper amount or to obstruct this order in any way shall be subject to the King's justice.

HENRY II REX ANGLORUM, DUX NORMANNORUM ET AQUITANORUM ET COMES ANDEGAVORUM."

Baruch was not there. Abram knew that he should go and tell his father immediately. Perhaps there was something that could be saved out or hidden. His mind raced with possibilities, and then he caught himself, thinking suddenly: Why, I am no better than he. This waste of our substance for a cause in which we do not believe is unfair; it invites deception and treason—yet . . . Rana had come to the crowd, and Abram, to still his own mind's turmoil, spoke with that false brightness which so distressed her: "Good masters, is it not written: 'Even in my bare flesh shall I praise God?' Now we are being given that chance!" The jest was in very poor taste and he knew it, but could not have helped making it. The men scowled at him. He opened his mouth again,

but his mother came up behind him and said, "Do not persist."
He broke away from her and ran to tell his father.

The Justices and the Sheriff came with their big feet into the houses. They turned with half-embarrassed, half-covetous smiles, into the clothes presses, the trunks, the private pots and pans. Some of the jewelry stuck to their hands, but more than ever they were fascinated with what they saw in the Jews' houses. The Sheriff was a courteous man. He was old and had been long acquainted with the people of Northstreet, and he did not like to go sniffing into corners like a dog, but the others were looking out for themselves. Who, after all, had the complete authority over them? The King was far away, in London. The men of rank hated the power of the King and his protection of "his" Jews. The fathers and grandfathers of these Justices had once carved lands out of the wilderness for themselves, which were like little kingdoms, and they were not yet bound beneath a king except with the flimsiest of ties; but the old days had gone and now the King ordered from London and barons were obliged to jump in York. All this, while untitled Jews walked forth like princes. So did Richard Malabestia walk into his collections with a smile, and shake the sleeves of the ladies' garments, and of the mens', and when a spoon dropped out of Rana's gown, and two ells of purple cloth trailed alluring ends from beneath her gown, he made her undo her belts and her hair and he stood over her as she unfolded robe after robe to him from her cabinets and chests.

Rana was a woman not yet past her prime of life, and she was weeping. Malabestia liked to see women weep. When she undid her hair—a thing which she had done before no man save her husband on their wedding night—the thick, black heap of it fell down over her face, for she was frightened and ashamed, and this, too, Malabestia liked to see in women.

"Give up your treasures, you she-dog!"

"But Baron-Justice, even your own lady has beloved jewels, the dowry and gift of the past. . . . These things I got from my mother, and would give to my children. What have I with them? . . . I am only a guardian . . ."

Northstreet knew that the order of one-fourth could not be trusted. The King demanded one-fourth, but the Justices took what they would, for the kingdom was happy so long as the King was well satisfied.

"Be glad I do not take your lives as well," Malabestia said. He said something else under his breath, but they could not hear what it was. "Come on, Jew woman. Give up the rings . . . come on, come on . . . give the Pope back his treasures!"

When he left the house, he carried with him not only the glimpse he had seen of the wealth that Jews could accrue, but of the woman also. He remembered Rana, with her tears and her fear and her shame, and the lustrous black fall of her hair.

Rana began to cry again. "That little spoon I had was my own. My mother fed me from it when I was young. I knew the little worn spot at the handle so well, and the little design it had. Now it is gone. . . ." She covered her face with the now bare fingers.

"Be still . . . be still," Baruch said gently, and he touched her shoulder very quickly because he was not a man given to show and he was ashamed to have been outfaced by someone whom he could buy and sell. "There will be other spoons!"

Rana left his side and walked to the outside hearth, murmuring over and over again the memories which lay heaped in Malabestia's hands.

Had the Baron even been grave about this duty, they would have forgiven him and the sight of his heavy hands among their treasures, the slow accretion of their years, but he had come with contempt, he had laughed and been lewd, and in their sudden defenselessness they cursed him in bitter whispers.

"They laughed!" Rana moaned. "They were joyous because of our grief. That Christian carried my clothes and the jewels warm from my body as if he had owned them and it all of his life." Once more, because of the little spoon of such long memory, she began to cry. She looked at Abram as he came in the door, and all of her bitterness exploded toward him. "Where were you, then, when that pig was looking at me? Do you know that the presence of men itself is protection!?"

"I—I was with Bett—I thought—well, you know that they hate to see Christian servants in our houses—perhaps if she were seen——"

"Who is she, my son, that you should concern yourself!" Baruch was angry, and even though he had not noticed Rana's face go white at the mention of Bett's name, he had heard enough of the gossip of Northstreet to be angered.

"She is defenseless. She has no one!" Abram answered.

"Behold!" Baruch shouted sarcastically, "how my son deepens his soul with works of holy charity!"

Rana ran forward and put herself between the two angered men of her house. "Please," she said, and put her hand on Abram's arm. She was shocked once more as she saw her own hand; she had forgotten for a little while the loss of her jewels and her hand's bareness.

"Never mind!" Baruch said. "I give him leave." Abram bent and made his obeisance, kissing his father's hand in the etiquette prescribed, and Baruch did not know why he did not strike his son as the young man bent before him, for even in his acts of submission, the rebel will made his cry as loud as thunder.

Yomtob lay in his bed, thinking thoughts as cold as the night which bore the hated fog of these islands. Was I ever warm then? He remembered the countryside of the land to which he would never return. Strange, that for a landless Jew, exile is also bitter. Maybe it is wiser, as the joke goes, to keep out of the eye of God. It made him think of Abram, that hot young soul trying so hard to keep out of the way of his calling. Indeed, this new trial for his people would go hard with him. He would have to still his blatant questioning and retreat from the proud and lonely stand which he had taken. The community would have to draw together into a single body of belief and dignity for the test that might come. The *I* is a luxury of peace. And the Rabbi rolled over for sleep, saying to himself, "If he is to be one of our strengths and not one of our weaknesses, the good God will have to drag him, kicking, into greatness.

September, 1188

FAR more than the absence of jewels, there was **18** ⌀ something moving over Northstreet that made it harder to laugh and stretch wide on a sunny morning, emerging from a house into the good daylight. Somehow, for no reason that could be pointed to, it became more comfortable for the women to use the small and ill-adapted well near the Community Hall than to take the washing to the river with its flat stones and open spaces and talk, far away from the sewage troughs and city mud. Because they did not go to the river, Denicosa and Anna were not able to learn in the old daily way who was ill in the Christian community and needed healing herbs, and thus they stopped offering to do their medicine, but waited until the people came to them in trouble to beg help. Northstreet was growing away from the rest of the city. It was a slow growing, a series of small, private severings, natural and without hatred, but those who did hate drew their mouths harder and began to speak of "that nest of Jews near the river."

Abram felt the pall on Northstreet and one day, at the end of summer, he went to Foss Isle because of it. He had thought often of the crusade camp, speaking to Simon and letting his own memory move him toward hope yet again. The years had ground on with delays and turmoil among the souls massing for the great assault on Jerusalem. Now Henry was fighting with his own sons for his crown. If there was any love and sweetness, any charity (the paradox of a crusade), it would be there on Foss Isle. He asked Bett to go with him, but she was afraid of provoking Rana to a fresh uproar and bade him go alone. As he left, she said, "I shall be waiting for you. I shall be here, waiting when you come back." Her words and tone puzzled him, but he did not connect them with the fact that she had been to the crusade camp some few times since their afternoon together. He walked on a rickety bridge, pleased that the day was so right for going to the encampment and almost glad that he had been despairing these weeks and months since "the gift" and his forlorn commission. He needed a change of feelings and an ease of the pain of being Abram —laughter, silence, prayers which were not his own to judge.

When he reached the encampment on Foss Isle, he thought that he had been mistaken, or that the camp had disappeared, and was now somewhere else. There was no longer a single group, but many small huddlings of two or three men alone, sprawling or sitting on the hard-trodden ground. They were filthy and ragged and numbers of them wore parts of religious habits, hiked up or belted for comfort. Pots of food bubbled over fires here and there, but it was random and makeshift, stolen or begged, by the sight and smell of it, and its guardians hunched over their little pots with curses and looks of bitterness and fear. Abram remembered that there had been great communal fires and food brought out by the women of the city for all who had come to listen to the words of wonder. Now he saw men's hands patting for reassurance at the grips of knives beneath their rags, and he found himself going with his own hands closed, clasped before his mouth in a thwarted anger at what York and the world had lost in this waiting and waiting. Whores turned as he passed, greeting him with exaggerated looks and joking about him to one another to shame him. His mind knew what had brought these people to Foss Isle, many to die when winter came, belonging nowhere and outside the laws of faith and nation, but the knowledge was for his head only, and his loyalties felt sickened and betrayed. The King's beloved successor-son had died and the younger brothers had been battling the old and tired father. After his defeat, perhaps they would war against each other. Another year's delay, and yet another, and the bright-burning sun of ambition and the thrust for glory had drawn away from this encampment, leaving it in a cold twilight without hope. "The Armies of the Living God" had left its remnant: an unled rabble of whores and outlaws and fallen monks, scattered and exhausted, thralls of their empty bellies.

Some coming spring, the patient and the wealthy would take ship for Acre and forget that it had been so long between the first stirring cry to destiny and the final lift to the horse.

Lost in his thought, Abram did not notice where he walked, so that he came suddenly upon a low-built canopy affair of rags stretched out on poles and he almost tripped over it. A voice inside the shelter bawled a curse and a hand came out holding a sharpened spike and stabbing the air with a tumble of obscenity at every thrust. Abram backed off hurriedly and was gone as quickly as he could go, but all night he lay tossing in his bed, remembering the mindless, brutal, hate that had guided the hand under the rag flap of the lean-to, and the gush of obscenity with the jab of the spike. At last, he thought, the warriors will go off on their horses and leave their ruined ones behind . . . with us. . . . And when he finally fell into a drowse, its dreams were full of lurking shapes.

Of "The Young Kings," only the bastard, Geoffrey, chose to ride with his father. England stood back and watched. The Church, cheated of its English and French troops, tried envoy after envoy, begging for reconciliation between the two great Kings. The armies of the Netherlands and the Rhine were at keen pitch, France East was ready, Norway at pitch, Flanders chafing. Holy Church knew better than any how delay cools even the reddest ardor. Here stood the jealous princes, and in spite of the good efforts of all, Henry, looking tired and full of despair, took ship for France with only one son.

Father Odo, the priest of Allhallows, watched the death of the crusade camp's fervor and the oncoming of the restless defeat of faith. He preached as well as he could for patience and wisdom and begged Our Lord for a beginning soon. He watched this war emerge, still another delay, keeping Christendom from its duty and its glory. The way to God is found alone only for saints, he told his congregation . . . wait, take counsel, be patient; but he pitied his hearers too much. He knew that they were, after all, remote Christians, living an isolated life on a cold island. They shrugged at a war of sons against father and of brother against brother because the dying would be done across the channel. He had been to Acre and Jerusalem on one of the dozen ill-planned and diverse crusades of thirty or forty years ago and he knew that Christendom was what his Christians needed above all. He told his congregation to wait for some sign from God that would assure them of their cause.

The Jews, knowing that they were helping to finance this war and also the war to come, saw the old peaceful bonds beginning to shake apart about them and wondered if the trembling would not perhaps shake loose some of the stitches of their own allegiance. Some hid their remaining treasures, some tried to put them in the hands of Christian friends to be taken out of the country and reinvested. Baruch doubled his rates of interest, and moved, through a Christian intermediary, to buy up lands from his debtors.

As the news from France came more and more clearly in the color of defeat, more and more mouths forgot Henry's name for those of the sons, Richard and John. The King, it was told, half dead of sorrow, raced against the overtaking powers and ran starving into Anjou. He had hoped for gratitude from the mass of people, for homage gifts and feasts, for Anjou was his province. Instead, the crowd came in rebellion, with flails and with stones, and the King wept like David on Absalom's body, to have, added to the bitterness of his sons' defection, the sting of the infidelity of his subjects. A man of dignity, a king, was now being cursed like an animal and given up to captors with sticks and foul language. "I shall stand at Chinon," he had said. Soon the war would be over and the more important business of the Crusade could be taken up again. The Church moaned with impatience.

Summer had passed. The creeks drained away and dried, the rivers slowed. The lands of Yorkshire were cracking dry under the autumnal winds. On a night of faint stars and no moon, the bells of the city suddenly went wild over the sleeping houses. Some awoke, remembering the war and France, and cried, "Richard has won!" Some, shaken from a dream of crusade, cried, "Jerusalem again is ours!" but those who were wise and knew autumn and dry timber knew what to cry, and that cry was "Fire!"

It was St. John's Church which was in flames, perhaps from a torch whose sparks had crept into the dry planks, or fastened on the waiting thatch. St. John's was a parish church so that the leather fire buckets and other equipment, ladders and staves had been stored there. Materials had to be gotten from the neighboring parish, and men ran quickly to get them, and as they ran, the fire clutched still deeper at the body of the church. Confusion multiplied their errors. Some ran to St. Elene's, thinking that it was closer; some to Allhallows, beating on the door and trying to wake Father Odo. The father could not be stirred. He would regret the deep, peaceful sleep of his that was like death and would pardon those who broke the doors down to get into the cellar where the fire tools were stored, but precious time had been lost forever. By the time the heavy buckets, pikes and ladders had been taken out and brought to the church and mounted in place, hope of saving St. John's was gone.

The fire fighters noticed a man haranguing the crowd which had come to see the wild blaze and to fear with them that it might set the neighbor buildings afire. The crowd about the speaker began to close tightly as he spoke. They were keeping the fireguards from saving anything out of the burning church. Then, someone looked into the fire-brilliant night above the burning roof and saw the heavy jewel-encrusted casket, which contained the prime relic of the church, the bones of St. Brithonus. They cried out at the casket, hovering like a bird over the blazing building. And at the sounds and the pointing and excitement, the men looked up with a great "Oooh! A miracle! A miracle!"

The Baron Malabestia had come, in that rumor-mad and uncertain season, to York to see how the city was taking the news of Henry and his sons and the toil for Jerusalem. The proud landed lords were bitterly angered that now the cities had a voice in the making of law, and that the tides of custom were beginning to run against the inheritors of the great names and holdings. Malabestia was no more bitter than the rest, but, unlike the others, he found it wise and not against his dignity to fall in with the new way and work it to his own advantage. He had brought with him Richard de Kuckney, still his squire, thinking perhaps that something could be done to turn him to a little profit. They were lodging in rooms kept for them at St. George's Church, which the Baron supported.

Malabestia heard the bells and leapt from sleep, leaving his unroused squire and going alone into the street. People were running in the darkness. He called to one who only had time to shout, "Fire!" "Where?" No answer. He followed the excited men past churches, houses and alleys, up the Walmgate Road, over the bridge and then he saw the light. They ran on around the corners and up to the blazing church. He felt immediately that he had arrived at the perfect moment. The church was a mass of flames and there was nothing more to do but watch it burn and hope that other buildings would not be lighted by some greedy random spark. Fires were common in the cities, still mostly wood and straw thatch, and the nights of alarm were many in the autumn. Excitement was at its highest pitch and people wanted to act; the blood was up.

The Baron stepped to the front of the crowd and turned his back on the burning building, so that he seemed to stand against it. As soon as he had seen the fire and realized that it was near the Jewry and that it was a church, the possibility of having, now, all that he sought, dawned on him as sudden and real as a sneeze and he had laughed and run on. Now, in the position of exhorting, back to the fire, he raised his hands and began to strike with his words against the sight-drugged faces of his watchers.

"At last the Jews speak their intention!" he shouted. "We had begun to wonder how and when it would begin. But now they start this fire. After it will come a plague!"

"Plague . . ." One of them had caught the word. Several others turned around, for autumn also had sickness hidden and waiting in the arms of the bounteous harvest.

"Yes, yes. The way is clear—the terms have been drawn and the debt signed in blood. Now they begin. They will start a plague. Burning churches is the first act of faith for them; a gift they make to their blood-drenched heathen god. After fire, plague; after plague, famine."

A group was listening now, half to the fire, half to the burning words. "Were there none about the church?" one said. "Who has seen the Watches? Perhaps they——"

"Who is seen in the pocket of the night?" Malabestia said, lowering his voice so that they must strain to hear him, putting their own effort to his purpose. "Black-cloaked, the Devil's dark ones come walking, shielding the sparks with their bosoms. They are acolytes in the Devil's faith and we must strike them away or die ourselves!"

Somebody cried, "Then they do sacrilege!"

"It is their faith! It is their life! They pray with hands covered in blood!"

"We will stop them! Stop them!" some cried, and "Yes!" and "Yes!"

A little further and they would be taken into the rhythm of his will. They would soon be ready to move, without reason, in the middle of his power.

But then, unexpectedly, as he spoke, a cry went up from the corner and a great shout close by: "The casket! A miracle!" and then "Where? Where?" rustled among the crowd, and minds, eyes, dreams strained toward this more immediate manifestation of divine will.

Malabestia tried to interrupt, but he knew even before he started that it was useless. The great idiot-child mob had been turned to this newest toy, forgetting what had been so vital to it before. He turned away from the holy rapture of some and the frenetic confusion of others. His head ached because of what he had almost had and had lost by such a narrow minute. In the Baron's rhythm, for the Baron's reason they might have poured down the road to Northstreet and killed every Jew in York, those men who had almost been his hounds. Most of the authorities were not even in the city and Henry was in France. How easy and how lucky it would have been for him—the quiet, unobtrusive passing down one deserted street after another. The Cathedral—he could have forced his way to the vault where the debts and contracts were kept. The debt-rolls would have been destroyed and no Jew would have been alive to stand against the Malabestia, a King's Justice, and declare before the King what was owed in hundreds of marks.

His head began to pound and he had to force his feet on the road back to his lodging at the church house. He would see blood on De Kuckney's face. He would see fear and paleness under the blood. He would see the pleading in the eyes for this failure, this shame. Until he could get his hands to grips with his frustration, he muttered over and over to himself, soothing, "It will come. It will come. It will come."

Morning brought a leaden hand on York. The streets were slippery and the skies heavy and chill. Rats, caught in the choked sewage troughs, looked even uglier in their death; choking on the very filth which they sought so greedily. Early in the morning, the two helpers and the eager little Servant of the Synagogue ran with fuel and fire to light the great ovens which baked the Jews' special Sabbath bread. Already fires were being lit in the small Jewish bathhouse (for souls which would be blessed to look out from clean bodies). While these fires were being tended, the Christians eyed their neighbors with the beginnings of mistrust and went about their work with the remains of their own fire. The ashes of St. John's were being sifted for anything which could be saved from the ruins left by the flames. There had been the miracle also, which kept the curious standing about in spite of the weather. This gathering at the church hindered the work of the priest and his men, picking and sifting for bits of metal in the wreckage, but gossip flowed about it and rose with the smoke. Could it perhaps be the work of certain Jews?

Two monks, clothed in the white habit of Praemonstratensians, stopped and spoke to the ash-blackened priest. They looked, the three of them, like a vision of angels and devil. Brother Simon and Brother Norbert were on monastery business. After hearing about the fire and the miracle which had lifted the Saint's bones to safety, the Brothers prepared to go on their errands. Turning, they saw Malabestia, and Richard, the squire, coming toward the crowd that stood around the church. The small body of Brother Simon recoiled almost imperceptibly at seeing the Baron, but in the six years since the newly admitted novice stood shyly in the sheepfold while a Jew spoke to him, Brother Simon had learned much. His eyes and face showed no change, his hands were still. Malabestia greeted the Brothers, asking the questions correct for him to ask. When he was finished, the standard form of repose was pulled across his face.

"Tell me, Sir Baron," Brother Norbert said politely, "what news comes from France? Our father Abbot would like some little news if there is any."

"The King will lose this war of his. He does not know how many are against him."

"What will he do?"

"What can he do? Now he is confident. He will fight, he will lose, he will surrender, he will accept the terms. The terms will be hard. He will have land enough only for a grave."

"The King is old and not sanguine," Simon said, half unbelieving. "Surely his own sons . . ."

The Baron turned his suave face blandly to the monk. "You are Brother Simon, are you not? Simon the Jew? . . . Do not imagine that age gives any safety or prior claim to mercy. The world is not easy, Jew."

"Sir, do not call me Jew"—the warning flash from Brother Norbert's eyes made him add—"I beg of you."

"Well then, Jew's sweetheart. Do you love this fire-making also, Jew-lover?"

"What did the Jews have to do with the fire?"

"Ha-ha-ha." Malabestia laughed, as if Simon and he alone were sharing some rich joke. "You know, sweetheart dear, that they set it."

"But what to gain?" Norbert asked, perhaps truly believing and truly curious, Simon thought.

"Relics," Malabestia answered him. "They have noses for gold and jewels that lead them to the caskets of the saints like vultures to the ruins of a lion." His eyes were sparkling.

"But . . ."

And Brother Norbert's eye caught Simon again in mid-answer. Disciplined for these years by rod, by rope, by voice, by eye, by hand, Brother Simon stopped, cleared his mind of thought as a peasant brushes the heavy snow from his roof, clasped his hands together and waited silently. Abbot Adam would have been pleased at this discipline—Simon's mastery over himself was so complete and so prompt. The boy had come to the Order full of eagerness. His mind had been one to run ahead, daring anything, going anywhere, followed too far behind by a panting will that strove to catch up with it. Now the will, trained runner, had finally won the race. Abram of York, Jew, would have been shocked sick and speechless by such a discipline. It could not have been told to Abram, that, without a sharer to wait, to listen, to dream of using thought as a way to answer questions, speculation becomes lost between "spiritual laxness" and "willful self-exaltation." It turns this way and that in its loneliness. Its hints and openings are never taken up. It finally weakens enough to be put down by the ordinary exercise of the faculties of the mind, as a yawn is put down by the ordinary faculties of the body and, once put down, is forgotten. Monklike, Brother Simon had not used his feelings or his thoughts to speak himself. He cleared his mind of its wishes.

At that minute, Abram was not far away. The synagogue was around the corner and up a short street from the ruined church. Overlooking the walled court, in his room off the balcony where the women worshiped, Abram was busy with his writing. He was working on a copy of a new religious tract which interested him only a little. Because of the work done in the upper room, a window had been made there, to provide light for the scribes. Abram looked out over the figure of the busy Servant of the Synagogue, who was carrying his polishing rags to hang dripping heavily in the damp air. He looked over the stone wall, over the low roof of a house, to the little green square, which called the eye to it again and again because it was without its spire. His view of the wreckage was hidden by houses, but he saw Baron Malabestia and his squire rounding the corner and two monks in white were with them. Abram looked closely. Yes —it was Brother Simon there, talking with the Baron. Abram was glad to see his friend. He put his brushes down, threw a cover over his desk with all his pens and inks and the copy just as they were, and went down the steep stairs to the sanctuary and out the door. They were ahead of him, probably going to the cathedral. As he walked, he wondered how he could get the young Brother's attention without creating what would surely become a scene if he gave his greeting straightforwardly in the presence of the Baron. He would follow them and when the Baron had left them, he might give his friend a greeting or have a few words with him. It had been a long time since he had seen Simon.

Ahead of him, the Baron spoke his words, and as Abram came up, he could hear fragments of them in the rise and fall of talk. Was it not enough that this dog was called a Justice, that he adjudicated and was called upon for mercy? Was it not enough that he had ransacked the Jewish homes with malice and cast lewd eyes on mothers and wives—must he now slander the people in the streets! Abram's throat was dry with anger and his heart was pounding. Prudence cried to him that the man was a noble and a Justice. To strike him would mean prison, if not murder first. So intent was he in his anger, that he did not notice the four ahead of him slowing down until he nearly collided with Richard de Kuckney, who was walking slightly behind. No more than two abreast could walk easily in the narrow streets. They both recovered their balance and glowered at one another.

Young De Kuckney was over age for a squire, and he had borne much shame because of it. He should have been knighted long ago, and back with his father to learn his own lands and estate and to marry and father. But Lord Robert had been impoverished by these very Jews, and was not wealthy enough to buy the ceremonies, pay the taxes or give the gifts which attended the making of a knight. At nineteen, Richard de Kuckney was an embittered misfit among the high-voiced pages and squires, and in his anger at being jostled in the street by a Jew, he saw the trampling of the rags of his dignity. Suddenly he was desperate for his grandfather, the murderer of Thomas Becket; for his father who was too poor to buy his son the place which already by law belonged to him; for himself, growing old in service to a lord who had scorned him into impotence and dried up the joy of life in his veins.

Abram saw before him the repudiation of all his beliefs, a hired retainer whose code was battle and death; who could kill by a hundred ingenious ways but could not read; whose pride was rape and looting, not conjugal love. And there was envy, too, of the name he bore and of the honor and of the lands and titles that were given freely to this vandal by his birth alone and to which no wisdom, no bravery, no courage, skill or wealth could ever give Abram claim. The fists of both knotted on their anger as they faced one another in the narrow street, realizing that they could not fight here—that they would be jailed and shamed, that quarters were too close, and that others would be taken up in their fight, but they could not help themselves.

A person, going through the street on his own business and not noticing anything but his own haste, brushed past Abram and pushed him forward and the clenched hands flailed into one another. The slippery street made them stumble and soon Jew and lordling were both rolling about in the reeking place. Abram caught glimpses of the crowd; he thought he saw the Baron, and Simon, white as his habit, and someone in a robe of Jewish cut, but he did not know who it was.

Richard de Kuckney was thickly built, well muscled and used to fighting; but at these close quarters, the slenderer, quicker Abram had all the advantage. The squire, in all of his extra years of training, had been shown too often which was the dignified and which the undignified blow, which was the honorable stance and which the dishonorable; and Abram, sensing this, let his untitled arm go as free as he would, glad and laughing with the irony of his enemy's weakness. At last blood came from the squire's nose, and the Jewish cloak whipped into the cleared place and bore down on the wild-eyed Abram. As soon as the young man saw Josce before him, the strength went out of him, and his anger fell away. Without a break in stride, Josce caught Abram up and propelled him on down the street. He held him at arm's length, a stained, stinking creature of the sewage trough.

Richard de Kuckney lumbered to his feet amid the jeers of the town boys. The anger swelled in him like a great wave. He was blind with it. Worse than defeat was his dishonor: a noble, a man trained for battle, beaten by a soft heathen scholar! Would the house of Kuckney never know honor? He knew that the worst was yet to come. In the Baron's scorn there was no hiding place for honor, no refuge for his spotted name. "Damn them! damn them! damn them!" the squire said, muttering. "Someday I will kill them all!"

WHEN Simon and Norbert reached Welbeck and the monastery, it was quite late. The gate had been left open for them, and through it they went, forgetting to still the tiny bell, which tinkled after them and somehow reminded them how late it was, and how dark, and that the vast clear sky was full of stars. They looked up, and Brother Simon said "Oh—" in awe and the sweet chant rose in his mind: A *Salve Regina* in the warm voices of his brothers. The night had suddenly opened for them and though the cold remained, it was not a leaden chill, nor a damp whine in their cloaks, but a clean, hard cold with the vigor of the spare arches of the monastery court.

A figure appeared before them, framed against the dark bulk of the great House doorway. "Come in, come in, my Brothers!" It was Abbot Adam.

Brother Simon was moved that the Abbot himself should have waited up for them, giving his own greeting and not one sent them through a yawning lay Brother. The young man stopped for a time, wishing to keep this moment among the others of great beauty which he stored in his mind so carefully against dry seasons of boredom and melancholy: the rest after the journey that was now ended, the bell, the stars, the dark earth beneath cool winds of autumn, the smell of the cold, the deep voice of welcome, the shadow of the chant serenading in the mind; and all of these somehow were part of the very darkness in which they had been hidden. The Brothers went into the icy vestibule and shook off their bundles.

"Come," said the Abbot, "I have set aside a repast for you. Tomorrow will be soon enough to hear how things went with you."

It had been Brother Simon's first trip outside the environs of Welbeck, and now this added novelty of sitting late with only Brother Norbert and Abbot Adam had a pleasure all its own. He felt like a little boy again, allowed a special privilege because of a fair. It was special because it was a single gift, to him alone. Now the adventure was over. He would lose himself in sleep, and rising teeth a-chatter in the darkness long before dawn, would be back with his Brothers in their common life and work. As he said his prayers, noting, however sinfully, that there were but three voices, and that one was beautifully pitched, the Amens breathed together, and the three went wordlessly to their beds.

Brother Norbert stood before the assembled Brothers and spoke of monastery business. The fire at St. John's was not mentioned, nor were the roads, beautiful with burning leaves this autumn, for these were out of the purview of their community. He spoke of the new lands which had been deeded to the Order and of plans for taking their wool to London rather than weaving all of it themselves. They had also purchased a few things which the Community did not make—pitch and barrel hoops and some crude iron which the smithy needed. Abbot Adam asked several questions and after a prayer and the confession of Faults, the Brothers rose to leave for their work. As they went, Abbot Adam called to Simon and he turned, monklike, the full turn to face his superior, and came the full distance back and did obeisance again before responding, "Yes, Father Abbot."

The great bulky man smiled. "Sit down, Brother, and tell me what you saw in York and in the towns along the way. Is there health in the air? What did you sense and what did you hear? If we listen, we can mark the future walking to meet the present."

Brother Simon did not want to speak, and the hesitation showed so plainly on his guileless face that the Abbot knew it at once. He asked a few simple questions, discreetly, and heard from Simon how loud the people were for crusade and how they blamed King Henry for a war which he was going to lose so badly. That war seemed a wall to them, keeping them from the holy destiny at Jerusalem. Adam asked about the raising of armies, and Simon answered, speaking of prices and lands and jewels mortgaged, and Adam said at last, "What of the Jews?"

It was a logical question, seeing that they were the lenders of money and would finance part of the venture, but the young monk began to stammer until finally the superior said smiling, "What should you contrive to hide from me? Have I not always been well disposed toward you?"

In his grave way, Simon told him of the fire and the miracle, the tax of the Jews, and of other things which he had heard at the edges of the fight between Abram and the young Kuckney. The Kuckneys were prominent patrons of the Welbeck community, and the Brothers prayed for the continued glory of their line. Simon told of how Abram had almost beaten the heir of Kuckney's house, and had been whisked away by another Jew, after having drawn blood from the young nobleman who still was the Baron Malabestia's squire. The Jew had thus heaped shame upon both houses before the people of the city.

When Simon finished his telling, he said, "Abram does not belong to that life—he does not know nobles or the servants of nobles—he has been town bred and in the town there is a different face put on these things. He has wrought a small havoc, but he does not know it."

For a moment they were both farm lads, watching the embarrassment of a noble house to which they were not connected, and they looked at the faces which they saw in their minds with the merriment of the ploughman who sees in a pratfall and a loss of dignity that the meek are one step closer to their inheritance. Then they sobered.

Abbot Adam had seen Jews, but he had never known one.

Now he listened to Brother Simon with only the wish to know so that he might plan his wisest course or send word to Premontre so that they might know to plan for him. Almost absent-mindedly, he gave the Brother leave and each went back to the sure routine of the monastery's day, happy in The Rule which would stand so strong. Let the waters churn—this rock at least would not be moved.

As the Abbot went to his place, he could not help turning over in his mind the extra news which Simon had given him: that unrest was stirring everywhere, that Geoffrey, Henry's bastard, might be being given the Archbishopric of York, that brigands and bands of the hungry were making travel hazardous through-out the land. Anguish piled on anguish. He sat down on his hard pallet. Geoffrey of England was no Religious. He would take hasty vows, but such "ten breath" clerics seldom did well for their communities. York was the second most powerful See in England and the princes were giving it away as a pacifying sop to Geoffrey. Adam was glad that the charter of their order forbade its voice in the politics of the world outside. Enough Houses and factions were a-toil. For his own sons in Christ he felt the fear of these strange times. The restless desire to see new things, to belong to a great, overtaking commitment like this Crusade, was making many a Brother turn runaway. He must try to tell them all—the guileless Simon, the headstrong Lewis, the passionate Unam Sanctam, the lay Brothers, with their feeling of endless poverty—that the world outside was brutal and that they had forgotten how savage its hungers could be. He slept at last, still wondering in his sleep if he could paint the long and daily sacrifice at Welbeck in colors as rich as the sword-silver, flame-red, blood-crimson moment of Jerusalem. . . .

He spent the early part of the next day stock-taking for the winter: both stores and the raw materials which would give the Brothers work through the days of rain and snow. When he was finished, he walked from the storehouse to the outer gate, thinking to see the Brothers hard at work piling winter food for the sheep, hauling water and sharpening knives and scythes. Instead they were standing in a small group, clustered about Brother Lewis, who stood upon some wooden beams, speaking.

The Abbot stopped, waiting to hear what the speech was about, but he did not want to be seen. He moved back until he was half hidden by the gate. More than once the mad, stunning eyes of Brother Lewis seemed to meet his, but he stood very still and they moved away, not having recognized him or a real world, so fixed were they on the stranger vision of private devils and angels.

"If we are to deny ourselves Jerusalem, Our Lord's home, the least that we can do is to bring the Holy Land to us, for we have infidels enough close by at Norwich and at York. Christ's killers there are thriving; we can cut them down like standing grain. The Jews have gobbled up everything; they are the wolves among Christ's sheep, and now they claim the lives of two Cistercian Brothers! Little by little they break the edges of Christendom until they weaken and destroy it. When mankind takes banners against the Devil, shall we turn away? When Christ calls his Sons of Light, shall we excuse ourselves because of sheep? He bids us purge ourselves of the unfaithful. He loves His guardians, His hawks who see sins from above and plunge upon them, root them out and destroy them even if they be within the darkest canyons of the world. How dare the sinful Jews live with their deviltry exalted to the light? They crucify us daily, shall we not denounce them? Shall we not bring our Crusade against them? We must go with armies and offer them the Light, and if they will not have it, we must slay them, slay them as a man cuts off a dead limb, lest the very death of it pervade his healthy body and destroy it!"

Abbot Adam could feel the words beginning to thrill through the group of standing Brothers. Brother Lewis's words about the two Cistercians was a mark in memory, a scandal over which the Brother was still agonizing. In the spring of the year they had left their House and gone to Lincoln and been converted to Judaism. When he had heard of this, a shock to every White monk in Christendom, the angry Lewis had taken his mortifying scourge to Brother Simon, shouting, "Your Jews! Your Jews!" until the others had stopped him. Now the passion of his loud, hard voice was beginning to be answered in their knotted fists, the tensing of their bodies. Abbot Adam stepped out from behind the wall, but the voice went on:

"We have holy work to do. We know what God's will must be. We know what He awaits—we shall not let him wait! We shall not let Him die again! We shall not let His Holy Breast be pierced!" Louder and louder: "We shall arm against Satan! We shall stand against the heathen! We shall kill Christ's killers! We shall . . ."

It seemed too late for intervention. Already the knuckles were whitening under the austere skin, the shoulders held rigid. Even from the back of the group Abbot Adam could see that they were beyond a gentle reasoning. In front of him stood Brother Norbert, his back stained with blood. He had been wearing, for the honor of his namesake, a studded belt about his chest under his habit. Without his feeling it, the three stud-wounds had wetted the back of his grey garment with blood. Mind left Abbot Adam and feeling took its place. He did what he did without thought, animal-like. He began to roar with laughter. He laughed until he wept, until he was weak and sick with laughter, until his own penitential ropes bit hard to him, and when he stopped laughing, he found that the wild voice of the Brother had stopped also.

The listeners were standing stock still. They had turned to him in amazement and breath was held. It seemed to be only their heartbeats sounding in their heads.

Abbot Adam gasped for breath. His voice seemed very soft. "How dull is a labor of sheep compared with the sure glory of Brother Lewis! Shall we Chosen Messiahs of the world pitch up the daily manure, or is work in God's courtyard too mean a thing for us? A crusade at York, and for the murder of the King's Persons . . . how saintly! How practical! I shall be replaced by Premontre, who will give you one more capable of Holy Discipline, and we will have as next Archbishop someone who hates us. Feel for Jews what you will, but touch them not, for they are the King's property. Go on a crusade if you must, but the punishment is excommunication, fines and probably a good while in one prison or another! Excuse me, good warriors, but since I am not delighted with these futures, I beg to be leaving, for I have work to do. . . . Brother, will you help me?"

He turned away with the Brother he had chosen and went slowly to his work. It would not be good for him to stay and see the others go to their duties thick-faced with embarrassment. It would not be necessary to give any more than a light punishment to remind them of obedience. No more would be said. It was better so, but to Brother Lewis what? Abbot Adam's mind wound around the problem. His taut companion in Christ was either pious beyond the human degree of it, or else just mad. To feed his piety and starve his madness—it was the problem of doing the first and second things together. Well . . . he thought, I shall let him be with the rest, and make no difference between the speaker and the listeners in disobedience. It is a worse punishment for that particular soul, than the saintlike grandeur of a solitary penance.

Let it be, then. He knew that he had learned something from that ring of Brothers. It was amazing to him that their zeal should not be from the message, but from the ardor of its delivery. The terrifying Brother had been speaking neither piety nor sense, and yet their hands were aching to begin that which had never been important to them before. Brother Simon had a Jew as a friend. He himself was frightened by hate and violence, and yet he had stood as deeply enthralled as any of the others. Had the order come to slay the Jews, might he not have run a mile before he realized what he had meant to do?

Abbot Adam fell upon his knees in the dust, and he was not sure whether he was thinking or praying. It was well, he was sure, to take up swords against the infidels who steal treasures, burn and desecrate, but where was there a rest between Saint's salvation and Satan's vengeance? Murder would stain the hands of pious men and iniquity would be their portion as part of the winning of Jerusalem. Rape and pillage go with any conquest, be it by rabble or The Armies of the Living God. Daily he had read in the Offices of his faith, which all men said, was love. What had this to do with fire and the sword? "Lord God and all the sweet saints, help us," he said, as the winds of autumn sharpened out of the north. He turned, for mortification, into the wind, shivering with it. "When the righteous stop thinking, even the angels run for cover."

December, 1188

20

THERE had been a fall of snow, and when it stopped, the people of York walked out once more to look at the changed world. They wished to save the perfection and yet to print in it, both at once; to keep it virgin and white and to mark themselves upon it, with the identities of their feet. When someone walked, then another followed, and soon they were all despoiling it happily, a small wish to ruin what was beautiful. Upon the door of the Community Hall of the Jews a notice had been nailed, and Bett read it, fearing that her eyes were faulty or that it was a joke or that her mind deceived her or that some strange mistake had been made:

All Christian servants who do not arrange to leave their Jewish masters and houses before the first day of January, 1189, are to be presented with a bill of Excommunication from the Body of Christ, His Church, and a service of this Excommunication shall be read against them from a suitable secular place in the city.

(And this was so that such unclean persons should not defile holy ground.)

Racing to Allhallows, her only Christian haven, Bett found Father Odo and heard that the order had been posted by an emissary of the Pope himself and was, indeed, true. All she could say was, "My house—my home!" And she bolted for Baruch's hearth, leaving the saddened Father Odo behind her. Bett's allegiances had never been questioned. She considered herself a Christian without thinking of it at all, but at the same time, she saw at last, how much of her life was the life of Jews. Unable to believe that she would really have to find a decision in all of this confusing morass of hopes, beliefs and habits, she let her work blot out the final choices for her. Somehow, vaguely, foolishly, she waited for the order to be rescinded. Such things did happen sometimes. With the rumored troubles of the King and the rounds of the day, with the rumors and speculation attending the courses of Richard and John, with the Archbishop-elect, Geoffrey awaited in York at any day—with all these events and the unchoosable choice blocking the way before her, Bett pushed the ideas and dread facts away and waited.

One by one, the Jankins and the Joans, the trusted servants of a lifetime and the pert little maids earning their dowries, slipped away from Northstreet. The changes were so gradual that Bett could still ignore them. Without Christian servants to light and tend their fires on the Sabbath, when Jews were forbidden by their Law to work, fires were banked to last as long as they could. It would be a misery soon to greet the holiday in an icy house, teeth a-chatter and fingers blue. The laws of a warm desert land where no snow fell and only the nights were cold was hard mercy, indeed, in the chill islands of the North, and too long had Jews been living in an exile in which they were made to depend on a Christian world about them. Those whose servants had left sat pitifully huddling through their holiday until at last, some Christians saw to it that "favors" of fire-lighting were done on the Sabbath eves and days, and Northstreet paid dear for these services. A note of disdain came to the voices of Christians as they spoke of their Northstreet neighbors: "They would die without us—though they have gold and are fat even at the end of hard winters, yet they are weak and would die without us."

The days moved on toward Christmastide, and still Bett could not leave. She became thin and her face hardened and her eyes sorted out restlessly over the objects of the world for one familiar one. In kindness to her, Baruch had called for her and had spoken to her of leaving. She could return to Kuckney where her parents served, and there would be generous gifts and marks of his gratitude. She would marry perhaps, some widower or so, for she was advanced in years: twenty, was she not? It seemed as if he were talking to a ghost. She did not see him or hear him. It seemed as if her waiting had gone too deep.

Gossip in the street passed over her head and she knelt at the Eucharist stunned like a sleepwalker. Her strangeness was noted by Jews and Christians alike, but there were so many other things to gossip about that her predicament got short rehearsal on the tongue.

Jerusalem's loss had blown the vision of crusade full yet again before them. Richard would be King—gay, courteous, chivalrous Richard—and he would lead them to wealth in this world and to Paradise in the next. For those who wanted another hero and who loved old Henry, there was the tragedy of Geoffrey. Commoners saw this great story played out in its simplest form: a bastard son (oh, the sweetness of a little stolen honey!) who loved his father not for Kingdom nor for prize, but for love alone and respect; riding with his ailing, weak old lord and sire even to death. Never mind favor, never mind the practical necessities of tomorrow's position in the world. The poorest miller in the most remote little village thought on this and loved the King's bastard for it.

Prince John was clever enough to see the value of such favor by the commoners, and the foolishness and danger if he and Richard should try to harm their half brother. A few words in Richard's ear settled the case: Geoffrey, cloaks flying in haste, would take Religious Orders and be made Bishop of Lincoln. As soon as Richard was crowned, Geoffrey was to be invested Archbishop of York (on the understanding that he would also be given estates in France, and that the management of these estates would keep him so busy that he would not, on any condition, return to England before the passing of three years). By that time, Richard hoped that good news from his victories in Jerusalem would make the populace forget a son's defection. Geoffrey, wishing to look over what had been given to him, made arrangements to arrive in York very early in January.

York had much to do for its visitor. The streets were washed, work in repairing the cathedral was accelerated, and all of the possessions to be seen and later claimed were found, cleaned, fixed and repainted. A see which has been vacant for so many years has much to do, not the least of which is finding all of the movables listed on the rolls as belonging to it. Let it never be said that a Christian soul would steal from his archbishop, but enough of the misplaced articles showed up in questionable surroundings to give the Dean of York Cathedral pause. He wanted no one's head to turn and no one to be able to smile any smiles. The Dean was a new broom. As he walked about, inspecting the cathedral grounds and making remarks to his clerk, the snow began to fall. It whitened the ugliness of the grey streets as sleep erases memory, by changing it. But to the official it was an inconvenience, a hindrance for his plans, and he cursed it.

Through the fall of snow Bett walked, with a veil of it settling on her hair, and she was numbed by wonder and fear. Toward the end of Northstreet stood Allhallows Church waiting for her. All of the Christian servants of Northstreet prayed at this church, some had married in it to save themselves from being excluded forever from its graces. Now she felt herself alone before the familiar entry. There were the saints, surrounded by their symbols and their attributes. They were crude but strong, and she stood looking at them, mindless of the snow and seeing in them a vision of her forebears—the English part of her. She went up the steps and into the church, opening the small door cut in the great one. A blast of icy air, colder than that outside, caught her and she gasped. Her eyes passed down the aisle, over the cold smooth surfaces of the stone columns and to the altar and the crucifix above it. How can it be, she thought, that they could say I am untrue to this? She knelt, feeling the slight rises and hollows of wear in the stone floors. Patient Christians, she thought, and deliver us from evil, Amen.

She heard Father Odo coming, limping toward her. His battered leg was an agony to him in this cold and the still colder dampness of the sanctuary. "Come, my dear child," he said. He led her to a

143

room off the side and back of the church. Its floor was not stone but packed earth and the stone of its walls was rough. There were two stools there and a rough table. Father Odo was a simple man and did not demand that laity of common birth kneel while speaking to him, but neither of them knew how to begin. Each in his own way felt blindly for the saving sentence, the answering thought, and as they searched in the darkness, each came to an end, a precipice beyond which there was nothing but the fall.

"Excommunicated . . ." he murmured, "cut off—it is worse than death, my daughter."

"I am a Christian!" she said, too loudly. The words rang off the damp wall-stone with a hollow sound that made her shiver. Her heart began to pound inside her with the terror of an aloneness so absolute that it overwhelmed speech. At last she said, "For eleven years I have worked in that house, and it was not a sin. Why now, suddenly, is it so—and worse than sloth or greed or murder!"

Father Odo did not know how to answer her. The Church had been many years trying to convert these heathen to the True Way. Perhaps She had seen how obdurate they were, and had at last relinquished them to their own deaths and an eternal damnation. He also knew from his distant years abroad, how sweet and alluring those false voices were. The shire had been shocked and then angered at the conversion of the two Cistercian Brothers—perhaps there had been more throughout the country and Christendom. Perhaps the Crusade was forcing a last drawing of the battle lines of allegiance. The Holy Church would try to protect her own from pitfalls in the way, and so must he. There were all these things that were perhaps and perhaps. . . . What could he say to Bett of them that would make good sense to her soul as well as her mind?

He began to speak quietly, of what mattered most to him, and thus, perhaps, to her also. He spoke of the love which Christ had for His Church, and that the Church had for every soul. He wanted to be as fiery and convincing as the traveling preachers were in setting before their hearers the visions that were almost to be reached out toward and touched in the awe-hushed air. He spoke of early memories and the peace of prayer and the sweet promise of Heaven.

When he finished and looked at her face, he saw that he had moved her, but only to himself—not to the truths which he was speaking. He had hoped to stir again the fires of her love for her past, but he saw that she had taken this as a playing upon her love, a using of it. How is one to know what will move a soul to tears and contrition, and what will harden and embitter it? She sat before him, burning with rebellion and indignation. She had been won to him more than ever—she was even grateful to him that he had taken his time with her and used his heart to save her, but she had been angered, perhaps beyond reconciliation at the Church which had provoked it. The ancient cry of servants was welling up in her: You can command my body, but myself is closed to you forever. He had violated something of herself, and had lost his case.

"It is well enough to love," she said in a controlled voice, "but where will I go—what will I do?"

"Is your family not in service at Kuckney? Why do you not return there?"

"My sisters and brothers have forgotten me. My father, who loved me, is dead, and my mother sits by her cottage door drying up with hate for me."

"But you could have service there . . ."

"I read, I write, I cipher!" she said. "I am no longer a part of that world. I can reckon in four currencies and write in three. . . ."

"There is marriage. I know that you are no longer young, but some one would be willing to take you. I know many another who marries a second time at twenty-one."

"No," she said.

"And religion—there you might someday be able to use what you have learned. You would be acceptable for many a convent right here in the shire, and your master would furnish a dowry, would he not?"

"No," she said again. "I cannot. I am too old for that also. I would not lie or dissemble to make myself fit for it. I am not fit for it—I have no joy in contemplating it." Suddenly she thought of Abram and a wave of loneliness swept over her so that she almost cried out, but her answer had angered Father Odo, for his loss and for hers.

"Proud girl!" he said, and the words released more anger than he thought they would, "take off the clothes that Jews have given you and return to your true life and God, or if you will not, get your master to furnish you a dowry and enter religion and be a daughter of Christ. There you will learn humility! Do you not see, blind one, you have eternity to risk in this!"

145

"I could have served my father, stranger though he was," she said, "but he died two years ago when the Throttler swept by like the wind that follows a galloping horse. What comfort there was after his death came not from here, although you were kind. I said the prayers and I was grateful for your own public mention and for your words to me then, but"—she was trying to follow her feelings without knowing where they would at last lead her, for she had never thought of these things before or made comparisons—"after my father's death, my master came to me and said, 'Mourn for him, and give him full measure of your grief, but do not mourn for yourself, for you will always have a place here, and we are fond of you,' " and she smiled, remembering the easement that had flowed to her, and the knowledge of what proper mourning was.

"I did not say that they were evil . . ." he persisted, "I said that they were doomed."

She remembered then a conversation that she had had with Abram and the cross which she had drawn in the air, saying, "Then I, too, must be afraid for the Jews." She rose and thanked Father Odo with the dreamlike expression which she wore so much of late, and as she left him, he sighed and uttered a prayer for the safety of her soul. He had never had a chance to help her. She was like smoke in his grasp, this servant with the speech of a scholar. He, who had thundered loudly against the errant Cistercians, now had a member of his own flock poised on the rim of heresy. He crossed himself.

Bett walked down the three steps of Allhallows, knowing in her Christian mind their echo of Trinity, and her thoughts were filled with a new note, stubbornly repeating itself: If I am half Christian, am I not also half Jew? She had never thought of it before. Her understanding of herself had always been as a Christian, but now, with every step down the familiar Northstreet, the certainty grew in her mind what she must do. She returned to Baruch's house, begged a purse-lipped Rana for the afternoon off to go and see Rabbi Elias on a most important matter. Rana raised her right eyebrow, as Bett had known she would, and then, with a shrug, gave permission. Perhaps it could be—perhaps it might be—that she would belong at last to those with whom she had lived, those whom she served, and—thinking with a sudden tightening of her throat, of Abram—those whom she loved. She suddenly saw herself dressed in the odd, lovely clothes of these people. Abram was by her side. Before she could stop, she saw the bridal wreath and the ring and the embroidered coif of a married woman. She tore the picture out of her mind, suddenly desperate at the hunger and the doubt and the terrible complication for both of them. That will not help me, she thought. My case cannot be made on that desire. But the heart was not prohibited from its vision, even by decree of the head.

The familiar wheels of discourse and decision began to turn and she spoke to Rabbi Elias, then to Yomtob. Before her was a week to the blank wall of her future, and she hurried like a mouse in the bins, to get done what had to be done before the great end should come for her. But they would not hurry. She spoke to each of them again, and then together. Elias greeted her in the street with an especially warm smile, and Yomtob saw her before the door of the synagogue, passing, and smiled; and they talked the matter away, up one street of inquiry and down another, until the idea, gutted and boned, lay beside the fish of a dozen suppers.

Thursday came and went, and then the furious cooking and cleaning of Friday, crowned by the Sabbath. This time, when they sat about the table singing, Bett, who had often hummed along in the other room, sang aloud, words and tune, and they were surprised at the familiar, well-used Hebrew coming so readily from the Saxon mouth. There was no other servant to reproach her for her heathen ways; they had gone. Sabbath eve opened into Sabbath day. Bett ran here and there, in service, but her mind was on the Sunday before her. Christmas Eve was Sunday night. There would be the Morning Mass, which she had attended even as a tiny child, carried by her mother to the small peasant's church at Kuckney. If she was really to be a Jew, really and truly, she must not go to this Mass, nor to the wonderful, dark glory of the Midnight Mass, so full of bells and beauty. Her heart felt tired with her decisions.

On the Sunday she did not leave the house. Baruch and Rana looked at her strangely, and she thought: Perhaps it is a mistake . . . perhaps they cannot even see me as a Jew. She knew that these people, so alone in an island in the sea of Christendom held family hard, and suspected the stranger. On Sunday evening, she lay down when master and mistress took the rest of a common day. All through the icy vigil of the streets of night, voices rang in song, candles and torches flamed. She lay awake, tight with loneliness and sorrow and, finally, she heard the bells: not wild, as for a fire; nor sorrowful, as for the death of a king; nor prosaic, as for the turning of the day from cool matins to warm vespers, but mystically, majestically, each tone of each bell of each church rang full time, full voice and the streets were empty. Every Christian soul was in church, and *Christus Natus Est* was being said, sung, lisped, laughed, whispered, shouted. Is God's Son to be born in the midst of winter, when all things sorrow? The woodman freezes in his tracks, the cold reaches into the very most secret bone of the body. Fly from us, Death; He is born. Begone, Sorrow; he has come.

Bett lay in her bed and wept. She had given up trying to comfort herself with thoughts of the sweet and wonderful Jewish holidays. Now the worshipers would be leaving the church and going home, singing, even as she had sung so many, many times *Laetatus est Angeli et Archangeli*. Mothers in poor shacks, beggar women who had come mother on some icy road, would, this night, hold their tiny ones, blue with cold, to rock them before what fire there was, and they would think of That Mother and That Child, and poverty would be like a crown of roses blooming in the snow, and death would be like a diamond without price, and suffering would be their offering to Her.

Monday followed, and Holy Joy turned easily into earthly joy. Men walked wide-legged in the street and women danced, and it was said that many a woman would lie in labor in September because of a little stolen honey in December.

Through a Northstreet trying to close out the revel of this, just another ordinary day, Bett walked to the house of Reb Elias. Her feelings were suspended, like the tiny cross of terra cotta which hung about her neck and which she had not the courage to take off. She went in quietly, humbly. They who had sent for her were sitting and waiting.

After a pause, Yomtob said, "We are happy that you should desire to become one of our people, considering as you surely must, that we no longer hold positions of such honor in this land —that we are, perhaps, in danger. You have worked long at the home of Baruch, long enough to have learned our customs and beliefs; long enough to know our Laws and our truths. He has told me that you apply yourself well, and that through learning and sympathy with us, the Natural Horror of the unclean has become instilled in you."

She was amazed that they had spoken to Baruch about her, and even more so that Baruch had answered in that way. Of course, those observant eyes could never be closed, those eyes that could tell by the way a man wiped his nose, who he was and what was his errand; they would have seen, even without meaning to, her weaknesses and strengths. Most of all, that anyone should care enough to inquire, to weigh her merits and find them good, moved her to tears. In confusion she put her hands before her face. Suddenly, she wanted to be one of them more than anything in the world.

Rabbi Elias's voice was gentle: "Young woman, had you come to us ten years ago, five years, even three, and asked us to let you join our people, we would have been as glad as we are now —and we could have accepted you. Now we cannot."

She was stunned. Looking down at him as he sat, she could feel her throat constricting. It was dry and her head was spinning. No safety. . . . My God, my God, no safety! went turning over and over in her mind.

Denicosa, Rabbi Elias's wife came then and brought a chair, and given the sign from the Rabbis, Bett sat.

Yomtob spoke now, and his voice was slow and grave: "You do not know how shakily we sit, we Jews of England. Richard will take the throne, and he is not strong, really, even with the plum of Crusade. If we accept you into Judaism now, the Barons and Church may jump on the scandal. Have you not learned painfully enough that we are heretics to these nations? We cannot risk the panic and fear and the desire of envious people to crusade at home, here, on Northstreet. Those who have not money to outfit themselves for a Jerusalem any further away hunger for our bodies as their way to grace. Now, to yourself: could you marry? You are without family in a faith whose foundation is family. Could you, as a Jew, help us and yourself as you do now as a Christian? No. In a year when excommunication dogs the steps of Christians who have Jews for friends, even, where would we find such a one as you? We know that your motives are high, but the way of wisdom is not always the way of happiness. Stay with us in all the safety which we ourselves enjoy. We sorrow with you. Perhaps later . . . in years to come . . . We sorrow with you."

Rabbi Yomtob raised his hands and let them fall, and in his gesture she saw all the hopelessness of her desires, and of his wish to grant them, and his helplessness to do so. There was silence then. In the midst of the silence, and carrying it with her, heavily, she left them. The two Rabbis looked at one another.

Finally Elias looked across at his friend and laid a hand on his arm for comfort. "The decision was right, my friend. When the snows come, prudent men go inside."

"But must we die, fearing to live? Must we build rooms without doors, fearing attack? I know that this was prudence, and oh, Elias, Elias, we are all slaves to ourselves, but the bonds pinch only occasionally. How much harder pinch the lighter chains put on us by the world!"

HE was like a mountain, the White Abbot. Bett's eyes were blurred with anguish so that she could **21** not see his face, but Abbot Adam remembered a certain Saint's Day some three years ago, on which the Kuckneys and their servants paid the annual visit of respects. There had been to Welbeck then, a proud young fox of a girl with a high head and a triumphant way of wearing her fine clothes. Was this that girl, this thin, sorrowing creature? He looked at her closely. Yes, it was she, but greatly, greatly changed. She told him— pushing the words from her with her flat, work-hardened hands in an agonized mockery of the Jewish gestures she had learned— what had happened. He listened with great attention, and when she finished they were both silent.

At last he said, "Are there many others whose service is to be ended?"

She answered almost with disbelief, "I have not seen anyone in York stumbling about as I do. It seems not to trouble them. The men go into other service and the girls run about scratching for quick husbands and the end of worry over whether to say Benedictus or Baruch."

Abbot Adam thought a little sadly that suffering of mind was not to be the lot of these young servants. Perhaps suffering of body was all that the Good Lord expected of them in this life— God knows they starved if they lost one place and could not find another. To some few—to some very few out of all the many —God had given that they should lie awake instead of sleeping through their hours of hunger, thinking of what the reasons were.

This pitiful girl, brought so low from what she had been, was one of these, and he felt his heart move toward her in pity for her that was also pity for himself; in pride for her which was also pride for himself. He knew that she had been cowed and frightened: too many voices, too many insistences, and so he took her arm as if she had been an invalid and led her to the cluster of tiny rooms that were reserved for visitors to the House and left her with an ancient blessing and a benediction of sleep. It was strange to her in Latin, but she knew better than he how ancient it was, for she had heard it spoken every day of her past years, in the tongue of the Jews.

Abbot Adam was restless himself that night.

Maybe the world hung in the night like a bell, he thought. Every hour it rang and God heard the sound of it. When last had the sound been pure? He lay on his pallet and listened to himself repeating the troubles of the day. Were there ten thousand other abbots also recounting? God, how the world must ring! Now also there was this Jew-Christian that the city and its strange demands had made. What would he say to her? There was only sympathy, only pity. When a wheel rolls over a man's leg and crushes it, no advice in the world can mend the broken part; and when the world, the unseeing wheel of the world crushes its men, there is only sympathy to be given, only pity. . . .

Even before Lauds he was awake, thinking of the Jews— strange people, indeed—who could barely live at all without a Christendom about them, and of the Christians who needed them and hated them and gave them an odd kind of reverencing, too, because they were so ancient and so close, even in their heresy, to the all-reverenced Christ.

But Bett slept well. For the first time since the Proclamation, she felt a certain safety and peace. The bells that rang for prayers did not stir her and she rose only when the servant of the day came with his holy greeting to wake her. As she went to the chapel for prayers, she passed a tall young monk and something about the tilt of his body made her turn and look at him. It was Simon, her cousin. She stopped in amazement, and so did he. They had seen each other last almost as children. The shining, eager look had lasted in both of them longer than usual. Innocence, and pride in innocence was gone. She remembered that Abram had come home not long ago and said to her, "I saw your cousin Simon." She had laughed and said, "Your friend Simon, Master Abram," and as she had spoken there had been a silence and an expression of sadness in Abram's face, and she had wondered at it. Not having seen Simon in so long, Bett had wondered of him: How could a boy like that hurt Abram? Now she knew that they were all grown up—men and women together in the current of the world, turning and fighting in their separate eddies. Simon looked safe and strong in his White Monk's garb. He seemed to have all the Church's strength to guard him. Abram, too, was safe; there was in Jews a sense that they, not the whole world of Christendom, were one with God, and that it was they who were to be shown salvation, not the mass of others whom they so disdained in heresy. There was only she, caught between the angry wheels, each complete in its own motion.

"Cousin . . ." she said, and he looked again. She thought that she saw surprise in his eyes and then recognition and then pity. She wondered if he had heard of the edict or if it were just the look of her that made him so.

The bells for work and prayer rang and stilled over them, but they did not seem to hear. She spoke of the years of service and of the knowledges of those years. She did not tell him of her love for Abram or of her dreams of him in the bare nights of the servant's house, but Bett was not meant to equivocate with her own kind; the love poured out in her voice, her look, her eyes, and loveless Simon was embarrassed by it and a little envious.

"What will you do now?" he asked finally. They were by the sheepfold where he and Abram had met so long ago, it seemed in the youth of the world.

"I do not know," she said, "and what I see is nothing but sorrow and blankness."

"Do you know just how blank, how sad?" he asked knowing, of course, that she did, but wishing to wake her up to it somehow, from the confusion of all of the loyalties that he felt himself. "You may never have congress with any Christian soul for as long as you live. You will never speak to a true Christian. You will be denied the barest rights of law and protection. You have no sanctuary in the Church. You will not have the right to contract a legal marriage or sign or witness a legal paper. Your Will is null. The whole thrust of Law and Rights will be against you. You will be forever an outcast, classless, outlawed and alone." She shivered. "Can you not join a Religious Order, one whose code is not too stringent? There, at least, you would be safe."

"I do not know if safety lies that way or destruction," she said.

He was suddenly frightened for her, and his fear showed in her face. Under it she broke and cried, saying over and over, "I am not a heathen! I am not a heathen!"

Vespers rang. They heard it, and suddenly heard again and realized how long they had been away. The oddly mild day was turning cold for evening and the light was going. What ease had he given her? He wondered. He looked at her face in the mellowing light which gives its fullest beauty to everything, and saw her beauty by that light. It was the beauty of the lost, a desperate, almost mad vividness, and he knew that all he could do was to befriend her. There was to be no quick *Ego Te Absolvo* and then a tranquil sleep. He remembered that he had left Abram with something of this feeling. Against his friendships and loves ground the wheel of Right and Duty and State, and his ears rang: Submit! submit! But he could not submit entirely; he could never renounce Abram completely, nor Bett, nor even the world which contained them all. He looked at her again, and they began to walk rapidly back to the Chapter House.

"I was supposed to have spoken with Abbot Adam this afternoon," she said.

"It was a waste, then, to speak with me, for he is wiser than I, and is better—and perhaps *he* . . ." And she saw that it was a true humility and not a style, cut for monastics with their clothes and tonsures, and it moved her.

After the simple meal the Abbot did call her and they walked along the chill corridor. To her surprise he did not add more to the voices that told and counter-told the confusion over and over in her head. He merely said, "I have a friend, a distant relative whom I have not seen in many a year. She is Abbess in the Nunnery at Lincoln, right near the cathedral. I would be most pleased if you would take my greetings to her—to go, if you could, and visit her and perhaps stay awhile. She would be happy to hear of me and my doings after all these years. She is a woman of great kindness, and perhaps you could go there to rest and think after you leave your service"—he added—"should you decide that way."

He smiled at her as he gave his benediction, and went down the corridor.

She thought of his gentleness as she moved back toward York on the slow little donkey. That great ham-handed man . . . but the animal's feet kicked at the stones in the road, and it suddenly occurred to her that this very trip—a two-day journey out of the shire just to discuss a problem, was a Jewish thing to do. Her mother would have thought it unbelievable; Lord Robert de Kuckney, her mother's master, would have thought it absurd. Only Jews sought wisdom farther away than the parish—only Jews would have given leave with such generosity—and yet the very grace and dignity which told these wanderers, living on sufferance in lands not their own, that they were Chosen and Beloved of God, and must live to a higher degree of perfection than other men, made them disdain charity to those who had received them. The knowledge of self which had let them stand as a race apart for hundreds of years stopped short of mankind as a whole, and drew the line of their kindness, charity and love hard around themselves, shutting Christendom outside. It was a fatal flaw.

Jews and Christians—Christians and Jews . . . and she—how did she feel? Again the old voices crosscut each other with argument and rang and rang in her head and her eyes were dulled with their noise.

From a high window in the Chapter House, Brother Lewis Fauconbridge watched the passage of the girl on the grey donkey. He watched her head as it got smaller and smaller. He laughed at the strangeness of it—the disappearing of man into the distance —into the earth—into nothing. Suddenly it occurred to him that it was prophetic that he should have been at that window at that particular time. Some message was in it for his eyes alone, some call, some mission. Already the Devil's armies were moving in his own body, the microcosm in which the battle would finally be waged and the decision of which would be the first victory in the great Last Contest for the world. A bell rang in the House. His years of obedience made him turn to obey it, but the Will in his mind was stronger. He must watch the dot of mankind out of sight. Destiny, Grace, the Sainthood of Sainthoods rested upon it. His eyes burned as he stared without blinking after the vision. With infinite slowness she grew smaller and smaller until she became air, a shimmer over the curve of a hill. He was fit then, for the Holy sacrifice, for the Destiny. He went down on his knees in a prayer of thanksgiving as the bell below called the other ones to their other prayers.

January came, and with it Geoffrey the love-child, Archbishop of York elect, on his fine horse. An unpopular enemy one slays; a popular and powerful, one buys away; and thus the royal sons contrived for their half brother. He was to be Archbishop of York, but never to stay there, and for assurance, they had given him an earldom in France on which he could lose himself. Nothing of this second gift was known except to a very few, and the people were wild with excitement. Purple and pomp the procession moved through the Walm Gate with the faithful son, now to be their Archbishop, leading his retainers. Banners whipped in the wind and cloaks flapped about the crowds who came to cheer half-noble Geoffrey as he rode in triumph. Since before noon they had been waiting; now it was growing late. To the crowd that pressed close in the narrow streets he gave his Bishop's blessing, and they laughed, for they knew that he was soon enough to be elevated beyond all bishops. Over the Foss Bridge they went and the wood creaked beneath the weight of the mounted men and of the welcomers who went with them. The old ones in the crowd marked this bridge over which the young Geoffrey rode, and remembered another bridge two score years ago over which Archbishop William, now St. William, had ridden in such a triumph. As he had crossed, the bridge had trembled, groaned and then splintered with the weight of the crowd. The spring current had been swift. Standing on the swaying end of the broken bridge he had lifted his wonderful arms in benediction and had obtained mercy for his flock, for every man, woman and child had been prayed to safety. York had had its great days, many of them, and with this Richard and this Geoffrey, how many more yet to come?

As they left the bridge, they heard the bells of the cathedral sounding the vesper service. A great roar of laughter went up. People were shouting: The smiling bishop still rides outside, and with him are all his loving congregation! They continued through the maze of streets. The beggars had been warned away, and so nothing but the sweet smell of wind blowing down from the hills might come to the hero on his day. They drew up before the cathedral at last, and Geoffrey dismounted and went up the steps. Even with the noise of the crowd one could hear the faint, sweet notes of the choir inside. Geoffrey's face darkened: the Archbishop-elect, late for vespers and closed away like any servant girl! The others came up the steps, and hearing what Geoffrey heard, whispered among themselves with confusion and embarrassment. With a roar, Geoffrey ran down the steps, seized a mace, flew back and pounded upon the heavy door. The crowd cheered. In a few moments the door was opened and a large nose and half an eye appeared in the shadowy crack. "What do you wish, Sir?" It was the Treasurer.

"What do I wish!" Geoffrey flung the door open and stalked in, his spurs clinking on the stone floor. "Who is responsible for this?" he thundered. The last "Amen," like smoke, rose slowly into the vaults of the cathedral.

"Be silent!" he roared. The final "amen" continued along with his shouted order, echoing in the high spaces over their heads. The Dean of the Cathedral, attired for prayers, appeared opposite the angry Geoffrey.

"It was time for Vespers and Vespers were said, my Lord Bishop."

The Treasurer had been flung back against the wall by the force of the door. He picked himself up and began to extinguish the candles. As Geoffrey strode down the center aisle, the man went up to the altar and put out those lights also. Geoffrey gripped his mace hard.

"The service is concluded, my Lord," the Dean said turning to the mailed priest. Grinding on his heel, Geoffrey strode out of the cathedral. When he came out into the fast fading daylight, the crowd cheered again. Geoffrey held up his hands for silence. Standing in his magnificent clothes, his gesture one of command, he was like a king and the crowd stilled immediately.

"I call upon God and man to judge my case!" Geoffrey cried. "I have been denied the Vespers, the candles snuffed out before my eyes. Though I am their superior to be, their father and guide, the ungrateful sons will not attend me!" The crowd roared again against the Dean and Treasurer. "Richard, soon to be King, has sent us to you. The envious, disdaining his will till it be vested in the virtue of a crown, denies me hearing and service!"

Another roar, a roar of anger and hatred from the sudden mob.

"Know then my will," Geoffrey shouted. "I hereby suspend all services, be they public or private in this cathedral, till I have my satisfaction. I am sure that it will not be long in coming!"

The crowd laughed and cheered. The favorite dog of this crowd was a little poodle, who would attack a crazed wolf and thrust its yapping mouth at that great throat. Its favorite man was a bastard who would stand, even against Heaven, and press his rightful claim. Dean and Treasurer drank no toasts to Geoffrey that night, but long after the ordinary hours, Will the Owl served up the good ale and mead, the wine and the second-press brews, while toast after toast named Geoffrey hero.

Abram left his home, knowing that on this night the curfew was sure not to be kept, and went across the Ouse Bridge to the synagogue. He had left his work undone, having run out when Geoffrey arrived, to see the splendor and to enjoy the revel. As much as he had laughed at his fellow Jews who had gone out to cheer an Archbishop, he knew that it meant much to his people to have some event of joy which they could share with their neighbors. The wonderful Geoffrey was, after all, not yet Archbishop, and so Abram had cried welcome along with all the rest, and he had admired the splendid horses and the impressive cortege while his pens dried with the ink on them and the expensive pieces of manuscript parchment lay scattered about. Now, as he passed through the gate into the courtyard of the synagogue, he wondered how long it would take him to straighten up his table. A light on would be noticed, so he intended to hang a cloth over the window of the balcony room where he worked. As he went toward the door, a light figure ran to him. In sudden fear, Abram's hand went to the knife at his side, but the voice called out, "Abram, Abram!" and he recognized Josce's youngest son.

"What are you doing here?" he asked, smiling.

"I was excited," the boy said simply. "I wanted to break a rule."

"You mean in honor of the Archbishop's coming?"

"It was as if there was a fever in the air. I felt like Passover. I could raise the cup right now and sing out, 'Glory, Glory!' "

"It is good to be so young," Abram said drily. "I came to work, or rather, to finish working."

They went in together. As they entered the sanctuary, they saw that someone else was there in the shadow.

"Who is that!" said Abram, again hand to knife. The voice which answered, let the words go as if they were birds, freed by mistake from a snare. "Oh! oh! I did not know anyone would come—I was not near the Ark—I have been in the back all the time!" It was Bett, moving toward the door like a thief.

The young boy, standing next to Abram, was astonished. He had never seen a woman in the main portion of the synagogue before, and this a Christian too! Excommunicated or not, the Jewish community had said, she is still what she is.

"I . . . had wanted . . . to be alone for a little while," Bett stammered, "as I was sometimes in the church. Now——"

"It is no matter," said Abram gently. "I was only coming to set things to rights."

The boy's high voice sounded stridently: "You have profaned everything!"

"No! no—" She hurried. "I must go, really—I touched nothing, nothing, master Abram!" and she darted away. His hand had been held out to stop her and her brushing by it seemed to the young witness almost like a furtive embrace. The two went into the loft and, covering the window, they lit a candle and Abram began sorting his pens and putting his parchment in a chest.

"You were very rude," he said after a little. "She is lost and in trouble and you made her ashamed."

"She is not one of us," the boy said righteously, "and you should not walk with her. Already there are whispers about the two of you, and scandal."

Abram ground his teeth in anger. A few short walks, an afternoon spent watching the birds and studying a Hebrew lesson, a little joke passing in the streets. The price was scandal and disgrace, and yet he knew that Bett would have died without these little grains of sustenance which a few, so very few, friends gave her. She was like an invalid now, with whom one walks slowly back and forth. The excommunication had struck her down like a shaft of lightning, and she was sick with it, almost to dying.

She loved him and now he knew it, and he, too, was thinking of her more and more in his dreams and thoughts, but since the blow had fallen on her, he had been like a father or brother, and not so much as seeking her eyes.

"How, scandal, how?" he burst out, and shook the boy.

"Abram, my sleeve—I am not at fault!"

"How!" Abram shouted, and then lessened his grip and stepped away.

The boy straightened himself as if he had never once touched temptation or known an evil by conquering it. "Your mother went to a practitioner of magic, a dealer in the Cabala. She went because of you and that woman."

"What?" Abram was dumbfounded. He turned and seized the lad again by the sleeve. "What is this? How do you know?!"

"Everybody knows," the boy said matter-of-factly. "My mother told my father how your mother had gone to a conjurer, well versed in the mysteries of the books of The Sword of Moses.

She had paid this conjurer, and they went through the book to select which charm to apply. As the conjurer turned the wonderful pages, reading off the names and types of curses and charms, your mother became frightened. She thought (my mother told my father) of all the ills that were written there, and to every one she added your name in her mind, seeing you, with her imagination, in such a suffering, and such, and such. Makers of spells delight anyway in showing their power: '. . . to such-and-such broken bones, death by invisible fire, and a penny extra I will read it so that the corpse turns blue!' All this your mother saw as clear as truth before her and ere the conjurer had settled on a charm, your mother jumped up and ran weeping back to her house."

Abram's feeling was first one of terrible anger. He had been cheated by his own mother. Behind anger walked shame. What would poor Bett think if ever this got back to her? And it was sure to do so. What had yet to be done to her in the hard world, that quiet, kind little dreamer, who was still so gentle in return? Behind shame walked the Jew's Angel: laughter. He imagined Rana, running as if pursued by the very devils of which her money had given her choice. The more he thought of it, the more he laughed. The boy beside him looked on in horror that such things were being taken so lightly, but Abram knew that he was missing the reason for laughter as he had missed the reason for anger. Finlly, seeing the amazed face through his tears, Abram rose and took the boy's shoulders.

"You will learn," he said, "at least, I hope that you will learn."

Josce's son, beyond his depth, fled in haste. Still laughing, Abram completed his work, cleaned his table, put it away and crept through the indifferently guarded streets to his home.

The next day was Epiphany. "Our Lord's life," Father Odo remarked in his morning sermon at Allhallows, "had the order of all holy things. On this day we celebrate the vision of the Magi, Baptism of Our Lord and the miracles of Cana. The day is like a book in itself, a small Trinity of the Happenings of Truth."

This was said at dawn, when each parish went to its own small church. Later, after the simple services, the men and women of York dressed themselves in cathedral finery, and stepped daintily through the streets on their way to the Great Event of the day. Now, with an Archbishop, the cathedral could be used on this Epiphany. Surely the Dean and Treasurer would have backed away from the fire of Geoffrey's interdict. Arriving at the cathedral when the great bells of the parish churches called the time (the cathedral bell-tower had not been rebuilt from its fire twenty years before), they saw the heavy doors closed against them. Standing in the Close, they whispered and muttered. Was there to be more of a spectacle than this feast itself?

Through the crowd a rustle passed: Geoffrey is coming! Geoffrey is coming! They parted a way for him, and soon he appeared, and his garments and jewels took the breath away. He was the brightest of priests and from his studded belt a sword hung ready. He smiled to them. They cheered. With his youthful, sprightly step, he walked up the cathedral steps, mounted the porch and stood before the closed door.

"Break it down!" the voices cried, and "We'll help you, and break the bones of them who try to stop us!" Geoffrey took his heavy sword, still in its scabbard, and pounded it, hilt-first against the door. The crowd fell silent. He banged again, making a loud, heavy sound. Again.

At last the door opened and the Treasurer stepped out.

"Send us the Dean!" the crowd yelled. "We called for the horse and they sent us the droppings instead!" The air was full of jeers and laughter. The Treasurer retreated through the partly open door. Geoffrey remained outside, cool and smiling. This amusement encouraged the crowd. After a moment the Treasurer again appeared, followed by the Dean. Geoffrey raised his hands for silence.

"We come to pray here, good men. The see being vacant, and I soon its head, I am willing to assume my dignity aforetime."

"Your office is not that of Archbishop at this time," said the Dean. "The cathedral is not open. No service is being given here." The crowd growled. "When you are enthroned, properly, we shall hold it an honor to show you to the Altar."

"Thank you, Sirs, truly," said Geoffrey sarcastically. "Do you hope to wait until Prince Richard returns from France in the autumn? Indeed, we hope we are not to stand here with our stomachs growling until you relent and give us satisfaction!" The Dean's answer was unheard in the general roar. Finally the noise settled enough for Geoffrey to ask again. "Do you intend to refuse me here?"

"You are not Archbishop of York. The see pays you its compliments. It does not give you its cathedral."

At the sound of these words, uttered so defiantly by the Dean and seconded by the grim look of his underling, the crowd surged with aggravation. Streaming up the steps, they grabbed the stout Treasurer and the angered Dean and began to beat them wildly. The Treasurer landed a heavy blow on one of his attackers, who fell like a sack of meal to the ground, but now the feeling of deep violence was heavy in the air, and men, once careful of their good clothes, were mad for the melee and eager to kill the two stubborn men who stood against their hero. Quickly, Geoffrey saw that this anger would do him no advantage when the heat of it cooled. He had all he wanted, and beneficence would put the cap on his claim. He quickly stepped into the thick of the mob around the two now bloody men, and raising his hands, shouted for silence. The fists relaxed slowly, the breath went out.

As the noise of the crowd subsided, the battered Treasurer looked up at Geoffrey. "They will kill us, my Lord—they are angry at themselves because they are children. Law does not come and go, to be given or taken at will. Conscience will be put to rest in our blood."

Geoffrey lifted his arms over the heads of the two. "These men must not be harmed," he shouted.

The crowd muttered again, pressing forward: "He is too good to them. He is too merciful. We must punish them."

"Not be harmed . . ." Geoffrey was shouting again. As the crowd let itself be stilled by the powerful man, the Dean fell down the cathedral steps and ran into the deanery. His officer slipped into the cathedral and ran to St. William's tomb in the cellars, but Geoffrey's words must have reached both of them where they hid, for he was shouting at the top of his voice, and with the thunder of the crowd behind him, he excommunicated both of them until they should relent and he closed all services in the cathedral until he, Geoffrey, should call them into use again. Then, Prince and Archbishop to be, having won the day, he stalked off to inspect other of his possessions. The group waited for a while, enjoying the added interest of the skirmish and wondering if any more of import would arise to fill the tankards of future conversation. Soon, when it became clear that nothing was to happen, they wandered away, one by one, no longer held together by their hunger to prove themselves alive, if need be, by watching someone else die. They went to their homes happy. Geoffrey, for all his princely station, seemed suddenly closer to their own lives (conceived as he was by passion and not by protocol), than were Church bureau-men, with their niceties of law and precedent. Thus had Geoffrey triumphed.

Will the Owl and his wife served up good French wine aplenty, as the victory of the young half-prince lit the night, but thinking men saw dark portents at the bottoms of cups. Mob and master had answered one another antiphonally across the bodies of the upholders of the law. No issue had been studied, no just way decided, yet all feasted as if some towering truth had won the day. What they were toasting was forgetfulness, release, and the relinquishing of all the heavy ropes of responsibility and ancient law. Geoffrey would go soon enough, all jewels, the golden sun of their popular dreams, but a hunger had swelled in them and would remain, and they would be distraught once more, hopeless of the patient worth of law, of their own single thoughts and memories, and they would respond more quickly still to the blood joy of rabble and the glorious power to inflict horrors at which their single selves would shudder.

August, 1189

The autumn sun had set and the Brothers were awaiting their evening drink and the last sweet prayer. The bell rang in the court and the Brother who kept the gate went to answer it. There were low sounds and then the Brother returned, walking as fast as was permissible. He left with Abbot Adam, and again there were voices, and at last the Abbot returned with the message. He signaled them to their knees and said gently, "The war is concluded, and our King defeated."

He thought: Such terms, such mean terms to fit the dignity of a King, the dignity of a father. "Richard is to be declared King one year from this date—not John." (A murmur of approval from the Brothers.) "Philip and Richard will hold the captured lands jointly. Henry is to pay France twenty thousand marks." (An "Ooooo" from the Brothers.) "The barons of England will see that these terms are enforced."

At that word a strange racking sound cut rudely across the path of Abbot Adam's voice. The Brothers looked up, astonished, and saw that Brother Lewis was shaking and that the sound was his, a kind of laughter, crudely torn out of his throat. Brother Lewis was possessed by the sound, and with the terrible shaking he seemed almost to have disappeared beneath it. His great voice echoed through the stone hall and down the stone corridor, sending threads of terror and wild thoughts whipping through the silent men. But as suddenly as he had begun to laugh, he stopped, so that while still the laugh went beating echoes up to the tops of the high walls, no one could have told, coming in, that it had been he who had caused it. In the silence that followed him like the pause between the lightning and the thunder, he said, "The barons will see that he keeps his part of the agreement."

Brother Simon was very frightened. He felt almost like screaming himself, but in the same thicket where one can hide from a friend, one can take refuge also from an enemy. He pulled The Rule across his mind until he was completely safe behind it, and when his pulse stopped hammering and his blood accepted the balances of humors, he murmured, "Poor King—he is eating the stones of the road."

Abbot Adam had gone to Brother Lewis and had taken him by the shoulders and said, "You are not a member of the nobility. You are a brother of the very poor. What is your allegiance? You are only a member and servant of the Church of Christ, and thus you should be a man of charity and love. The King was invested in Christ's name and pledged to love and defend Our Lord and His children. He is ordained by sacraments. Why then, this unseemliness?"

Brother Lewis was silent, but his eyes were burning in his head, and he looked as if he might strike Abbot Adam. The Brothers stood; the breath was taken in very slowly, but the Abbot was a good deal larger than Brother Lewis, and his bulk had the further advantage of stability. He was like the House itself: sturdy, plain and unornamented; earthlike, mountainlike. The only danger was that Brother Lewis was one to hurl himself at mountains, and the more insurmountable they were, the more he was compelled to pit himself against them. This time, however, the ingrained discipline of years and habit forced itself through to him, and Brother Lewis brought his eyes once more under the control of his Obedience to Rule.

The brief time of comradeship remaining was filled with awkward silences and odd, unappropriate bursts of laughter. Other Brothers felt the same way as Brother Lewis, for quite a few of them had been members of great families in the three counties and had not shaken off old thoughts with their fur-lined garments. Many a monk saw in his dreams, where he could not put them out, sights of a baron's table, pleasures of a knight's spring morning, and only upon waking to *Deo Gratias!* did the monastery walls around him become the real walls. But those Brothers whose noble birth made them happy to see their cause advanced at the expense of the King smiled at their triumph, when they did so, privately. Abbot Adam was not above insult, and he was not of the nobility, having risen by capability and strength. Some part of him knew this, yet because of the difference in their original stations, Abbot Adam did not remonstrate further with Brother Lewis, nor did he assign the rigid penance which he would surely have given to another. He merely closed the embarrassing period of recreation, composed his face and his thoughts and led the Brothers to the refectory where their evening drink was being set out for them. They sounded the prayers, the sweet and gentle anthem of sleep in Christ—then each to his narrow bed in the wolf-cold solitude, to quiet sleep, or to dreams, or to the temptation of thought.

In the sound of rhythmic breathing lay Brother Lewis. He did not know whether he slept or was yet awake, whether he was lying down or standing. He seemed to have no body and no mind, except to feel the strange sensations as they came and went; a lifting, a lowering, a kind of purpleness growing rounder and wider inside his head. He seemed to be turning around in the center of this purpleness, and then he seemed to be standing, and the vision or dream came sharply to him and thrust him into it and he was drinking in a tavern. The haze was still there, clouding his vision, but a voice said by his ear, "Have another, your Excellency." He looked down and saw that his robes were those of an archbishop. He heard himself saying, "Pour another, pour another!" The drink was put in his hand. It was thick-looking and greasy against the brass goblet, but he felt somehow that he had to drink. Something was beating in his head. It was the sound of a word, perhaps something like *pom, pom, pom,* over and over. He looked about at his host in the evil world of this dream. "Is this the way you serve the Archbishop of—of . . ." He could not seem to think what he meant to say. A whore walked by his bench, motioning to him, and suddenly anger and lust burned together in him and he reached out for her, but she was gone. He got up clumsily and grabbed the jacket of his host. The whole tavern began to roar with laughter: women's shrill laughter, men's deep bellowing laughter. "I am very important!" he cried, enraged. He looked down at his clothes once more. The lacy embroidery, as he beheld it, turned into rags; the gown was greasy and full of filth. "I am the Archbishop!" he thundered. "I have come disguised, the better to catch you in your sin!" The laughter was louder, but it began to change, even as his robes had changed, and it began to be fear and soon they were screaming. The host said, "They are here!" and there was the sound, *pom, pom, pom,* growing louder. He looked helplessly about him and suddenly he knew what was coming. From thousands of holes in the walls, the floors, they crawled, ugly spiders all making the same sound. It was not *pom, pom, pom,* now, it was *vint, vint, vint.*

He tried to remember that sound, that awful yet familiar sound. sound. They were coming closer. Yes! yes! In the terrible second's dawning of truth: he had been a little lad, and the Jew had come to visit his father. The Jew had been a German, pronouncing the French oddly: I come: *jo vint.* When the Jew had left with his assistant, the father had said, "Those cursed lice, those spiders, they will strangle a man!" Now the spiders were coming to strangle him from the earth which multiplied spiders. He tried to scream; he had to escape them. *Vint, vint, vint . . .* They oozed like a living blanket down the street and, behind them, nothing stood. Down another street he ran, and from a crossway they cut him off and he could hear the terrible *vint, vint, vint.* He listened hard. Now, with great effort, straining all of his senses, he could hear them thinking. They thought in a kind of hum, a one-tone song: Strangle with hate—strangle with hate! The thought repeated itself, now simple, now symbolic —vivid with metaphors, but always in the deadly hum: here to strangle, here to hate. They came forward to him to engulf him. He fought, holding them back for a while by the strength of his will alone, but he could not stop their surging, and they flowed up to stop his mouth with their bodies. . . . Already he was wrenching from the dream with the long cry of terror still shattering the icy night.

He was awake now, shivering uncontrollably, with his rough, reeking sheet over his head. The hum could have been a bell. It rang again and again. He tried to sort himself from the dream, for the bell was a call to act, but he knew not in which world. At last he struggled to his feet, and looking about in the dark, saw dimly the walls and partitions of his monastic cell. It was an hour or so before the regular time of waking, and the Brothers had always been brought from sleep by the voice of one of their number.

Now, with the bells and the strange awakening, they stumbled from their narrow pallets confusedly pulling on their overcloaks and went into the main hall. They saw the Abbot standing there. He said simply, "Pray for a King and for a King." They went on their knees where they were. Henry's reign was dead and Richard's was born. Although this news might be no more than one of the hundred rumors that were given credence in these days of fearing and hoping, the substance of a reign a generation long was now mere shadow and Abbot Adam wanted the moment of passage to be marked; a separation in the hours of sleep, lest it be lost.

Back in the penitential bed for a short time of rest before the ordinary hour of waking, Brother Lewis lay with the ugly ravelings of his dream. "It warns me truly," he said to the cold night, stuttering. "They will come in hordes, and I shall have to fight them, to be powerful and full of fire. Their plan is as wide as Christendom. Why is the Devil always outwitting us? Why is he awake while we, and the saints, sleep? It must be for me to thwart alone, for I was warned awake. For my own special grace, that I am alive with righteous wrath against these spiders. My grace, O God," he whispered. "My glory!"

The second dream, the dream ended by the familiar *Deo Gratias!* of his Brothers was filled with splendor and his own voice saying, "It is I who will conquer! It is I who will be glorious, and even against the Devil and his legions, be they as wide as Christendom and as deep as Hell itself!" and his robes once more were the robes of an archbishop.

September, 1189

22

THE turning of spring to summer and summer to late summer was alive this year with a growing sweep of excitement. On August 12, Richard, Prince, soon to be King, landed at Portsmouth from a forgotten battle and his father's death in France, and his adoring crowd cheered themselves dry. He rode to Winchester to see his old mother and throngs lined every step of the way of his fine white charger. White horse and silver of sword, lance, spears and spurshoes, he burned in the sun like an archangel. No one who was so blond and so burning and so young at last (for the old King had been with them thirty-five years) could but be perfect; and he had courtliness about him, too, with its love for honor and politeness and liking the look of one's self riding on a righteous errand. Everyone was mad to meet and serve this flower of Great Britain, who loved to please his subjects.

When he invited the Jews, his Persons to his coronation in London, Northstreet York took fever in a red eagerness of haste. They gathered, from secret stores, jewels and gold; they wrote a parchment, Abram working far into the night to have it finished on time; they gossiped the pros and cons of each gift; they outfitted themselves, Rana and Bett working as under whips to finish a sumptuous Baruch to honor his King. Although some knew that the gifts were only the beginning of a major job of finance for the Crusade to come, there was little bitterness among the Jews. The invitation had seemed to give them the illusion of state and rank for which they so desperately hungered. They would walk with the lords and knights to whose number they felt they really belonged, and would tell, with their presence, that they, too, served this history. The heads of every Jewish community in England were coming to show their honor. The coronation was set for September 3, and Northstreet looked toward that day as if it were the beginning of more than just the reign of another king.

On the thirtieth day of August, outfitted themselves like kings royal, Jews from Newcastle and Durham sat on their prancing horses while Josce and Baruch were mounted with their groaning weight of splendor, of robes and gifts and cakes and chicken for the journey and the thousand endearments of friends and relatives to distant ones in London. Yomtob had last included a sack of medicinal gems, and Anna the extra shirt—"Another Moses for another forty years in the desert?"—and they had all laughed. Josce handed the paper of divorcement to Rabbi Elias for safekeeping, for his wife still shrank from touching it. The crowd outside the Walm Gate applauded as Baruch prepared to turn his horse for London, but he stopped suddenly, almost as if he had forgotten and been reminded, and he called his son privately to him for the farewell blessing.

"Do you have the parchment, Father?" Abram asked, and it annoyed Baruch that Abram seemed more worried for it than for him. "As safe as death, every last flourish," he said caustically. "Here." He took the divorcement paper which he and Rana had signed and gave it to his son, saying gruffly, "Here—and see that she is true and does not change the date for a little sip or two while I am gone."

Abram's mouth fell open. He was used to his father's gruffness. He knew that Baruch would never be able to bid good-bye to his wife and son, but this crudeness amazed him.

Yet Baruch was not finished. He leaned down toward his son and said, "Look at your clothes! You could at least have dressed suitably for my leave-taking!" Before Abram could answer, he gave the gesture of benediction and turned his horse.

"Go carefully, my husband!" all the wives were shouting.

The horses began to stamp. Women and children, sons, daughters and friends said farewell in the formal words of public speech, and like the pictures of kings and magi which the Christians painted on the walls of their churches, the beautiful procession left on its way. The group cheered them off, and some remarked how moving a thing it was to see so important a man as Baruch of York take time for a private good-bye to his son. Laughing and talking, they turned back to Northstreet.

As the handful of days slipped by before the third day of September, astrologers and learned men sat down to their predictions. A great Doctor of the Stars, casting the day of the coronation, discovered that the third was a most unlucky day. It was called Egyptian day and it had a forecast of very poor omen. He called his colleagues together, and they found that their readings agreed. The astrologers in London tried to convince Richard to set the coronation ahead so that his mighty and long reign could start under the most auspicious of circumstances, but Richard was not to be put off. Too many delays had already ground the patience of the people fine, and though the young prince believed the mighty oracles of the stars, he had no faith in their human interpreters who made and remade auguries and reburied the dead a hundred times with their hindsights. Yet for some demands he had ears. A convocation of churchmen and nobles persuaded him for his own safety that he must publish notices excluding from the coronation ceremony witches and Jews. Some felt that both of these would be amiss in a cathedral, and it was well known that Jews would not kneel there. It was therefore posted that witches and Jews were not to appear at the cathedral or nearby.

On September third, astrologers or no, Richard was crowned King Richard of England. At the minute that the crown sat firmly on the head of the smiling young King, and London's cathedral bells announced it, church after church up the coast and into the midlands, took up the echo and beat it farther north and east to the ends of the Kingdom. From little village to town to city to town to village again, the bells sounded, so that before London's feasting citizens had stopped their dancing, York's had begun. It was French wine at Will the Owl's that night, for those who could pay for it, and a drink extra at Will's expense. York was happier than it had been in a long time, happier even than when Geoffrey came, with his fine spirit and his sword at the ready. Now, at last, God's Will would, indeed, be done. Now, at last, the agonizing wait was over, and the armor need rust no longer, nor the soul hunger for holy adventure. The winds of spring would find the willing martyrs, swords drawn, in Jerusalem.

The curfew that night was thrown to the winds and the dancers in the grand dance found breath enough to swing and swing as the bell did in the belfry, until it was dawn and the sobering Mass caught them up again in their web of days.

They came to it dry-mouthed and weak with wakefulness. Some, whose legs would not be trusted, sat outside and fell a-snoring where they sat, and the frost formed on them, indiscriminately, if they were little sinners or great. Inside, the priests rambled through their observances. Even the candles were tired, and the clothes on the women hung slackly. Those who could still think thought: Oh, what a night that could end in such a giant yawn! From *Ite Missa Est* to sleep was so short a space that few remembered walking to their beds.

The York Jews had danced in the streets and feasted with as much fervor as anyone else, and they had double reason for doing so. There were few times enough when Jew and Christian could both laugh at the same celebration, and the crowning of a king was one such time. Northstreet was also planning a feast for the returning emissaries, and now they were eager to decorate their Community Hall with autumn fruits and flowers and to have pranks played and riddles told. All who could play musical instruments were practicing, and, of course, there would be singing. They supposed that the London Festivities would be three days, then three more for visiting in London, one or two days more for business, four days home if the weather was good —two weeks then, and they would sate their eyes and ears with all the gossip, fancy, fashions and changes going on in London, that fast-growing capital where every language on earth it seemed, was spoken, and where minds and money moved as fast as quicksilver.

Rana had sent Bett on an errand to Rabbi Elias's house, and the old wife let her in, smiling, and stayed awhile to chat with her. Denicosa had always had a fondness for this girl, who loved learning like a man, and since her excommunication, with its terrible sentence of eternal damnation and a life apart from any community of Christian souls, the Rabbi's wife had taken special pains to give her kindness and company. Slowly, that tragic, blank look, the look of having been struck, was moving from Bett's face.

"The edge of autumn's foot is in the door," Denicosa said, handing Bett a cup of spring mead. The drink was very cold to the lips and in the mouth, but it went heating down into the throat and chest. Bett loved the drink. She sat on a stool holding her cup in both hands like a little girl. If Denicosa was not too busy today, they would talk or perhaps read from one of the scrolls of philosophy which Elias kept about the house and traded with scholars who traveled by now and then. When a knock sounded at the door, Bett sighed with disappointment. She rose, but Denicosa got up before her, as if she were a guest, respected in the house, and opened the door, and there was Abram. "Is the Rabbi here?" he asked, and then he saw Bett and dropped his eyes. "No," Denicosa answered, "but you may come in and wait for him."

They sat together, not knowing what to say to each other, but glad to be where they were. The Servant's Face had been removed from Bett and she smiled, and Abram thought how lovely she was. Denicosa, missing children alive and dead, was glad to have those about her who could have been her children, and Bett, when she was with Abram or the Rabbi's wife, could forget as if it had never been, her memory of her own bitter mother, and the hatred she had poured from her tight body at the father's funeral. Sometimes Bett thought of her father. The excommunicated could not say: "In the Name of the Father, and of the Son, and of the Holy Ghost. Amen," but Bett said it, and in the deep places of her loves it echoed and was not to be cut away from her by edict.

They drank another cup of mead and then a woman came to the door to speak to Denicosa about the plans for the welcoming of the emissaries on their return. The holiday season was nearing and perhaps there would not be time to get everything ready at once. The woman came in and Bett leaped from her stool as an adulterous wife, caught, covers her nakedness from her husband. She pulled her blankness up before her, and Abram, having seen her in such guilty haste—for whom? for what?—was covered over with his own shame. Bitterly he thought: Anyone can use a woman and bring her to disgrace, but it takes a scholar and a genius to bring disgrace to a woman without having used her.

So they stood rigid and apart while Denicosa's guest chattered on about the plans. As soon as Abram could, he made his excuses and left, and a moment afterward Bett also, and Denicosa chattered and chattered as if she might drown with words the knowledgeable look in the eyes of the other woman.

Abram was waiting for Bett as she came around the corner, and he pulled her to him out of the wind. "It was too soon," he said. "You were in mourning for your father, and then there was this anathema, and after that, it was too late. See how I have made you suffer? You have taken so much misery—you would be only beginning to suffer if you joined yourself to me."

"How could that be?" she said, knowing but not wishing to know.

"You have been too long without belonging anywhere. There would never be anyplace where we might be safe and calm out of the wind."

They began to walk over the bridge and toward the hill that overlooked the city. In the grove the trees were still late green, and just beginning to turn and so they did not climb the hill but stayed in the grove with its protection, for they wished to be housed against the world.

"When my father returns I will tell him, and he knows that I will leave if he does not let us marry. How can they deny you then? They will take you in—they will take us both in together; in the home as man and wife and as Jews. If not here, why somewhere. You are no longer an embarrassment to the Church you served, and besides they know that you are lost to them; there was no choosing done that could inflame them——"

"Oh, now, please . . ." She was pouring out tears, this plain girl who was so beautiful, and the causes for them were so many that she could not stop. He held her as she sobbed until she was too weak to stand and they sat down on the mossy roots of the tree while she cried still longer and until she seemed to have sated herself for all the years. All of the weeping that Abram had ever seen women do, had had a certain ritual quality to it. The Jews believed in crying out their pain and ridding the heart of its weight, and so women accompanied travail and men and women the burial of the dead and songs for the lost Jerusalem with great rending dissonances. Over the generations the sound had become a style with them and they hid behind it and poured into it whatever their feelings were, and thus for all the crying, Abram had never seen crying or heard it.

When Bett had faltered against him so long ago at the side of the house, he had been too much with himself, too flustered and put from face to hear her truly, but now, listening to her and holding her so that even the shaking of her body and the pounding of her heart was immediate for him, it seemed as if he beheld and knew an intimacy as much as that in marriage. And he began to yearn for her.

Abram had not been a man for sweetness, and even this marvel, this revelation that he could love, had some of the bitter flavor of the rest of himself. How many lovers had he seen or come upon at the Foss's side or under the river bridges, "leaping and groaning" as he had said, in the generous months of summer? "Christian pigs—animals," he had said, and passed by, surprised that a feeling against Christians should come where he least expected it. He had never known that there was stored in him, also, the grain of hatred. Now it came back to torment him. He embraced her gently and kissed her a long kiss that came to him with a passionate reminder of life, but he yet reserved the secret coil of doubt or discord that would not let him love with his whole self. They rose and walked together as betrothed ones do, across the bridge and into the city and down a whisper-buzzing Northstreet to home.

"Shield me, O my God, with Your darkness, or I may be murdered in the light of the moon! What have they done to us, Your people? There were such flames, such burning swords, such anger! O my God, my stomach hurts still from the blows, and my head is beating like a madhouse regiment. Shield me, God of

Abraham—at least let me die among my own people. I will never see the doors of York—I will die outside the walls like a dog. Oh, my death, my death—were you meant to be so ugly? I have blood in my mouth!"

Behind the houses, stumbling against the walls, breathing so loud that the guards who walked the streets must have been deaf not to have heard it—Josce. When he reached Northstreet, the world was heaving and spinning in his brain, and with safety almost in sight, he stumbled and fell, unseeing, against the door of Elias's house.

HE did not die. When his eyes opened, it was **23** not on the Plain of Darkness, but on the familiar, homely faces of Elias and Denicosa.

"Are we all dead, then, all of us?"

"Dear friend," she said, trying to calm him, "do not say anything now. Rest. Misfortune can wait to be told. . . . Oh, those robbers in the road; they are worse than animals!"

(She could not know then, what it was . . . I must tell her. . . .) He tried to get up.

"No, no," she said gently; "you will recover, but you are ill and need to rest. We will call Anna the first thing in the morning."

(Of course that was what must be done. That was what was sensible.) With a shock once again, he remembered this last week. Who had thought of sense then? Who could be merciful? He lay back, twisting and moaning. Elias came with some cloaks in his arms and Denicosa rose and took them from him and the two of them whispered briefly together.

"It will soon be dawn," Elias said, coming to Josce. "At least rest until then. I have told the sentries to keep your horse for you if they should find it wandering outside the gates. They are good men. You will have your things intact and soon all this will be forgotten." Elias could say no more than that to comfort him. Laying the cloaks over Josce's ragged and bruised body, he and Denicosa watched carefully. When they saw that he still turned and opened his mouth in an anguish to say something, Elias came close and began to repeat a Psalm in Josce's ear, in Hebrew. As he went on, he lowered his voice gradually until it was very, very soft and droning. By the time the Psalm was finished, Josce had fallen asleep. . . .

When he woke again, Anna was there, and the children, but he would not let her try to comfort him. He made them lift him up.

"Help me to walk. I must go to see Rana, now."

"What is the matter?" they asked him. "What has happened?"

He did not speak to them any more, and at last, wondering what it was, more than his weakness that made him look so ill, they helped Josce out of the house and toward the stone mansion of Baruch at the end of the street. Rana was sitting on a bench outside, preparing some flax. Yomtob came and took Josce's arm from Anna, and the three men walked with a deliberate, slow step over the cobbles of the road, closer, closer. When Rana saw the three of them coming and still coming on toward her, she dropped the distaff and rose, still clutching a stray strand of flax tightly in her hand. (Pass by, oh, pass me by with the news you have!) She was praying for them not to stop. Pressing her eyes as tightly closed as she could, she prayed with all her might: "Oh, let them be an apparition that is gone. Let them be a vision. Let them walk on. Let them turn. O, God, let them turn!"

She opened her eyes, and a sudden wave of anger rose in her. Why have they not turned? Why are they before me, when I bid them pass by?

Josce, leaning weakly against Elias, made obeisance.

"Call Abram," Rana said hoarsely to no one in particular.

"Madam——" Josce was trying to speak.

"Call Abram!" Rana repeated. Yomtob raised his hand, as if to gentle her. The street is not the place . . .

"Call Abram!" Rana demanded, and it was as if she knew that she could be imperious, and protect herself for a moment with her will.

Rabbi Yomtob walked to the nearest house and told the woman, standing half-curious, half-horrified at her door. She went quickly, and Rana waited in complete silence, standing before the three as if she would face them down. Abram came at a run from the synagogue, his hands still white with smoothing dust. When he saw the men and his mother, stopped in time, like the statues at the doors of churches, he could not seem to make his legs move quickly. He suddenly felt very ill. He went to his mother and held her arm.

"Tell me," she said to the men.

"Madam"—Josce could not bear to look at her—"inside, per-haps——"

"Tell me," she said with the same dead-level voice.

"Baruch is dead," he said. "He died in London."

Of course she had known, even as she had prayed that the men not stop before her, but now that words had been said, she could no longer stand the fact. With a cry, she put her arm across her face, and for a moment she stood that way. The men waited, swaying, feeling the sorrow that her body could not con-tain, so that it seemed to overflow from her. Then, lowering her arm from her face, very pale and changed, she said, "Where did he die, and how, in London?"

They saw that she could not bear to go inside her house, to be alone, even with them, in the middle of her life with Baruch. It would have to be told here, in the street, and Josce knew that the worst of it was now, not with Rana, but with the knowledge which could no longer be hidden. "Many are dead," he said, forcing himself to speak loud enough for them to hear, and for the passer-by to stop and listen. "Many are dead. It was a massa-cre—it was a massacre in London. A horrible, horrible——" Yomtob's hands went up in shock. Elias let go of Josce and put his hands to his head.

"Where? How?"

"In London. At the coronation."

"Oh, my God!"

"My son!" Yomtob turned to Josce, trembling, cut away from his duty, his people, his scholarship, his holiness. "Where was my son? Did you see him? Was he hurt? Please! Please tell me about my son!"

Some had seen, from their doors, the gestures of anguish, but the cry of despair that had come then split the air, and soon the street was crowded with questioning people, standing in the street with their hands wringing their questions. At last, Yomtob regained himself and motioned the people to come with Rana into her house. The children were sent away. Through the glass win-dows the bright sun shone, and the sounds of the children's play came in through the door.

Josce whispered, "Give me the strength to tell it!" and then he started where they had all been, at the leave-taking, with the gay colors and the festival in the air and the gifts of tribute. They had come into London with about thirty in the party. Kinsmen in London welcomed them, but had given strange news. Richard had published an order excluding Jews and witches from attending the coronation ceremony in the cathedral. Some had been a little bitter, having traveled from afar with gifts and good wishes only to have the door slammed in their faces and to be left as one with witches, outside the pomp, and more, outside of the King's consideration of human beings. The sage Rabbi of London had counseled humility. After all, the ceremony was but one part of the great celebration week, and there had been no notice posted to exclude the visitors from the banquet following the ceremony. They had planned to go to this banquet and there to present the letters and tokens and gifts, and no mention was to be made of the slight by the new King.

"Excluded as we were from the coronation," Josce continued, "we hoped to present such a dignity and fine stature and gifts that the King would find us to his pleasure and would ask our pardon. Forty of us went to the banquet. There was such a pack of people outside the hall that only a few could get in at all. We chose ten, and began to move forward, excusing ourselves, saying, 'Please, step aside; we have gifts for the King.' Your brother," he said, pointing to a man in the group, "went ahead. One of the Norwich men was ahead of me and we were trying to get through the crowds and into the hall to present ourselves in a group. Baruch followed after the Norwich man. It happened then—I do not know how or why: someone pushed the first one and he stumbled and fell against another man. The Rabbi turned to see what was happening. Suddenly, some were yelling, 'Help, murder!' Men grabbed hold of us and began to force us out of the hall. There were hundreds out in the courtyard who could not get in. When we came out, someone inside yelled, 'Here are the assassins! The plot is foiled!' and 'Here they are!' The crowd fell upon us with hands and stones. People were shouting like madmen. There was no time to call out our innocence in the wild rain of fists. Standing in that rain, I saw the Rabbi. He was trying to tell them, to reason. There was no reason in them.

"They beat him to death on the spot. In and out between the mad faces and the wild fists, I saw Baruch, and though I tried to call out to him, I was pummeled and kicked, and he was borne away in a mad pack of people, and I was left where I fell, thank God, in the corner of the courtyard and forgotten."

He sat for a while, silent, in a sea of wailing, and the babble of voices in question: "Where was my brother, my father, my son?" "And what happened then?" "Was there more?" He waited a long time, until they had stilled, and his mind was groping over the parts of the happenings as an old woman gropes over the threads of a torn gown, seeking to find the way to mend it, to save each strand. If there were only a way to tell it without the suffering—as a fact of history long past. He did not know how to save them anything, and so he continued as he had begun.

"How long did I lie there? I do not know, but when I woke it was almost dark. I went into the streets. A horrible insanity had taken the people. Although the King had soldiers trying to stop the slaughter, it overpowered them also, and drew them in, so that the massacre went on and on. The Jewish section was on fire and the old and infants were left to burn with it, and those who ran were slain. I saw the house of our eldest son"—he did not dare to catch Anna's eyes as he spoke, but he saw them in his mind all the same, and he faltered until the hungry voices goaded him on —"the house of our eldest son was gutted with the fire feeding upon it. I went close, but the fire was raging wildly and I saw no one of them there. I wanted only to find them, all of them, or some word . . ." And again he saw the face of his wife in his mind, but it was not the older face, the one that would have been there had he been brave enough to meet it—a young face, the face of a new mother, holding that child now grown for whom he had looked in vain. ("Surely you could have found a way, some way to save them," the eyes in his mind were saying.)

"A woman ran toward me. When she came close, I saw that she was a Jewish woman. I asked, 'Where are the people who were in that house there?' Her eyes were like a wall. She kept screaming something that sounded like 'Barley flour! Barley flour!' Poor, mad thing.

"I knew that I would not find them, that there was no one to help me, that murder was like a plague in the city!" he cried out against those accusing eyes in his mind. At last he looked for Anna among the women, and found her, daring himself to suffer at last the real burden of his love for her. She had not raised her eyes from the floor. He went on, doggedly, everything he remembered as if he would be held to account for every lost soul,

177

every forgotten act. He told of the dawn on the city, of the stinking, smoking ruins of houses, of the synagogue which had been sacked and defiled beyond belief with the offal of the drunkenness of the rioters. He had heard a noise in the balcony of women and had found the Rabbi's daughter, half mad with grief. They had made their way, creeping and hiding, to Richard's palace, where asylum had been offered to those who could get there. Baruch was there, he learned, being tended, and there were others, too, and he named them as well as he could.

"I obtained permission to see Baruch. That familiar face was like the Sabbath of peace which God grants even in Hell. We embraced. I saw that he was very ill and in much pain, but he told me that Richard was truly sorry for the madness of the populace, and wishing to protect us from further violence, gave us place in his courtyard, together with those others who managed to find their way there, and safe-conduct letters to all who wanted to venture out. I left Baruch and returned to the synagogue, where I found three: the man who came from Durham, the jeweler of Lynn—some of you here are his cousins—your elder brother, Rabbi Elias . . ."

They realized that in his recital of horror and death, Josce was trying, combing his memory for names and faces, for the smallest half-living bits of hope in all that wasteland of death: This one's father is yet alive, and that one's brother or cousin yet alive, yet alive. ("And where is my hope—my comfort, my brother, my son?" . . . "Your son I saw with his head in the river Thames and his dead hand playing with the water. . . . Your father a burning shaped like a man. . . . Your daughter stoned . . . Oh, God! . . . God!")

He sat still, stopped suddenly in the middle of his thought and stared out beyond them all to where the world was burning up in madness. Yomtob thought, with a shock of the paradox, that the world beyond their circle of familiar faces was the world that Josce had in his mind, and he sat in the very center of them all. A thought jarred Josce's mind and he woke to them and spoke again.

"We returned to the castle yard and found a few more who had managed to escape death, though only with their bodies. I must remember carefully who those people were. I am sorry for it, but I must compose my thoughts first, and so I beg you to wait—I know as well as you how hard that is. . . . We went to the King and begged him to assign takers of census to go about and find out who was yet alive, so that we might know. This he has promised to do. Lady Rana—at least you must know that I sat up with Baruch for his night and day. When he died, it was in peace."

Dully, she said, "Thank you," and was silent.

Rabbi Elias touched Josce's sleeve. "It is enough—come away and rest for a while." He saw that Josce teetered on the edge of the confusion of worlds that is madness.

"No—no," Josce mumbled. "There is a worse word yet to be said. The monster passions that were sated in London are slowly beginning to awaken toward the North. I myself had to leave in haste, and as I rode through the environs of London, I saw already the beginnings of fire and looting and madness. I traveled by side roads and at night, outrunning bandits and the armed and hungry wanderers of these strange times. The fever is rising against us, and though the King promises protection . . . I cannot forget what I have seen!" And he buried his seeing eyes, as if for punishment, in his dark hands.

They all sat for a long time, unable to speak. The children whom they had sent out into the streets were laughing and playing, and the sounds of the gaiety came strangely to the silenced people. It was true, then, what Yomtob and the others had said, that in spite of all horrors, the sky does not cease, as one thinks it must, and even the most fragile flowers along the way to death do not show a difference. Some were angered at the unconcern of the glowing sun, and in their hearts they raged against it and Heaven, feeling that if they wept, God must weep also.

Others saw the unchanging light and the unbroken sky, and had the bittersweet knowledge that life would go on, and even thrive, if need be, without them. Quietly the listeners rose and quietly they left, giving obeisances to Rana, now as with a crown, a martyr's wife. They went to their homes and there they called their children to them, and they hugged those children close, close, until they cried out and went pouting into the streets again to play in the sun, and the mourners marveled, how fragile as a breath was even the strongest of their blessings.

As Rana sat, still too numb and silenced to release the high, sharp wails of keening for the dead, Bett, her servant came and took her mistress's hand, and said, "Mistress Rana—the Lord heal your griefs." She was going to ask if the traditional things were to be begun, but she saw that Rana had not even heard her.

Elias and Yomtob helped Josce to his home. The sick, exhausted man, reeling with dreams, was watched from all the houses as he made his short passage across the street. All watched, but no one could pass him or catch his eye. Who knew if the horror could be transmitted to the victims as bloodlust had been to the tormentors, and no one wanted to see what Josce had seen. A man with such sights in his mind was like a man with plague; only the Rabbis had will and strength enough to help him, and even Anna, when she opened the door to them, averted her face. When they left each other after their errand, neither of the Rabbis spoke the ancient words of parting. It was as if they, too, were afraid to say another word in the same day that Josce had spoken.

At dusk, the long, heavy, ceremonial wail of grief arose from the stone mansion, and the women of other houses covered their faces to the eyes with their shawls and took up the plates of food for the house of mourning which, by tradition, would not cook or tend a fire during these days. As they left their doors, many of the comforters wondered if they, too, were not themselves in mourning for someone buried as a blackened scrap without a name, or tossed in a trench with a dozen other dead, and they shivered and hugged close the cooking pots still warm from their fires.

The winter is coming; see how early the dark comes on. The birds are going south already. . . . Who will never look up from London's streets to mark again what we send from York? . . . and they wept as they walked through the darkening streets to the house of Rana, widow of Baruch of York, Martyr.

As he had had wealth and power in life, his death was heaped with honor. A martyrdom carried with it the greatest praise and dignity which the community could give, and the rank of martyr's widow was so high that she could never think to marry again, and would be supported for her life long by the grateful community. The sons of a martyr were touched also with his stature, and would be heard with a special gesture of deference forever, and would take preëminence above others of their age in the ceremonies of the Synagogue and in the life of the people.

On the next day, Rabbi Elias saw Abram's pale, stricken face as he entered the synagogue, and the nagging doubt to which the Rabbi had refused to listen as it sounded itself in his mind woke again. Something that Josce had said—something he had not said

—a gesture perhaps—a look running across the face quickly and into hiding: What was it about Baruch in London and his agony there, and his death? Rabbi Elias had never liked Baruch. The financier had lied and cheated, yet he was wealthy, blessed with a son and with great power in the community. He was the president of the Synagogue, and his advice had been taken more times than Elias's had. Now he was honored for his moral strengths. Am I envious? Elias wondered to himself. He turned his feelings over gingerly, examining them, and still the tug of doubt was there at his sleeve, apart from his dislike and the little well of resentment which he harbored, ashamed, in his thoughts. He looked at Abram again. Very pale, he thought, and he is thinner, so that his eyes seem to be devouring his face. So restless, so brooding those eyes—and Elias was embarrassed before the young man. He had never seen suffering so naked and exposed. Later the Rabbi went to Josce to ask him for some more of the details surrounding the death of the martyr. There was going to be a memorial given. But as he was about to knock at the heavy door of Josce's stone house, he stopped suddenly, held with his hand in the air— What am I seeking?—and he turned and went away.

In his bed, guarded by the night, Abram wept. Through the day he had gone about the house, dry-eyed. The neighbors, bringing food and condolence to the blank-faced Rana, had whispered behind their fingers, "Miserable son—has he no feeling?!" "A stone for a heart." And they went away revived by their own righteousness.

Finally the night came and Abram lay quietly and wept quietly: If only I had loved him, I, too, could have the sorrow that would be a crown to him and a healing honor to me. The others weep their beautiful tears and then go to sleep. Does he see me where he is, Baruch Martyr? Does he say, 'Peace, my loving son'? I was a stranger to him and he to me, even from childhood. Why not, for I am a monster, not a man, who is called a human being because he loves. Oh, oh, had he only died less nobly, I could have given him my pity, because I could have understood so easily. In his hero's death, in his exaltation, I have nothing to give to him, and so can take nothing from him. It has always been so. My father, I shall bear my guilt as well as I may, and I shall try to mourn you truly . . . only, monster though I am, give me some sleep!

WHAT happens to the shield when the warrior is gone? Lacking a wound, does the soothing unguent soothe itself? In her mourning, ashes in her hair and her clothing disheveled, sat Rana, the shield between Baruch and the world; but Baruch was no longer there, with his terrible needs and his hard judgments. In the idleness enforced by the Law, Rana's mind wandered in strange channels, taking her where it went without resistance and winding on and on until she was tired as from a day of heavy labor. In the afternoons the women came with bits of dinner in pots for the family, and a little gossip to take the widow's mind from her griefs for a while. There, when she could, she spoke of Baruch, and her speaking gradually gave her a little ease.

A woman said to her, "Have you heard the talk concerning Rabbi Yomtob? . . . Why, he had planned to marry again when the exile came."

"Well . . . they say . . ."

"Behold!" And Abram came in from the gentle autumn rain and shocked them with the hardness of his voice. "Has even the great now become familiar, and the toy of tongues? Madam, if he had not done, or thought of doing something cut not to your idea of the garment, would you now not truly be disappointed? Where would one's tongue stay, madam, if not for conversation?"

They remembered former errands and fled in haste. Rana's eyes had humor in them as well as reproof. "Oh, my son," she said.

"I have come—and a timely coming, I might add—I have come with a message from Rabbi Yomtob to you."

"Abram, you are so careful for half of the world's morality, and so careless of the other half. What is his message, then?"

Abram told her what the Rabbis had said, that since the father's body had been left in London, there would be no burial for him at York, but since he had died a martyr, a pride to York, perhaps, if she were willing, there would be sermons given at Jewbury in Baruch's name.

When he finished, they sat looking at each other blankly.

At last Rana said, "I do not know . . . Would you feel proud at such a thing?" It was as if she did not care whether he were honored or not. Then she looked up, startled, and to placate the invisible hearer who had hovered over her for so long, said, "Of course we will do this—it is a great honor to the House."

"I envy him his hero's death," Abram said flatly.

"Abram!"

"Mother, do you always sit in public? I feel no reproach in you, yourself. I hear only your mind saying over and over. 'People will hear us; they will be critical of us.' Widow, the goblets will not hear us. The table will not reproach us. Let me speak truly to you."

"What do you wish of me!" Rana burst out in sudden violence. "Who understands my own solitudes? Everyone says, 'Let me speak honestly,' and then they tear the house down over us all! Are people so ruined in the world that only their cruelty is honest, and that what is honest to them is only cruel?" She heard herself shouting, and because it was unseemly, she stopped quickly and rearranged herself, as though sitting gracefully would give her grace.

"I am sorry," he said. It was the first time he had ever said this. He had made her a great gift of it because it had been sudden and he had meant it, and she gave him, carefully, as if from a tiny, secret store, some of herself in return.

"Strange . . . I had gotten into the habit of feeling always overheard. I used to worry over unseemliness because of him. He was so high that people always wanted to bring him low. I started to guard my words for him, and somehow it became part of me, and now that he is gone, it remains. . . ." Her thoughts began to drift again to another time.

"Can you decide if you want Rabbi Yomtob to say something?"

"Let him, if he wishes. I both knew and did not know that public Baruch." She saw the look of bewilderment on his face. "Why are you surprised? I am not clever enough to make you surprised."

"Why have you waited so long to show me that you are a person, with thoughts and wonderings of your own, apart from cups and a clean table and dinner on time?"

"Why did you never care to ask, or to wait until my work was done? Why did you never talk to me? When you wanted to drink mead, would you have settled for philosophy? Let me tell you something so shocking and unbelievable that I think you may not even imagine it: I was once young—I mean not only in body, but in my thoughts and mind. Now I am old and with different questions and with different thoughts, but try to remember that I am not dead. Standing between, just standing between, takes more energy than you will ever know. It is harder than to run or draw water or light fire."

"Standing between?"

"Between my husband and his enemies, his dislikes, his fears, his despair; and between you and yours."

"Mother, one person cannot really shield another."

"You say that now with a pride and a sort of joy. Grow older before you say it again, and when you do, it will be with despair and helpless grief. What we try and fail to do is counted against us by our children. What we try and succeed to do is not seen by them. We are known, then, by the quality of our failures."

"Madam, the Rabbi waits your answer. Is it to be yes? My father, I think, would have liked such a tribute by his people."

"Well, let it be, then," said Rana, and she lapsed again into her other thoughts.

Abram went to the house of Rabbi Elias, where Yomtob was now staying. The great Rabbi had heard no word of his son, who had been in London with his family and for whom he felt all of the guilt of his great preference. Yomtob himself had been like a fort of strength, but hate had touched the childish, selfish, vulnerable, poor and secret place inside him through his son, and now there was neither sleep nor comfort for him. Denicosa answered the door to Abram's knock, showing him the new words of courtesy which York's Jews accorded him now—first-born of a martyr. Wherever he was to turn for the rest of his life, was he to be reminded? He went in and greeted the Rabbis and sat down with them, then suddenly remembering his mourning, slid off the stool and onto the floor.

"What have you decided?" said Rabbi Elias quietly.

"It would be a great honor," Abram said, using formal language, "and we accept it gratefully." He thought he saw a look cross Rabbi Elias's face that was sorrow and something else—a kind of displeasure—but the look did not last long enough for him to be sure of it, and he thought that he must be mistaken. They made their plans and Abram left the two Rabbis with the chilling words of their respects in his ears.

He went down aimlessly across the Ouse Bridge and past the now full gardens that were kept by the shop men who lived on that side of the river. Beyond the gardens was a low hill and on it York Castle had been built for the convenience of the King and his court. They had not been in residence for many years, but Geoffrey had stayed there for his short visit and it was a pride to York. By the side of the castle was an older, abandoned watchtower, Clifford's Tower, where the boys of the city played sometimes at dying noble deaths. Abram wanted to go there and huddle to the winter-weakened sun and draw with a stick in the dirt the human forms and faces which were forbidden by the custom of his people, but the wind was blowing off the river, and when he climbed the little hill, he found it too cold. He walked around the castle wall, poking idly in the chinks with his finger. A boy had left a marble in one of them, and Abram took the little clay ball and put it in his purse and put a farthing in the wall in its place and then thought better and smiled and put the marble back on top of the farthing.

Down the hill on the other side of the Foss the fish markets were in full swing. He liked to hear the fishmongers as they cried their wares, and in the bargaining, even the spare and unpoetic Anglo-Saxon speech had a kind of beauty in the mouths of some. He went down and across the little fishermen's bridge and into the market. Not only were fish being sold, but there were also booths of supplies for the fishermen selling cork balls for the nets and bone bits that could be cut into fish hooks, and hooks readymade, and knives and oddments and cheap religious charms that protected against drowning and storms. As he passed these booths, he paused, looking at the wares, and then he looked up and without warning—there was Brother Simon and another whom he did not know, coming toward him.

With a gesture of welcome and friendship that came as naturally to him as breathing, Abram prepared to greet his friend whom he had not seen in so long, but suddenly the thought of his father's death came to him, and the massacre, the recent stillsmall incidents of drawing away each to itself that he had noticed between his community and the Christians of this city. He watched his best friend come closer to him as he stood covered with shame and anger for not being able to give him good day or take that blessing from him.

The Brother saw him then and there was the same play of emotions on the familiar face, so that Abram read them almost as his own. There was the instantaneous gladness and then the look of confusion and pain as the world's hooks bit deep—Remember who you are. Think what could be made of this. You have not seen each other in so long; perhaps he has changed—and then the anger and the shame that man is no stronger than the coward in him. Simon and the other monk passed him by and went on toward the center of the city.

Abram stayed in the market for a while, afraid to leave it for fear of having to pass the two again, and then he decided to go to the synagogue to prepare another copy of a work which he had finished. He knew that whatever parchment or roll he offered to Josce or anyone else would be bought right away at whatever price he chose to ask. Martyr's son! He ground his foot against the pebbles in the road.

He went to the synagogue, but his heart was not really in his work and soon he became exhausted with the effort of forcing his mind to the task. He rose and threw the cover over the helter-skelter of pens and inkpots on the table, muttered the prayer that ends the act of inscription of a holy work and went to find Bett. It had been a long time since he had seen or spoken with her except as master and servant in a house of mourning.

Perhaps she was down by the river, kneeling alone with her little pile of wet clothes; she was no longer welcome at the communal washing place. He went toward the river and as he saw the women washing and chattering together, Abram remembered how she had used to go there in the first years. Lately, he knew not why, the Jewish washing was done at the bathhouse, away from the Christians, as if it were part of the secret life of Jews. He looked up and down the river, but he knew that he would not find her there. It had slipped his mind for a while, how everything was changed.

He walked on aimlessly, past St. Margaret's and past St. George's, the church of which the Baron Malabestia and his family were patrons, past a new town house which the Percies had built and to which all the noblemen of the shire came when they were in the city. As he passed it, he saw the door open and the two Brothers emerge, turning to give their good-byes to someone inside, and he knew that he had only been waiting for Simon all this time. There was a little passageway opening on the street, which was the alley of servants' quarters, huddling up to the mansion as if for warmth. Into this Abram went, and as the Brothers passed, he called: "Pst! Simon!"

The Brother turned and then, seeing his friend in the shadows, whispered something to his companion who continued slowly down the street. The monk came into the alley, and again as he saw his friend, his face lit for what seemed a long and happy minute of recognition. Then the look left. It was as if he had wiped it away carefully, lest some scrap of it be left to damn him. Abram motioned with his hand, and Simon came gravely toward him.

"What will he say? Will this mean trouble for you?"

"He is new," Simon replied, almost shyly. "Can you imagine it? Now I am the fearsome and respected Elder Brother, and I come and count again the sheep that he has counted."

"We can greet each other then?"

"Yes." They looked a little rueful that they saw each other's weakness.

"How is it with you?"

"Well. And with you?"

"I am a Jew. Is it ever well with Jews? I went to visit you last month, but then they told me you had been sent to another part of the monastery to work and they would not let me give a message. When I came back, my father and his friends were leaving for London to see King Richard crowned. Then——"

"I heard of it just today——" Simon said.

"No doubt you did," Abram said bitterly, "but in a different version, I am sure—in quite a different version."

"Do you doubt what I made of it then? Do you think that the hate is why I did not see you? Because I thought suddenly that you were worthy to be hated, and a king-drunk mob worthy to be your judges!" Simon's voice was loud in the passage, and it shook with indignation. He was angered as much for what he said as for what he could not say: that he could no longer bear the veiled looks of questions in the eyes of his Brothers when the word Jew was mentioned, and that he had stopped arguing, even in his mind, with their prejudices. Rumors and harsh whispers of hate had begun to drift to the Brothers in Welbeck Abbey from the great rumoring and hating world outside, and at last the strange phantoms of their shadows appeared in Simon's dreams. Because of this, he had kept himself from his friend as one diseased secludes himself from those he loves, and sometimes less for fear of infecting them with his malady than for suffering the looks upon their faces as they see him ravaged and made hideous by it.

"I am sorry," Abram said, seeing how painful it was for his friend. The ghost of Baruch Martyr was standing between them and throwing a shadow twice as tall as himself. To the stranger he loomed even greater than he did to the son, so that there was no finding through him or seeing over him to reach the bitter, anguished Abram, whose friend this stranger could now no longer be. They were both wordless, yet stammering, desiring some binding truth, yet full of self-care and fear, dissembling, and hiding, and they could not meet each other even at the eyes.

"No matter," Simon said. "With us it must be the same thing, wishing to go or being sent. . . . In the beginning I had a great loneliness for you. Brother Lewis told me often that loneliness is just as strong when evil is denied the soul as when good is kept from it. Your friendship was a luxury—a very expensive luxury." His voice was very soft. "How many times did I do penance? How many penances were there, are there, will there be in all the years before I am forgiven . . . ?"

Abram was dumbfounded. "But you did not lie . . . you did no sin . . . why should you be guilty? Can a man be sorry for what he said or thought if he did so with the best of his mind and knowledge? Can he be guilty then? Is penance exacted for this?"

A glimmer of the old Simon showed on the young face, strangely ascetic. "Perhaps not for your people, but for mine."

"Forgetting what we said, or thought those years ago—or what we thought was forbidden, was it not good to be friends?"

"Yes, it was; but the price was great. Too great."

They stopped speaking then, with the painful knowledge that the words, the gestures, the expressions of face by which each one had learned what to expect from the other was not for them to know with each other any more. The understood word which priest gave to priest, the unspoken word which Jew gave to Jew, saying, "Stop" or "I like you" or "I am joking" could not be said by these two to each other across the barriers of faith, birth and way. Once they had had loneliness and their youth to help them, but the language they had made to bridge the barriers was a makeshift one, and now it was gone. With the special, separate looks, gestures, and words of Jew and priest learned yet three years deeper, they stared across the barrier sorrowfully.

"Good-bye," said Brother Simon.

"Good-bye," said Abram.

They walked away from each other.

Brother Simon turned again. "God be with you," he said.

And then Abram turned. "Peace," he said.

And they went their ways.

The light died, and it was as if the sounds of living things were a part of the light, for they were stilled also with its going. In the summer there had been a darkness in night, but it was rich with the comforting cries of little life in the trees and gardens. Crickets sang and the wind caught the leaves with sounds, and there were nests of birds with all their courting and their loving and their lullaby. Now summer was dead and autumn extinguished and the nights were chill-cold and silent. The Watches beat the cold out of their hands and stamped their feet like horses. Sometimes the guards on the gates looked down and thought they saw moving shadows and they shivered. In the deep forest to the north there were packs of lean-haunched wolves lurking. When they could not feed themselves with wild food, they would come from the grey woods and circle the city walls, hoping for the luck of a meal that men gave—a beggar cast out, a leper refused, the straggler of a band of travelers.

A Watch moved at his post. He saw nothing, but suddenly he heard the sounds he had been trained to hear. "Who goes there?"

"In the name of God, have mercy on us!" the darkness answered.

"Who are you and from whence come you?"

"In the name of God, have mercy on us!" came again, and the pitiful group came into the light of the torches. Jews.

"What are you?" The guard asked what was written into the law.

"Survivors."

"From whence?"

"From the slaughter at Oxford."

"What seek you here?"

"Asylum."

"Are any here who can stand surety for you?"

"The Jews of this city."

"Enter, then."

They entered out of the wolf-night into York, and a Watch took them to Northstreet and woke Elias out of his poor sleep to welcome them. There was nothing special about them—they had the usual look of the homeless and bereft, who had wandered without food or shelter for many nights; who had seen fire, murder and horror. What was strange about them was their number. The guard noticed it: before this night they had come by ones and twos; since the autumn time—and after the King had taken ship to winter with his troops in France for an early start on the Crusades by spring—the scattering cinders of spreading fires in the south had blown toward York. The people had drifted and rested, and some had drifted on again, unable to rest. Some had stayed, but now the occurrence was a commonplace, and the numbers were growing. The Watch went back to his post, but his mind was troubled by the look of the thing. They are moving in bands, now . . .

There were new names and new details, but the endings were all the same, and a man could stand in the synagogue and hear the ancient cries of pain of his ancient people until his mind whirled with confusion, saying, "Where was it, Babylon or Burford, where my little ones were slain? And was it two thousand years ago—or yesternight?"

RABBI YOMTOB sat at his studies, wrapped in his prayer shawl and bound with the ancient adjurations of Israel upon his hands and forehead. A young boy ran into the house and, knowing how sleepless all the Rabbi's nights had been, so driven for any news of his son, and knowing in his child's hundred ways that life was not as it had ever been before, he ran up to the engrossed scholar and pulled at his sleeve.

Yomtob turned in anger. "Who assaults the solemnity of prayer!?"

The boy hung his head in confusion. "Rabbi, they told me to run quickly and bring you."

"A prayer is not interrupted. Surely this much has been taught you."

"Rabbi, there is word of your son."

Yomtob found himself suddenly strong again after all the weeks of fear and despair.

"Behold," he said to the startled boy, "a man must move through his days in the order that imitates God's days of Creation. We have seen too many things torn asunder and shattered in these times. You may tell those who sent you that I have received the message and will come when I have ended my prayer." He gave the boy benediction and returned to his Book as if he had turned away only to cough. After the reading and the rites that end the reading, Yomtob, coats flapping, ran for news.

By the time he arrived at the Community Hall, everyone else on Northstreet was there, questioning and seething with rumors of a dozen things. The travelers of the night before had met a King's messenger on their way northward, and he had given them the King's census list of souls remaining alive in London after the massacre. To this there had been added a partial list of the dead and a few messages to relatives from the survivors. In one of these was another partial toll of the dead of St. Albans and a few of the towns beyond. As the refugee who held the roll explained this, the people quietened their voices, but their hands twisted with impatience, and the push of people breathed in great gasps.

The man undid the strings of the roll, and it fell on the floor. Another snatched it up and cried, "On the wall for all to see!"

"No, no—read it first!"

There was a mounting clamor and a scuffle close to blows near the reader, when Yomtob cupped his hands before his mouth and shouted through them: "Be silent!"

When they stilled a little, he came forward to the reader. "This man is weak and ill—let us be human beings and not cattle who in their insanity trample what they need for life." He lowered his head and made a gesture of self-reproach. "I know that my example has not been good in these weeks. Let us forgive one another. This man has need of rest, and my voice is loud enough to reach you all. If you will it so, I will read and then the list will be posted for a day, and then we must send it on to the sorrowers north and west."

The list was long. First the dead were read, and those who heard names of their friends or relatives cried out, or stifled cries while their ears were deafened by the cries of their souls and they could not hear what followed. At last Yomtob was obliged to read a name and wait, and then to read another and wait again. When he exhausted himself, he gave the list to another and sank down to rest. It was as if he had been flogging them with the names: a stroke and a cry, a stroke and a cry: Did I not tell you know you were sinning!? . . . God, my God, but this recompense is heavy!

The man who was reading was a refugee from London who

had seen much, and he added what he could to the names as they fell, but he had a hardness about him like the pride of a man who can speak of all horrors without trembling. He had endured beyond the range of common men.

At the end of the list of the dead, he paused. "One name remains," he said, "a York man." They all knew that it was Baruch, for his name had not yet been mentioned. "Benedict of York," the man continued, "called by his people Baruch, died in a room of the King's place of asylum. He is entered in the rolls of the King as——"

"No!" shouted Josce. "It is enough—we know already that our Baruch was killed!"

People looked around at him and whispered, but the reader cried that he was going to say the whole list as it stood, without interruptions, and the people silenced Josce and bade the reader to continue.

The man took a breath and went on. " 'Benedict of York, called by his people Baruch, died. He is entered in the rolls of the King as William the Convert, for he took baptism, abjuring his true faith and taking the Cross and a Christian name."

"It was duress!" Josce shouted. "It was duress! He later forswore it! It was on point of death!" He cried to their shocked faces, but nobody listened.

The people stood very still. The man from London continued into the lists of the missing. This one and that one . . . and Josce's son was among them. He clutched his hair, not knowing whether to rejoice that at least it was not death, or to agonize over another time of fearful waiting. He turned to his wife and let Anna hold him and vent her misery against his shoulder. The first-born. The names came on until the endless list was finished, for those who could still listen to the end. Now the messages of the living, and their words had a note of victory in them almost like vanity, but no one minded. After all, is not a talent for life a great talent? Finally, Yomtob heard the name of his son and the message: " '. . . safe and in health and will return and will rebuild.' "

"The Lord God, blessed be He, is praised above all nations. Thanks be to God, preserver of life!"

When the list was finished, the people began to leave the Community Hall. As they passed Rana and Abram, they turned away. Josce stood at the door and then moved and saw Rana and

Abram standing alone in the middle of the bare room. His wife raised her hand in protest, but he left her and went to the widow. Her face was a dead white, and Abram, too, was pale, but he was holding his mother and standing very tall. Josce moved to Rana's side, saying gently, "I am sorry—very sorry, widow. This will pass soon enough and be forgotten."

Rana turned toward him. Her face had the look of one struck.

"I will take my mother home," Abram said. "She will regain herself. I will help her."

Josce looked in surprise at Abram. He suddenly seemed stronger, taller, older than he had been but an hour before. Had he let himself believe it, Josce would almost have thought that Abram had been given a kind of glory at his father's dishonoring. To cover his embarrassment, he said, "Abram, you will have to live quietly under this scandal."

The look on Abram's face was triumphant. "I have been strengthened for shame all my life. I have already paid for my differences a hundredfold. Now, at last, I can use my gift. I will wear my father like a diadem, and his weakness like a jewel on my cloak. Now, at last, I can give him something. Now at last, I can serve."

Two stones fall: one from a roof and one from a mountain. It is to the same earth that they go, but for the one from great height the fall is all the more terrible for its length, and when the stone hits the ground at last, it smashes itself with the weight of its fall. Baruch had been high all of his life, and though his wealth and great power had been marred by many sins, his martyrdom had canceled even those in the memory of the people. He had been revered for everything, and now he had fallen so far that there seemed to be no end to his disgrace. A plaque had been placed in the cemetery commemorating his deeds and death, and in the synagogue the ornate silver pieces which he had donated had been polished with special care. . . . When Rana opened her door to begin the day, she found the plaque, broken and defaced at her feet, and in the synagogue, the silver had been placed in the background. Wherever the widow or the widow's first-born walked, a palpable silence went before and after. Some of the women, even those who had come with nourishing dishes, and nursed their babies in the widow's mourning house, veiled their faces to her now as if she were no longer one of them. William the

Convert's wife. Abram held his head high and his voice rang in the synagogue at prayer as it never had when Baruch was alive or during his praised month of martyrdom.

December came again, and with it, the obscuring snow. "Look!" said Abbot Adam, turning toward the courtyard, "God spreads a cloth to make this world an altar. Holy Jesus is to be born away from the ugliness that man has marked upon the earth." He crossed the courtyard, and with the snow falling upon him, he was white walking in white. Try as he would to be only a man, and humble, the holy snow exhilarated him, and he felt like a prophet or a great sage who has lived for centuries of time and has known everything because he is transfigured with the beauty about him. At the entrance to the gate he saw Brother Lewis and smiled at himself and at God's joke: two minutes omniscient and already a fool! The Brother was now completely beyond his reach. He accepted the words of the Abbot, he gestured the gestures and moved the moves, but Abbot Adam knew that he addressed himself to nothing more than a shell of assent. Brother Lewis was tightened on a secret rack, day after day, and his spirit was like the arm of a terrible catapult stretched backward to breaking. When the force that kept that arm was suddenly loosed, the catapult would heave its burden with the weight of a hundred horses. Where would he hurl his force when the ropes broke from him? As his mind and will pulled tighter and tighter, so that his words were like knots in his mouth, the Brother's body also took on the look of one who had been given to the wheel. From his chest, stripped bare by starvation, the cords of his neck pulled tight as if to snap. Daily he scourged himself until he spat blood and Abbot Adam had to stop him. The wondering man pondered at why Brother Lewis harmed his body at all, for he seemed to have no body left for injury. He was wounding himself for some inner form or propriety of his own, and his body seemed only a case for the two wild eyes that it carried.

As the Abbot came close, he called out to the Brother, lest he be startled. It occurred to him that he did not do this with the others—that it was like the charity which one gives to a blind man, saying, "Be not afraid; it was only I." Or perhaps the prudence of crying out in the forest when the bears are abroad to give them time to lumber away. "Mark you, Brother," he cried, "see how the careful Mother spreads the birthing sheets for her

Son that is to be!" The Brother mumbled what seemed to be an assent. "Here we are," Adam continued, "ham-handed shepherds, villains, sinners and misbegotten ploughboys—what a rabble to attend a queen at birthing!" and he laughed. The Brother turned toward him like a deaf man who senses comings rather than hears them. His face held nothing.

"*Benedicite*," he said in formal greeting.

"*Dominus*," the Abbot answered.

It was a beautiful sword. Richard de Kuckney had never been allowed even to touch it, and now his father had sent it to him on his Saint's day. He knew now that he might never be knighted in the beautiful ceremony for which he had always longed. There were no measures of money left for the making of a knight. Some could win a knighthood brilliantly on a battlefield, but Baron Malabestia had not left for Jerusalem, and was not planning to go, and he, Richard, was still the baron's squire. He knew that he was ridiculed by all the younger ones, and that many had gone out grown men in everyone's eyes, while he, their elder by four years, was still a boy. But now Lord Robert had sent him the sword and he would prove it and himself somehow, some-day, and redeem his house and his name. A flake of snow fell on the blade that was ever so slightly pitted with the wounds of rust, and he brushed it off jealously and took out his polishing-skin and began to rub up and down the long length of the blade. When he had received the sword from one of his father's friends who was journeying north, the Baron had called to him to show it, and had said, "Keep it sharp and soon there will be many fat necks to feed it. A thin edge will give a sword appetite—and a man-boy appetites," and he had laughed with that mouth-laugh of his. So Richard readied his sword for something that was coming, and he envisioned his triumphant march home to Kuckney, and he sharpened yet keener, yet keener, yet keener the instrument of his glory.

ABRAM did not visit at the houses of North- **26** ⁓
street. He knew that he was an embarrassment
now, and was not wanted, but one afternoon he
went to see Josce and accepted the cup of mead which Anna
offered halfheartedly. He said to Josce, "Behold—I offer a riddle: Who is it that was born an old man, lived a lifetime in three
days and died a father, yet had no issue while he lived?"

Josce thought and then said, "Indeed, I do not know the answer."

"It is William the Convert."

Anna suppressed a gasp and left the room hurriedly. Josce
paled and then said quietly, "Abram, do not joke of this."

"I want you to tell me," Abram said, with his hands pleading
from the cup, "I want you to tell me how he died and what were
the last days of that newborn old man, that William the Convert,
whose shamed son . . . I am at last content to be."

Josce sighed and gestured with his head that it was better past
and forgotten. What was to be learned, after all, from a mean
death? He had tried to protect the family of his friend and partner as he had tried to protect Baruch, and with all his evasion, he
had only made things worse. Those who had been really tested
by the hate and the fire did not blame Baruch for seeking to save
himself. How easy it was for those in the sunshine to say to the
one beneath the thunder, "Hold up your head." Even more unjust was it that they taunted and turned from the blameless wife
and son of the ruined man. But that was the world. . . .

"Please . . ." Abram said. "It is always worse in the imagination, and if you would spare me his suffering, know that it is the
only legacy that he left me. It is what makes me his son.
My mother will not be told. No one will be told, but I must
know."

"Very well," said Josce. "I do not know what happened to
Baruch when we were rushed away from the banquet in that mur-
derous crowd, but I went to the castle on the next day to find
him, and I found him in the care of the King's physician. There
was more than mere mercy in the actions of his nurses. He had
been broken with the impersonal cruelty that men have in their

crowd madness. The guards told me that his was one of the special cases and this I did not understand, so I asked how they meant 'special' and they were winking and making a sign with their fingers in some kind of mock piousness. I gave one of them a piece of flat silver that Anna had sewn in my tunic and he told me what had happened.

"He said that Baruch had been taken and beaten by the crowd, and that then they began to play with a sword to his neck and then here and there, laughing that he would die slowly. Someone half in jest said, 'Why not be finished with heathenness then?' and they all took up the cry—'Baptism or death.' Something of the great hunger for crusade was in the city. It was part of the anguish of those who could never go and seek and sacrifice, and they tormented him until he cried, 'I will be baptized, only let me rest!' Then and there they dragged him off to the cathedral, the whole muddy, bloody mass of them, and held him up for the Latin and then let him fall on his broken bones where he was. The King's man came by and recognized him and he was brought for care to the castle, but they took him to a place apart. At his religious ceremony, he had been given the name of William the Convert, and so he was called, as if the whole madness had been sanity and truth. The guard then took me to him, saying that the King had left word that we were to come before him as soon as this William could stand. What else is there to say? . . . So it was."

"Tell me all of it," Abram said, "all of the words—because—after you tell me, there will be no more."

Josce went on. "We came into the chamber where the King sat with his minister and the Archbishop of Canterbury, and the King addressed your father so: 'William, the Convert, onetime Benedict of York, Jew, yesterday you abjured your faith, submitting to the True Church and accepted baptism into His Body. How do you say now?' Baruch sagged in my arms like a man struck. Finally he regained himself somewhat and said, 'My Lord —I was taken under threat and forced to Baptism—'and then he coughed and said, as if he would remonstrate with them, 'Is this a way to make a Christian?'

"Richard looked at him, and I saw that he felt pity, for he said, 'Speak again, and without fear—which is your true mind: the heresy of the Jews or the True Faith of Christ?' And Baruch stood straight and looked at them both and said, 'I am a Jew, my Lord. I have always been so. It is my only faith.' Behind the

King the Archbishop stood and Richard turned to him and said, 'What punishment shall we give this rogue for lying for his life?' Then the Archbishop looked at our Baruch, our William the Convert, blind with pain and straight upon my arm——"

"Pitiless." Abram said. "They are pitiless."

"And the Archbishop said, 'See that he has been sorely chastised. Let him die of his wounds.' Then Baruch sagged into my arms and we helped him to his bed. Abram, pain makes some men angry, but it humbled your father. Abram"—and Josce looked hard at the unblinking eyes of his partner's son, trying to reach for the spirit behind them—"I know now why martyrdom is held so high by every faith. It is a rare flower, a flower plucked by very few. How would we stand, I wonder, any of us, under the agonies that broke him? If he was a coward in the streets, he was honest and brave before the King who could have had him tortured yet again. If he made one poor compromise in the cathedral, he redeemed it before the throne. York is frightened, Abram—too frightened to listen now. They made themselves a martyr and he betrayed them by being only a man. When they can reason, I will tell the whole story and the shame of cowardice will be drawn away from your house."

Abram said slowly, "How much worse I had pictured it! You know—I had visions of him offering bribes—rubies—bargaining for his life."

"Have you learned nothing?" Josce said. "Perhaps he would have tried to buy his freedom if there had been time. What would have been so terrible? Is not life worth money? Are not you and your mother worth the silver it would take to see you again? He loved you—this you know—and he wanted to stay in the same world with you."

"He should have fought bravely, not basely," Abram said. "As a hero he belonged to York—as a coward he belongs to me."

In the night, the night of refugees cold in their makeshift beds at the Community Hall, or in corners of the houses of friends, Abram, son of Baruch, at whose house no one would stay, lay asleep, and he dreamt a dream about the sea.

He saw himself standing on a barge that was moving down the Ouse. People were crowding aboard other barges, but no one would ride with him. The women had on their best shawls. As the river opened into the ocean, a spectacle of great splendor met their eyes. There, waiting a short space out to sea were great ships, a fleet of them, with sails of crimson and gold, and hulls painted with fresh colors. The ships glimmered; they were splendid and beautiful beyond anything that he had ever seen before. A man like a toll collector stepped in front of the eager people: "Fleet leaving! All aboard! Those perfect in faith to go!"

The people pressed close—everyone wanted to be aboard under the great sail, but as they went, one by one they were rejected for passage. Miserably the people watched the glorious ships leave empty, and fade with all their splendor out of sight. Soon a second fleet appeared, not quite so splendid as the first. The toll collector again cried out: "Ships imperfect; faith imperfect! Aboard! Aboard!"

And again, one by one they went by and each was rejected. A single rowboat put out for the beautiful ships, and in that boat, all alone, weeping, a tiny figure lonely in the vastness of the ocean: Yomtob of Joigny, taking ship. As the fleet disappeared, the people became angry: "Where is the fleet which will take us!"

And there it was, standing for them, and rowboats by hundreds to take them to the ships. The fleet was a pack of battered boats, full of leaks and holes; the sails were tattered and had been patched and tied in a hundred places. The original color had been beautiful, indeed, but now it was faded and chipped. The ships themselves reminded Abram of the first which they had seen, but so ragged, so picked and patched were they that their original form was hard to discern.

"To ship, Jews, to ship!" the toll collector cried.

Abram, as he passed, said, "Perhaps I am not a Jew."

The man was annoyed. "Were you born of Jews?"

"Yes."

"Do you live with Jews? Do you think of yourself as a Jew?"

"Yes."

"Then get aboard! Get aboard!" and they all went in boats toward the fleet.

As soon as they boarded the precarious vessels, they began quickly to fix the leaks and mend the sails; more bits and pieces were stuck and hammered here and there to keep out the sea and welcome the wind that it might find a home in the ragged sail. Abram looked about him, and beside him was Josce, fixing a split rail. "I am afraid of this ship," said Abram. "It will sink."

Josce laughed and said, "It sails well enough. We will always sail well enough to be in sight of the Perfect Ships, though none can ever board them. Patching, mending and fixing, we will keep our faith seaworthy to keep in sight of those . . ." and he pointed far out, and there they were, shining in the sea, beautiful beyond language. "As for Yomtob," Josce said almost a little sadly, "he is closer to us than he is to them."

Abram woke up and went about the day, but his dream seemed to enwrap him, and he looked up from his copying often, to the ships that waited in the mind. Somehow, because of the refugees and their refusal, even cold and hungry, to stay at the home of an abjurer, this dream, in which he was one with all of them, gave him comfort. He realized now that the men who had run away from the slaughters of the South were as frightened as Baruch had been in his nightmare at London. Faced by an abjurer, when they knew in secret places of themselves that they, too, could be weakened, their fear of Baruch grew until it spilled over into all that he had possessed. They were afraid even of the house, the grounds, the objects once his. His things had some residue of him, some power to drag them back away from their vision of courage. Yet, in the end, Abram thought, by his dream, even the abjurer and the rebel sails, patching and fixing to justify his faith and life.

During the morning, Abram looked for his real world out of the tiny window in the balcony of the synagogue. The light came in weakly. Below him he saw the to and fro of commerce, and the little rivulet of it, Jews and Christians who passed by the Jubbergate—the Jew's gate—where the synagogue stood. There was a bald pate of a farmer, carrying a load of hides on his back; a cleric so intent upon his book that he did not notice the heathen edifice to cross himself as he passed; and Bett, stopping at the door and knocking. The bustling Servant of the Synagogue opened to her and she came into the courtyard and stood waiting. He could see the top of her head with its meandering part, and he smiled to himself at the things which he called intimacies. Her straight, loud laughter and her cutting sobs, and the hair which could be braided and garlanded for a feast, yet still never achieve an even part—these signals of her were open to the world for all to see, and yet to Abram they were intimacies, for they led him somehow upon a course into her deeper life. The servant scurried in to give her message and Abram sighed heavily, frightened and miserable for what he at last must do to her and say to her. He rose and left his work.

"Hey!" the servant called up to him, "your maid is here." So the Saxon-speaking English were not the only crude ones in the world. A French-tongued keeper of God's House had also his hour, and Abram remembered that it had been but a day between "My dear master Abram, so please you" and "Hey!" Yet he had found that he liked the second better than the first. He went down to where Bett waited.

"Master Abram, a man has come from Spain on business with your father. He has just learned of Master Baruch's death and would speak with you."

"Does he know the circumstances of it?"

"No. He came to the door and I was carding wool in front and I told him. Although he knew about London, he did not know who died there." They looked at each other and smiled, both seeing the same thing in their minds: Rana, serving cups of mead to a respectful man, being listened to and told the latest riddles and jokes—wonder of wonders—Rana laughing; a rest from shame.

The snow was deeply gathered on their hill, so they went through the city, following the banks of the river, and then they climbed the low hill to the deserted castle. They would take a long time to get home.

He had waited for a long while to talk to her alone. Now that Baruch's death and disgrace had made him heir to a name, he knew that he could not disgrace it further by marrying a Christian—even if she was no longer a Christian. The wheel of circumstance had turned again, and as a wheel must, had made him rise by the same action as another's fall. For the first time in all his life, he was truly grateful to his father, and his gratitude called for sacrifice; but as he walked with her, he thought: Not forever —it would not be right to turn from my own way forever. Perhaps when the scandal dies away, we might leave and go south. When he said it for his mind, it did not seem impossible. They stood out of the wind, watching the clouds, like greyer smoke against the lowering sky. They were traveling so fast that they were beaten to wisps that formed and reformed in flight. "Rain?" he asked.

"How should I know? I am city-grown." They laughed, and then he took her by the shoulders and said, "You know what I have to say—it is so hard to say—since you know it, do not make me suffer the words."

Her laughter was soft and it was bitter and loving at the same time. "We Jews have a saying," she said to him. 'When is a

joke not a joke? . . . When a Jew tells it, for he makes you cry!'
God help me, you have made every plea, but not muteness!
My dear love whom I have loved so long, when your insults bit
with wit, I thought: What loving would come from a mouth that
had the gift to scorn so eloquently! When, at last, the loving came,
it was with muteness, and I forgave it because I loved so much.
All this I forgave, but I will no longer be stinted. I want
my denial in full measure, spoken out as if I were of some
account." She faced him, silent and full of pride.

Sweet Sabbath, he thought, she is beautiful! She had grown into
the privilege which she was asking, and he knew it and it made
the words harder than ever to say. He told her quietly why it was
that they yet must wait. Baruch would be decently forgotten, the
wave of hate would spend itself and she might, then, if she
wished, become a Jew in Law as in fact. After a time they would
marry, and Abram was now unimportant enough to do what he
liked.

He would not be a hypocrite either; they would walk together
and not avoid each other for the sake of form, and Rana would die
of this, but she would die a little less each day until she, too, forgot the causes of it. He looked at Bett covertly as they began to
walk around the castle wall for something to do. Baruch had been
proudly amused at his scullery maid who could write and read.
His amusement at a toy had turned to a wondering half-admira-
tion when the Rabbis had told him how learned and knowledgeable she was. How would he have seen her as a daughter-in-
law, with a bearing and pride that could have been bred of
princes?

"I wonder," he murmured, "how many times the dead are
repudiated to spare the living."

"We all do it one way or another; exalting or forgetting to suit
our needs or the fashion of the times. When old Kuckney killed
a meddling priest, he was a hero; a year later, the meddler was a
saint and old Kuckney a murderer."

"When is to be only human the fashion?" he asked, smiling at
her.

"Never. We will always hide ourselves from ourselves while we
live, and prudently prepare for a change in the direction of the
wind."

"Then I suppose we will forever be digging up our fathers to
change their cloaks."

"Abram—Master Baruch—I know what he was—that he was not virtuous as either faith writes of it, and yet to me he was always good and generous. We will both keep faith with him."

As they rounded the wall, his eye sought out a cranny between the stones, and he found it and reached into it and felt there, and he drew out another clay marble. It was crudely made but a little larger than the first one had been. He held it in his palm and laughed, and pulled out his purse before the astonished Bett and took out two farthings and placed them in the niche and put the marble back on top of them.

"What are you doing!" she cried to him.

"I am seeing in my mind a rare thing for this world," he said slowly, ". . . the face of one whose faith is not doomed—whose prayer will be granted without the little added irony that makes it itself obscure."

Through endless rounds of prayers, Brother Lewis stumbled; his chants and their chants, his offices and theirs, his routine of meanings and theirs, and the life of the monastery and his own secret life and world parted and fused—now one and now separate until he began to doubt even his own corporeal self. At times it seemed to him that he had already traversed the boundaries of mortality; that he was invisible, a burning spirit, bodiless and yet capable of great physical force. The more empty of body he became, the more desperate was the insatiable need to wound himself, which he said was to subdue his carnal shell. He had subdued it, for he never felt the blows as pain, and though he glowed in his triumph over flesh, there was a strange, deep terror in him at the distance that the world was from him. Then he wanted to prove that he was alive, and there was no way to do it. He felt certain that he was a saint, but the world was dissolving before him and soon nothing would be real.

Yet there were still the dreams, the brilliantly vivid dreams, with their every motion and sound heavy with transcendent meaning. Some were wild and horrible; some had a bizarre, bursting grandeur. The world would swing toward day again and in dawn wakefulness, he would be a formless smoke, bodiless and grey. One early dawn as *Deo Gratias* rang at Brother Lewis's cell, there was no answering sound such as he was used to make. The Caller sounded a second call and then a third. After a long time, the Caller went in. The cell was empty, and those few possessions which the monk had were flung about as if a storm had blown them wildly into heaps. There was a searching and a shouting for the missing Brother, but nowhere was he found.

Rumors such as entertain men hungry for speculation, which appear like succubi to draw them into sin, flew about the House: He was carried off; he was a saint called bodily by God; he had a woman and ran away; he had a visitation from St. Norbert. The very Christmas season which celebrates the Word Made Flesh, and which is the great hymn of reality, now fed the currents of terror and superstition in the brothers. Omens were seen, and crosses in the sky, and lights gone suddenly prophetic, and knowledgeable birds in strange formations, but Abbot Adam thought to himself: Who cut that holding rope so that the tortured machine let go and sent its burden out?

Still tight with the corded muscle, the teeth clenched and the spirit a sinew pulled to snapping, so that if a note could have been sounded upon it, the sound would not have been within the human range, Brother Lewis walked. He did not know why he had left the monastery except for the persistent message of his dreams. He had been circled about by shadows. He no longer remembered, even faintly, the faces of the Brothers of his long years, but he knew that they had held him from his mission—the mission of his dreams. Nothing of that duty was really formed yet in his mind, but somewhere, misplaced or changed in form, or lying in a net of symbols was his Calling, his Vocation, his Destiny. It must flower and grow and become apparent to him in the smallest detail, what was to be done and how. He was sure only that it was the True Cause, the Holy Cause, and that, through it, the Devil himself would be vanquished, and that he, as had been told to him in the great dreams, even he, like Christ the lowest and poorest of men and at the same time the most exalted One of all the saints of Heaven, would bring this cause to its conclusion in the greatest victory of all time. The dream had said, "With death, Death shall be vanquished." Soon it would be answered to him. Approaching a wood, he felt his strength failing. Earth's Answer cannot die because of earthly hunger. He hurried on.

At the other side of the wood rose Kuckney with its great house and turreted guard towers, under whose stone stewardship the mud-and-wattle huts of the landfolk clustered. Their smokes rose straight into the windless day, and as he saw Kuckney from the edge of the trees, it was like an island of brown and grey, rising between white snow and white sky, a lone division, and he went toward it out of the most basic of human habits. Perhaps he was a saint or mad or invisible, but the age-old ways of men had not been wholly lost. He began to run.

The monk had been without eyes for the present world and for himself for so long that he did not notice how raggedly the clothes hung on his taut, leather-covered skeleton of a body. The guards at the walk jeered at him as he approached until he raised his eyes—those eyes at which no one could laugh. As he gave his name and ordered the guards to call their master, they heard his speech and knew at once that he was, or had been, a man of noble house. They hurried to fetch Lord Robert, leaving one of their number at the mercy of the monk's bitter and intense face, and the haste they made was not for a beggar in a ragged cloak, filth-encrusted, but for a baron. When the guard returned it was with De Kuckney. For a moment Lord Robert did not recognize his distant relative; he could not place the man in his life of castle or the hunt, and he was about to ask him what he wished, as a stranger, when the name and the place suddenly lit in him and he held out his hand in welcome.

"Kinsman! Come in and take your ease; you must have suffered much cold and perhaps you are weary. Stay with us awhile, then!"

Brother Lewis did not recognize the place or the man, but the cold was beginning to make him dizzy and he permitted himself to be led into the great hall. Soon the Lady came and he found himself astonished at her youth and grace. It had been a long time since he had seen a woman who was not an alms-beggar or a grief-aged penitent. She gave him a warm welcome when she heard his name, for he was also a distant kinsman to her family, and she sent her servants a-scurry for wine and warm cloaks. While she was gone, Lord Robert tried to converse with the strange monk, but their talk was more like a duel with the guarded thrusts and parries of the Brother turning Lord Robert's words this way and that away from their mark, as if his courteous questions were attacks against the Brother. Lord Robert did not wish to mention the Brother's having left the religious life—to slip the cloister was against the law, and the penalties of harboring such a man were heavy.

In desperation he asked, "Where are you planning to go on your journey?"

"Somewhere I can wake the sleepers before Satan gives them up at last to sleep."

"You are going preaching, then?"

The monk roared and leapt up from his stool by the fire, overturning it. He was shuddering with rage. "I will not preach—I will do and conquer, and no Jew will stop me with his devil power!"

"Is it against the Jews then that you plan to fight?"

It was as if he had struck a spark to a dry hayfield. The Brother's eyes opened wide and he began to curse and howl imprecations. It was a conflagration of hate, conjuring burning Hell, the Devil and the enemies of man. The gaunt and starved-out body was suddenly possessed of a frantic strength. The hall was filled with his sound until guards and serving wenches clustered at the entryways to listen with eagerness, awe and terror to his words.

Lord Robert was afraid of his strange kinsman-monk. He stood under the shower of words as a ploughman stands under a torrent of summer hail—tiredly, patiently, fearing for the harvest rather than his own life. The world outside of Kuckney was far removed from the rhythm and pace of baronial life. The only real bond it had was with the seasons, and but for weather, the world outside was only of passing interest in the lives of a Kuckney and his workers. Lately, the subject of a fee and money paid to the outside had intruded upon the estate, and now, Lord Robert found himself wondering if this strangely inspiring man was well let out into the towns and cities with his burning words of hatred. He had heard travelers and preachers cry for the Crusade both in this very hall and in cities where they spoke from street corners to crowds of listeners. Some were moving and some were not, but there was in the good and worthy speeches an appeal to a logic and a love which illumines men and separates them from the brutes who are their slaves. Of this there was nothing in the Brother's shouting and hard rage, yet Lord Robert saw that his household crowded in the corridors and pushed into the gallery to listen enthralled, wringing their hands and biting their lips—and hating. This man held them almost in a thralldom until his own body's weakness overcame him and he sank down half fainting to the straw. Perhaps he had realized that there were no Jews here who could be victims—that there were no heights to which to lead the burning torches of those who had caught his hate.

Lady Agnes de Kuckney came quickly with the wine and they lifted the muttering Brother to a chair and rubbed his feet and hands. The Lady sent a servant running for a decoction from her cabinet of medicines and herbs, and after the Brother had taken it, they carried him to a bed which had been readied on their own bedstead. He was in a deep, exhausted sleep.

HE slept for so long that they thought he must be ill, but when he woke, he wolfed a tremendous meal, and the second sleep which followed **27** it was closer to that which reasonable men have in their ordinary beds at night. When he came down to the hall to join his host, he did not look so unreservedly mad as he had the day before, but Lord Robert was still afraid of him, and knew that he would not mention money, Jews, or the devil or religion, or crusades, or . . . By the cross! Was there anything safe to speak of?

Now that starvation had been averted, the monk's strange asceticism returned. Sometimes he fasted and sometimes he gorged, but it was always without pleasure, wildly, as a dog does. When he ate, it made Lord Robert think somehow of lust; to watch him eat was to share in an obscure depravity.

At every turn Lord Robert placated his kinsman. He saw how his wife venerated the monk whom she thought a saint, and he knew that she hated her husband for cowardice even in this. He could not bear the power of one in whom the Holy Spirit flowed. When, after a week or two the monk mentioned travel, Lord Robert heaved a sigh of relief, although he knew that it was impossible at least until the spring thaws came. Perhaps the wide world with all its intricacies would diffuse the passion raging in this Brother, whose presence at his fireside was becoming a wretched trial to him.

"Kinsman, you cannot leave until the springtime—and in what? Your clothes are ragged and foul. You must let us provision you."

Brother Lewis looked at him sarcastically and said, "With what could you provision me?"

"We could at least give you new garments," Lord Robert said when he had regained himself. "I have cloth in plenty and would be but shamed if you did not take some of it."

"It must be white," Brother Lewis said, "and a cross worked over the heart, and an alb of white also. I doubt," he added, "that you have any such garments in any chest or storeroom."

Lord Robert was proud of his name and his house. He took Fauconbridge's words only as they were, and overlooked the taunting voice. The monk had implied a criticism no less cruel and humiliating for its subtlety: Why was he, Lord Robert, not away to the Crusades, packing among his armor and the necessaries of war, a humble penitential gown for pious observation in Jerusalem?

Answering only the words, Lord Robert said, "I will tell the Lady and she will make you such a robe with her own hands. She will find it an honor to please you." He was angered with himself that he bore the edge of these taunts, except that he was warned somehow, to placate again and again, at any cost, this strange kinsman. No other man of his state would make such mollifying gestures but, because he saw something in all of it that was not seen by others, he found himself submitting to his inner orders. "Rest well, kinsman." And he gritted his teeth, walking as if he were a stranger from his own hall.

For weeks of winter isolation, Lady Agnes and her maids wove and sewed the habit of their new saint. It was a costly garment, but in the style of the Order of Premontre, for the Brother still considered himself a monk in that brave Rule. Cloth was expensive and they did not stint. When the garments were ready, they were the worth of two fine horses, and when the Brother took them as his due, with neither thanks nor courtesy, Lord Robert was ready to speak the hard words that he had choked aside. His eye caught the face of his wife: long thankless labor, the tedium of spinning and weaving, the special demands of a capricious lunatic—all this, and yet her face showed only awe and contentment. She had been reared by the baronial code and loved it, and was true to it. He had been reared to it and hated it, and yet had not the courage to play it false; he only skirted all the questions and waited while his youth passed and his age came on and his son rose to a patrimony of which he was ashamed. He turned away and left the hall for the stables and a satisfying authority over the lives of beasts.

On the afternoon of the presentation of the garments, Lady Agnes called a servant to her. He was young and clever, a cut above the rest, and she gave him a message that he was to remember: "My Lord must not know of your leaving or of your return, and for that reason you must buy a horse on your way and not take one from here. Go to Acaster and give Lord Malabestia my message and he will pay you well."

She took a brooch from her gown and gave it to the youth. It would buy a horse and provisions to Acaster and would see him back also. The Baron Malabestia was as strange a man as ever lived, but he was a baron, one of her own kind, and she felt that he would act his part and make restitution to her, for her message to him was perhaps of very great importance. A saint had come to them when they most needed one—surely it was the Will of God. This burning one could move a stone to wrath—could light the dullest mind to fire for their cause. She knew not how this fire could be turned to best advantage; that was man's knowledge and not for a woman to reckon, but here he was, a glowing saint before them. Let the Baron but see him, but hear him and he would plan how, in this kingless kingdom, the best use could be made of this holy weapon.

After the Morning Prayers at the synagogue, most of the Jews of York went to their work, but Elias often stayed behind to visit the school and lecture or advise the young students on some particular part of their lessons, breaking the monotony of the loud rote chants of question and answer by which the young learned sums, letters and a few of the laws of nature and God. On this one morning he stayed longer than usual, and he returned to his home through foggy streets whose pungent sewage smell closed out the hints of the thaw that hung in the air. He saw Denicosa sitting outside the house carding and he wondered why she was not before the fire on this chilly day. As he came close she made a sign and rose and came to him.

"My dear, they are inside—the leaders of the community, and something is on their minds, for they came right from the synagogue. There is a setness about their eyes and they would not take anything that I set out for them."

Elias thanked his wife and she went about to the back of the house.

He hated subterfuge, but he had lately found himself resorting to it more and more. There was a fear among the people that had shown itself in these few months in fits of envy and anger, and that resisted the sensible adjudications of humor and forgiveness. Something new was working in the no longer peaceful minds of Northstreet's Jews, and Elias did not like what it was doing to them. He had often said that Yorkers were too complacent and should be shaken from their secure and rooted sense of rightness. Now that it had come, he saw how wrong he had been. Fear was making some of them vainer and more cruel than ever. He went into the house, and as if surprised, greeted the assembled men. Since Baruch's death, a new President had been chosen, and still a bit tentative and cautious in his newness, he greeted Elias and raised the subject: His argument was for closing the doors of York to the homeless of massacres in the south. For all his indirection and care, his picking and choosing of the most advantageous words, his proposition was still as blunt as a fist to the face. When he finished, they all said their little words. Elias groped for a stool on which to sit, for he could not take his eyes from them. "We are all in accord," the President said.

"It should have been done long ago," the Singer said.

"Even you agree to this?" and Elias looked hard at Josce, at Josce whom he loved and respected ahead of all of these men.

Josce looked at Elias and said, "Yes. Even I."

The Rabbi rose again and turned to leave. "I will fight you all," he said. "Rabbi Yomtob and I will fight you all. If it comes to it, we will let the whole community put forth its decision. If the vote goes against us, we will leave. I am going now from my house. Be gone when I return."

The President raised a hand in a gesture of assuagement. "Come, Rabbi—we will reason together. When you hear——"

"Animals!" Elias cried, and ran from the house.

Even as he walked through the street, shaking with indignation, he knew why he was so angry. He had helped to sow a seed of iniquity and a field of it had grown up before his window to haunt him. A year ago he and Rabbi Yomtob had turned away a young girl who had come to their people for succor; she had called upon them in love and need and they had turned her away for no other reason than that it was not politic, not safe, not fitting perhaps in the eyes of the Christians about them.

The men whom he had just called animals had only taken his example and Yomtob's. They had told him that the community must, for its own safety, offer no succor and no entry to the refugees who beat upon its doors. The hunted would stand shivering outside the wall and the gates would be shut against them. How many would have persuaded themselves to live, to run, to endure one day more or one hour more, seeing York as a fortress, a safe island in the sea of hate? Elias knew all the arguments in the leaders' favor: It was prudent not to stir up any more of the fear and suspicion that was kindling behind Christian eyes in York. With more and more coming, there would be a shortage of food and place, and . . . "Rabbi," a man had said, "we ourselves may be fleeing, and will only be deterred by having to help others already starved and exhausted." He knew that they felt guilt for what they proposed—that there was desperation in their "reasonable" decision, or they would have approached both Rabbis together. It was Yomtob's wrath that they had feared, not his, and Elias saw that some of his anger at them had been personal, because they had lived with him so long and knew him so little. He was to have agreed with them, perhaps in a little time of coaxing, and with logic. Then he would have been the wedge, the wielder of their argument to Rabbi Yomtob. He sighed and the anger left him and the sorrow of it all poured into the gap, so that he found himself weeping suddenly, blinded in the street by tears and having to grope to a wall until he regained himself. Yomtob must be told, for they were undoubtedly planning even now, how to get the community behind them. As he wiped his eyes with his hands, he saw Abram coming toward him.

Abram stood in front of him and said, "And these are the men who slander my father!"

Rage woke in the Rabbi again. "Why do you make yourself as small as they? Very well, you are vindicated because your father is no worse than all the rest!"

Abram was shocked, and then his expression changed and he looked at Elias in surprise. "Is this the first you have heard of this idea?"

Elias seemed lost in his clothes; almost as if he had shrunk into them. Abram made a gesture of wonder. "Why, Rabbi, since the day that the London lists were read there has been a whispering and a questioning about the business: 'What will they stir up here and how will they hurt our position with the Christians?' After every arrival the flurry increased. I knew that these words were going around and what was being said—no one bothers to hide his true thoughts from me any more; I am not important enough to be deceived. I never thought that they would come to anything more than talking to the refuge-seekers and trying

to get them to go on of their own accord, but closing them out—
I never thought that they would lock them out!"

Elias clenched his fists against his forehead and said bitterly,
"What is the hardship? Before long the ground will thaw and
soon it will be springtime. Wolves seldom are a menace after the
middle of March!"

"You sounded like me just then. Don't worry, Rabbi—I told
Rabbi Yomtob as soon as I heard. You will have to organize your
forces and the community will be split and embattled for a while,
but I think that you will win this issue. Now, when I need to
weigh in the community, I am not held much in account, but
use my voice for what it is worth. The other side has lost what
would have been a strong voice in its defense, for my father is
dead." And Elias saw that Abram had tears in his own eyes before he turned his face away.

The thaw came to Kuckney with the small beginning drip-
drip of single drops from the ends of icicles. When the wind blew
in the middle of the day, it was not edged against the face and
there were scents and odors in it that made people remember
something long ago in youth—something that was not to be
touched or named, but only reached for in the wordless way of
man before God put tongue in him and bade him give his passions names. Although the wind came hard again and the nights
chilled the very soul into hiding, the thaw had begun and the waters opened into their courses and poured under the ice and took
it, breaking in chunks from the iron grounds of the banks. From
their posts of guard, De Kuckney's men-at-arms looked over fields
and woods to where the sky was a clear blue to the south and to
the roads already beginning to melt to mud.

When they saw horses and riders, they cried them and then
counted them and Lord Robert came up to a lower ramp to see
their approach: Malabestia, with his doe's-head banner and his
squires and several men-at-arms—ten or so. Lord Robert
stamped his foot and pulled his beard with the fury of his impatience. The mad zealot kinsman of his had almost been rid of
and here was a guest who would compound his mischief, against
whom kindliness would not prevail and for whom discretion
would be useless. He saw his son riding at the side of the
standard-bearer and, for the first time in his life, wished that he
had not come. Prudence was less than useless now—all his virtues
would be faults to drag him down and his son would be there to

see it happening. There remained only to act in the code and make the gestures which were so empty for him and in which he looked so false and clumsy. He sent a messenger to his wife to bid her prepare the hospitality for the Baron and his retainers and then he took his place upon the ramp, stiffening, and he gave the welcoming gesture that was called for.

The monk kept himself aloof from all of them until they were at their meat, and then he made an entrance with a flourish; bare, stark and dramatic in his white tunic and alb, thin as a winter-beaten tree yet tremulous with energy. Lord Robert looked at the others sitting with him at the table. Even the Baron was agape. He tried to see the scene before him as if he were re-membering and not living it now. I will let them all take me where they will, these happenings, he thought. I will submit and not suffer. Malabestia spoke to the monk as if with a great ad-miration, and Brother Lewis, whose audience before had been servants and women, opened to the flattery and showed his hands which had wrestled with a devil and spoke of the hells which he had seen in visions. "And are any of those hells," Malabestia asked, "in the shape of the city of York?"

They left the next day, going slowly northward by way of the estates of the important nobles in the shire. Lord Robert had told them that he would join them in York on their arrival. He saw the scornful look of his Lady when he demurred making with them the trip that was to gather up the gentry of the three coun-ties for an undertaking of some kind upon York city. Nothing had been planned explicitly, nothing stated surely, but it was meant for all of the nobles and must involve them all lest the blame be-placed upon one house and touch it with ruin. It had been so with the Kuckneys who had helped to kill a saint. The idea had to do with all of the nobles and all of the Jews, with the fact of no authority in York, with a taste for crusades and with the eradi-cation of the debt which was by now too great ever to be paid.

As he had waved them in, Lord Robert waved them out, his disappointed son giving him no nod of special good-bye. They were going to the Percies, like traveling troubadors with a trained beast that could be caused to roar. The young Percy was wealthy and well equipped for war or sport, but he never carried any-where in his baggage for hunt or home the flimsiest bit of subtlety. They would have to draw their pictures clearer for him, but he would go "for honor" and so would they all and so would Lord Robert, he knew. His wife was sure that the white-robed Brother was a saint, and Lord Robert was just as sure that he was mad, but if he had been put from reason, it was not so far that he did not know which was his benefactor's best horse.

Down the Walm Road into York, heads white and glistening, rode John Marshall and Henry Marshall and their armsmen. Henry had been elected as the new Dean of York's Cathedral, and John had been made High Sheriff of York. The old officials had been swept away to higher places and the King had swept himself away to France to wait for spring and his Jerusalem. The two men now to serve York were distantly related to one another; Marshall was beginning to be a name of importance in England, but not so great as some, and these two were anxious to lend their weight to its greater glory. Family pride was paramount among noblemen from the South as well as the North, but to this was added a second slight raise of the lip because of an opinion of the Southern men that Northerners were dull, provincial and drab, and so they rode proudly past the churches and whitened fields, over the Foss Bridge to their new lives. If Fortune was good to them, they would not stay in this "outpost" any longer than it took them to make their names shine in the King's eyes. Richard was their leader, their employer and the judge of their labors. As friends to him and to his reign, they were to see that nothing was done to harm the interests of the King of England. Richard, having given no orders, instructions or warnings to these two ministers of his authority and the authority of his somewhat brother, had ridden away to a glory less encumbered with ideas than with armor. The two men seemed confident enough in their fur wraps and sitting with dignity astride their fine horses, but for each man, this was to be the highest post he had yet held.

There was no hope of help from Archbishop Geoffrey, with all the magic of his popularity. With both King and Archbishop gone, there was no authority to whom John Marshall, as High Sheriff, would have recourse. He was a man of his generation, and proud of it, and he did not like taking action independently. For him and for all whom he knew living was seen as a series of responsibilities interwoven and inextricable—a garment of a million crossed strands. Even the landowners, the nobles on their estates, took counsel and all had always to answer to some greater lord or to the King or to the Church. The two men, as they reached the center of the busy city, comforted themselves with thoughts of rents, immunities, lands and houses; strips whose fruit they owned and the labor of which was theirs. They smiled to each other over the tossing heads of their horses. A very, very ripe bunch of grapes, indeed. The years ahead would be quiet, uneventful, rich ones, with the unquestioned interweaving of the strands of lives continuing in the ancient and prescribed ways, and they would be gone, if need be, before any of the faults in the fabric showed. They, the two most important men in the city, would bring honor to the name of Marshall. The hoarfrost greyed their winter-coated horses and the sound of hoofs was like a stone hammer, striking the sparks from its anvil. The air was cold, the sparks were bright; the entrance had a sweet and regal sound to it. The men sat straight upon their horses, and they were smiling slightly.

"LEAVE?" Rana asked. She looked at the guests in Josce's house; the tired, frightened guests, refugees moving north out of the way **28** of the hate that was coming and beating the reeds for them. The Jewry was choked with the quarry that had been coming by day and night into its streets for safety. Rana looked at them in wonder. "Leave? . . . Leave York? Where would we go—strangers, seeking the help of strangers? Here we are known and"—she lowered her eyes—"respected." She saw the doubt on their faces. "You people—do not be afraid. No one can stop you if you want to go farther north, but there is only Durham, and after that Scotland with its brigands and man-wolves. At Durham, even, no friends, no fellow Jews. These are the last real Jewish streets in England."

"Widow, were they the last on earth, we could not stay."

"Nothing will happen. Wait and see. My husband——" and they looked at their feet, embarrassed, and Rana remembered the shaming of Baruch. She had never realized how much she had used his name to give a weight to what she said. "Baruch

believes . . ." In April or May, August—in September, even—
it would have been of moment, of account what Baruch believed.
Now, like snow, the advantage had melted away and Rana was
left with whatever wisdom she might have had, naked and un-
adorned.

A few of the wanderers left on the next day to begin the miserable walk to Durham or Scarborough in the grey cold. Some
of the more feeling ones, whose minds had not been clouded over
by their own agony, saw the need for leaving the community to
whose peace their numbers were becoming a threat. Under the
surface rhythm of the changing seasons, beneath the dailiness of
bread, drink, prayer and the preparation for Passover, the tones of
loyalty and faith which had bound the people of Northstreet together were parting into discord. Suddenly it seemed that all the
ancient scandals had been rediscovered and were being lived over
again. Bitterness, buried through the years, woke bitter again in
the imagination, and many a wife, long since mother and grand-
mother, remembered the grudges of her youth with a vehe-
mence of which she thought herself no longer capable.

Hour by hour the great breech widened between those who saw
the threat of the ragged outcasts to their community and those
who saw only the pain in the exiles' eyes. The arguments were
as clever and subtle as Jews, sifted and sharpened on years of discourse and philosophy, could make them. "Behold," the Singer
noted, "it is only a choice between selfishnesses, for to the man
who calls me selfish for wishing to save the lives of my children,
I say, 'Is it not the more direct selfishness to peer at the exile as
if he were ourself and to think: How would I wish to be treated
if I came seeking mercy?'"

Elias listened to all of the talk and said to Yomtob later, "I
never knew they had it in them; such heights of wit. Why, every
undistinguished neighbor suddenly emerges as a gleaming logi-
cian! Is there not room enough in all that maze which they con-
struct for one—one—tiny seed of holiness, of love?"

Yomtob shook his head sadly, but he did not answer. Elias
watched him as the days ebbed by, and after a time he did not
mention his horror at what he heard on every hand. Yomtob was
trying to heal the awful cleft, to bring the warring factions to a
peace that was higher than either of their single wishes. When he
spoke to the congregation, it was not of his preference or even
of their conflict, but of the beginning things—the earliest defini-

tions which they had learned by the droning rote of the First School: What is Prayer? What is Life? What is Man?

The synagogue was small, having been built for the Jews of York alone, and as Reb Yomtob reminded Elias, no preparation had been made for massacres. There, pushed close as the seeds in a pomegranate, the pious observed the rites and the prayers which heralded the Passover. Yomtob stood before them, reading from the ancient Books which held their wisdom and the wisdom of their forefathers. The passage he read was triumphant, almost joyful, and when he closed the Book and looked about at their faces, he saw that many of them were struggling between the sorrows of their hearts and the joy of the Book in proclaiming the great wonder and beauty of God.

He smiled to them a little wistfully, and said, "The Jew looks at his observance and he says, 'How is it that at the height of the wedding, we remember lost glory and mourn Jerusalem? How is it likewise that we feast to commemorate an exile, and the portion read is one of triumph, of life?' Are we perverse, we stubborn Jews, who go on living in a world that hates us? Sweet Jews, this is the condition of reality. Nothing on earth is complete—in all the universe, nothing is complete except the Lord, our God. Neither joy nor sorrow is whole. Our Judge judges a life that has been lived, and he judges by the finished work. It is written! 'If life were taken by minutes, who would be a saint?' My people, let us pray that those who have been killed had good lives, and let us say to the young: 'Life is the gift which God has given. Let us not waste it. Let us not spurn it, but use it and live it as fully as we can. Charity increases life; let us be charitable. Prayer amplifies life; let us be prayerful. Love gives meaning to life; let us love. Thought informs life; let us think, and, thinking, let us glory in the gift of life. If we must sacrifice, it can only be with the full knowledge of what we lose.' Young men, breathing hard for heroism say, 'Let us join the martyrs!' When will God stop sorrowing to think: I gave him a treasure and he threw it away wantonly, like a rotten fruit into the street. Poor man—thought is a heavy coat, but forethought is the heaviest, and the hotter the fire, the more we must wear our coats."

Through the next days, Northstreet teemed with rumors and fancies. The Christians of York still saw hungry, wild-eyed refugees moving through their city to the Jewry, and they became more fearful, as they heard tales of the massacres to the south. With their thoughts dressed in the word 'crusade,' they began to stir with the same excitement as their countrymen of London, Oxford, Cambridge and Lynn—salvation here at home!

Father Odo heard these stirrings and shook his head against them. Had the simple never been told that salvation can only be obtained in difficulty, and that the sacrifice is blessed mostly because of its difficulty?

As he told them of their foolishness, he painted still brighter the picture of the glories won through true crusading in Christ's own land. He could not help himself, for he was afire with the hunger to share the soul-brimming grace of a Holy War. All the world was ringing with the virtues of that way to salvation, and some went to the limits of law and justice, forgiving everything in the wash of rapture. Let the simple think that poverty can be requited here, they said, that those denied Jerusalem because of serfdom or labor, illness, debt, laziness or fear might have, somehow, a way to overcome their world and have perhaps a share in Heaven also, along with those who met their victories in places whose names were burning brands in the imagination. Some wondered briefly if it were not somehow amiss to hate suddenly the friends of a lifetime: Denicosa, who with her bag of healing herbs was often seen at the doors where children cried: Rabbi Elias, whose trading was always concluded with a joke or a riddle to chew on; this other one, that other one. The streets watched each other carefully, and like figures in a dance, came together, went apart, came together and went apart with slow, measured steps, each with eyes seeking in the other's face for a signal.

When the wisest looked about for protectors or for the embodiments of law, either civil or ecclesiastical, in the city or the shire, they found a strange and frightening lack, an emptiness in the great seats of authority. Geoffrey, the Archbishop, who was popular and powerful, was in willing exile in France. From his great position to the parish priesthood stretched a long and empty plain of unfilled positions, all of which were waiting for the Archbishop's return and an investiture by an absent King. Richard, the new and vital keystone of all of their leadership was gone to his Crusade; his High Sheriff, John Marshall, was new to the post and to the shire, and he had been given his authority only on paper. He had not even had the advantage of the simple rules of thumb which the old politician gives the new—who is

218

to be seen to and who guarded against. The old Sheriff was in London, attending to greater matters as a regent's councilor. He had been twenty years High Sheriff in Yorkshire and there was no one else who could offer the strange new man a word of help. The shamed Dean and Treasurer of the Cathedral had recanted and been placed in Christ's service elsewhere, and Henry Marshall as Dean had no fellow to whom he could himself apply. Residence requirements were only in force when they could be upheld, and the upholders were away. The Dean intended to spend his time visiting. They had not thought to appoint a mayor.

And so at York there were no strong swords to raise against the violence men always seem to carry half at the ready. The people had always had leaders with set duties and a tightly woven place in the design of things. It disturbed them now that they were leaderless, that the very weave of their days had changed and that parts of it were pulling to ruin. A man had always gone in a familiar path of law and command—in faith: the parish priest, the Canon, the Bishop, the Dean, the Archbishop; in civil matters: the Watch, the Bailiff, the Mayor, the King's Justice, the Sheriff, the King. And these authorities did not make independent judgments for the single case, or frame up rough compromises on their own. In a life where every man was a thread in a fabric already planned, each single exception or complaint was passed up and down the entire warp of rule to the decision unanimous by all of the single threads. With neither of the great parts of the warp intact, people scurried back and forth like ants from a ruined nest, consulting, doubting, full of confusion. The simplest matters loomed tremendous in complexity before men to whom a single decision by one person was impossible; and in York at this time there was no one who had the experience even to know what any one of these decisions would be. Wisdom, reason, security, law and responsibility had marched away from the Yorkshire moors to the glorious war, and because they promised to return, nothing was put in their places. The ancient chairs gathered dust, and seekers after law, who came by habit to the places of judgment, found them locked and stood in fear and confusion under the eaves, shivering, in the open world.

On the first of March, with the weather like spring, some schoolboys hung a pig on the outer wall of the synagogue. It was cut down by Father Odo before it caused any distress to those going to the Evening Prayer, but in the Christian streets there was no laughter at this prank, only a bitter word of assent. It was justice, many whispered. Some days later, Abram of York, Jew and scribe, was attacked in the market place by a group of rowdy boys who pelted him with mudballs. Because no one spoke against the boys or stopped them, Abram was forced from his booth and chased over the Ouse Bridge. When he returned the next morning, he found his booth ruined. On the eleventh of March, Denicosa was reviled before the door of a Christian house. She had collected and sold herbs and simples to that family for twenty years. The door remained closed.

Josce knew that they should leave as soon as possible. The city was tense and full of murmuring, and every day new refugees came and added to the fear that hedged Northstreet. It was possible to go into Scotland and even west, and with the clement weather coming, they could make a long circular trip down to London where the fury against them had burned itself out. He spoke to the Rabbis and they agreed, but when Elias told Denicosa, his wife, and Josce told Anna, his wife, the women would not hear of it. "It is too cold yet for the children," Anna said, stroking the soft heads, "and what about Passover?"

It was the Passover that decided it. The feast was but a week away, and although it was the celebration of an exile, no one, especially in this much harder latitude than Egypt, could think of lifting cups of festival wine far from the sweet, familiar warmth of home. They would praise God with feasting, songs, wine and jubilation as they had planned to do all year, and then they would lock up their houses, clean and holy with the ritual care which they had taken, and turn their steps west and south to the remnants of a greater community than theirs. While Christian York relived Christ's anguish through Lent and toward Good Friday and the Tenebrae, the Jews were beginning to move into the season of liberation, the Passover. While the Church rehearsed His sacrifice with all its eloquence and tears, Jewish faces were smiling because a pharaoh and a sea and a desert were no match for their jealous God and his little people. This difference was marked by some.

"See how the apostates laugh as our dear Lord starts toward Calvary!"

"See how the cruel Christians frown at us because we once were free and full of power!"

The Law concerning the special week of Passover made great

stress upon the ritual order and cleanliness of the house. All the dishes, trenchers, knives and goblets were specially scalded and the corners of each storeroom shelf and cupboard were scoured and sweetened for the coming year. The women clucked to one another as they met and passed, or bent and straightened in their dance of cleaning—woman's second dance that replaces for a lifetime the short dance of allurement. In the old days when possessions were few and simple, it was a quick matter, indeed, to sweeten a house, but now there were a million things to see to. "Mark you," laughed a woman at the well, "who has time for exile?" And the rags went back and forth, and the old straw flew out from the doors in fifty separate storms, and the days of work rushed by from the whirling skirts of bustling women.

Brother Simon, Brother Norbert and one of the rough lay Brothers stood before their Abbot and heard his slow words as if he had spoken three separate speeches. But to all there had been communicated a sense of the worry and the deep sorrow that their Abbot felt in his own hidden soul. A message had come to him that a tall, gaunt man with red-brown hair and beard and dressed somewhat in the habit of a Premonstratensian, was riding toward York with a group of armed knights. The teller had said that the happening was very recent; perhaps only a day or so past, and that the one who gave the message to him had done so with much urgency. The Abbot looked at his three men. Brother Norbert was wellborn, well-spoken and a quick thinker. Brother Simon could feel with his every hair the rightness or wrongness in a situation and he could sound out a lie a half-mile away. They might need the tremendous and willing power of Brother Joseph, the servant Brother whose endurance was his way of praising God. If Brother Lewis was to be found and brought back, these three could do it.

The question turned over its rough edge in his mind: Armed knights—what could that be? If the Brother was under arrest, surely one or two guards would be enough, unless he had done something very serious, indeed, and was being taken to York to be tried. But there was not a canonical court in York; everything had been left scattered and confused by Richard's coronation and dispersal of the old court and he had left before another could be formed. Armed knights . . . ?

He shut the question away and continued his orders to the Brothers. They were to travel by good fast horses to York. He was breaking the rule against clerics using horses, but he explained to them that the sin was on him; they were acting only in obedience, and he saw that this, too, had its effect on them. The weight which the Abbot was bearing in the matter told them even more of its seriousness than their own knowledge of what it meant to abandon a religious order. Abbot Adam was feeling this mission rather than knowing it and he could not instruct his emissaries in the hundred invisible possibilities which were moving his thoughts so wildly about the figure of Brother Lewis riding toward York. At last he looked up from his hands and hard at them and said, "It may be that there is danger to others here as well as to the soul of our Brother. You will have to close your ears to the reasons that are given if you see evil done. Obey the Ten Commandments and do not suffer them to be broken by our Brother, even if his reasons seem full of truth.

"If you can bring him back, do so, even at great cost, for he is possessed and his devils may hurt the innocent." He found himself grinding his teeth and wishing that the Brothers could be attuned somehow to his thoughts that were so much more eloquent than his words. He sighed, gave them the benediction and sent them on their errand. They would be well-provisioned and there was a good choice of horses, for many of the gifts to Welbeck House this winter had been in kine and horses, some of which the Brothers had traded at the spring fairs.

Later, when Abbot Adam heard them beating away north, he wondered why he had been so sure; why he had acted so quickly, so instinctively. News should have been sent to Newhouse, the founding House: Our lost Brother has perhaps been found. From Newhouse to Premontre in France, to the Vicar General, to Premontre, to Newhouse, back to Welbeck in the ancient pattern of consensus and respect. Of course he would confess this overwhelming, sudden act of his, and the horses and all the rest of it. Back in Premontre, in green, sweet, long longed-for France, he would submit to discipline and a crisp, vigorous new soul would be sent out to be Abbot of Welbeck.

It was such a prideful act. Why had he done it? In many ways it would be a cause of dissension in the House. Dissension was the worst thing which could befall an Order. He had heard of Houses destroyed by the jealousies and breeches of discipline that had been given their origin in single foolish acts of pride. Yet . . . and he thought of the wild Brother and of coming down into the courtyard on an autumn day three years ago, into the circle of the fiery, frightening speech, and seeing the Brothers, even those who knew how wrong Brother Lewis was, enthralled, enchanted, hating with him. Now he was free in a world without leaders. Abbot Adam knew that to the south there had been great risings against the Jews, with murder, fire and rapine, and worst of all, to the Religious, the selling of baptisms in return for life. He wanted to convert the Jews, but though they were his enemies, he could not love them. They must not be instruments for the debasement of Christians. Murder, adultery, bribery, thievery, even heresy drowned Christian souls when they had this hunger for vileness stirred in them. The stirrings had been in the air, blowing like a perverse wind from the south. Its warmth was not springtime, but lust, and the burning of bonfires.

As he had done so many, many times before, Abbot Adam looked out over the lands which he had come to love. When he had first set foot upon this land, he had seen ugly marshes and stinking fens where the goblins of strange diseases lurked. They had battled it, his Order, and won. Sheep grazed upon the land and trees had been planted to hold the water underneath the ground; saplings that were tall now and full and awaiting another season in leaf. There was no pleasure in this. A dragon was loose and walking on its clumsy legs toward all of them, and the souls of men were shedding their years, generations, centuries of patient tilling and reclaiming, like the land, and were becoming primitive again for that dragon; and it would wallow, God!, in the muck that had always been waiting under the seeming green of men's Christian-sounding prayers. Ride hard, my sons, ride hard!

From London to St. Albans, to Hertford, to Colchester, to Northampton, to Cambridge, to Bury St. Edmunds, to Norwich, to Lynn, to Nottingham, to Lincoln, and then pausing slightly, as if to look where next, the Hate, dressed in borrowed clothes, whitened because of the need for righteousness, decked with banners and holiday, plunder and rape, turned itself still northward. Doncaster, with but a handful of Jews was passed over in an hour; Hull and Beverly were the quick wind after its passing, but whetting the taste for death, and by then the moving horror was at the doors of York, and pausing, it savored the numbers and the wealth.

They had heard, each, with his separate mind, the Abbot's message. They rode steadily and seriously, like men bound for a job of work, although only Brother Simon had a glimmer of what that might be, beyond rescuing their conspicuous fugitive brother. Brother Norbert sought to place this mission of theirs in some familiar rule. Brother Lewis was of his Order, his flesh, really, and he was ill and needed his Brothers' care.

If the House had been a large one, from which Brothers habitually jumped the wall and lost themselves, the affair would have been reported and forgotten, but this House were truly brothers and owed to one another the fidelity which they had sacrificed from their blood families. Brother Norbert had been a noble, and family died hard with him. My brother, he thought, and whipped his horse. The lay monk, gloried as he rode, in the horse, the action, the change, the challenge. He was a simple soul and honest and he thanked God for escaped Brothers whom one had to find on a good horse at the earliest moment of the spring. Brother Simon thought of a rescue, a timely arrival and saving, if only he and these could be the instruments; and the rescue in his mind did not concern the angry, hating Brother Lewis, but Abram, to whom he had forever said good-bye. . . . They beat toward York.

AT the entrance to the Walm Gate, four men dismounted from tall horses and breathed the hearty breaths of fighters and slapped their shoulders with exuberance. When they laughed, they shook with metal. The Barons Percy and their men. At the end of the Selby Road, four men dismounted and gave their horses to a keeper and eased their short, thick daggers at their waists and hefted from holders the heavy-hilted swords that were not for sport or litheness on some grassy jousting field, but bore their weight ponderous and slow for something final. The Barons Courcey, Tampton, Grimston and his squire. At the Mickle Gate five men dismounted from their deep-chested chargers and stretched, full of manhood and strength, and joked in the casually obscene way of men, laughing with the guards. One carried in great calloused hands a jewel-hilted sword engraved with the names of many noble warriors and sharpened to a shining edge of iron. The Baron Malabestia and his still squire, the young De Kuckney, and two other squires and a knight from Burroughbridge with a cruel chain-mace. The white-clad monk had ridden ahead of them, unable to withstand the fury of his calling. They walked through the gates into the city.

"My arms are as ten, my soul as hundreds. The sons of Satan swarm against the earth, infest the seas, darken the skies and rejoice because their day has come. The angels are being put to flight, but as they fly, retreating from serpents and spiders, they beg of Christ and Mary: 'Choose us a champion!' Christ answers them: 'The Lowest is High, the despised, Salvation!' Behold, oh, Christ, your champion.

> *Filia Babylonis Misera!*
> *Beatus qui retribuet tibi*
> *Retributionem tuam quam retribusiti nobis*
> *Beatus qui tenebit,*
> *Et allidet parvulos tues ad petram!"*

"Good ladies, how late it is getting! Have you swept again and spread the rushes? I hit my husband from the house with a broom, laughing as we always have—what preparations!"

The round, unleavened cakes baked with great care and ritual were doubled for the number of people and the necessaries of the rites had been counted off on the fingers of the housewives: the shankbone, the bitter herbs, the apple-paste that was a symbol of the ancient walls of Egypt that had been built with Jewish blood in the mortar. They appeared at their doors in the dance, flapping cloths, a greeting, a retreat. In the afternoon, the Servant of the Synagogue went from house to house, seeking what could be so familiar that it was overlooked. As he left each house, he made a sign on the door or the wall that the house was clean of leaven and ready for the Passover. The synagogue had to be cleaned, so Denicosa went with Rana and they carried cloths and buckets and scurried back and forth all day.

On the following evening, Abram, as master of his house, would rise from the table and go to the door and fling it open, speaking the words of welcome to the wanderer, the poor man, the stranger. Perhaps—who knows—to Elijah himself, the bidden guest, for whom the finest place was set in all the homes. Their doors would be opened, and if no one stood there to accept the hospitality of the house, perhaps a spirit would enter in to share; perhaps it would be the spirit of peace. When Rana returned to the house, Abram was dusting Baruch's prayer books and setting them in order. Rana was moved somehow with resentment. How quickly the dead were pushed aside, and how, begging no pardons, the young, living, put their hands upon the books.

"Today the windows must be sparkling clean," she said. "We and Josce's family are the only ones with stone houses in York, and with glass at the windows. If ours are not polished as clean as theirs, you know what will be said."

"I will see to it," he said.

"Now mind that you and Josce's boys do not get too spirited and start throwing those ragballs about——"

"Madam!" The tone was all Baruch, the Master of the House.

She stopped completely and assumed her old manner, and Abram, seeing that he had this sudden advantage, pressed on with it.

"Madam, I have decided that after the Feast, and when we return from London, I will marry Bett."

Rana looked at her son in amazement. "What a marvel of a sense of timing you have! My son, why must you tell me between pots and potlids at two in the afternoon, on the day before the eve of the first Feast, while I stand on one foot!"

"I have been trying and hinting for so long. Now it must be said and I am saying it."

Rana paled with anger. "Would such a marriage do anything but disgrace you both and add another blemish to your father's name and memory? Ungrateful servant! Not even the Christians wanted her, so they threw her out! What makes her good for our family?"

"She is good for me and I am a full man," he said. "I have told you and therefore is my duty done. You may rage if you like."

"Thank you," she said sarcastically. "Liberty is a fine thing. Do you suppose that you can get the boys and give them the ragballs to wash the windows? I am going again to the synagogue." He cursed himself as she left. With her, sometimes he could not, even now, keep from being a boy.

As the Servant of the Synagogue went in and out, marking the houses of the Jews, passers-by in the street and to and fro across the bridge saw the lines he had marked on the Jewish houses and they turned to each other with strange looks and with noses stretched for some peculiar scent in the air. For many years they had seen these marks and recognized the signs of Passovertide, the gaiety, the hurry, the strange round cakes, but now it seemed a new happening, a series of dark and sinister rites, and they remembered the tales of Christian blood—new leaven for Passover cakes—and the rumors of stolen gold.

Walking through the streets to the Percy mansion, they could not help but draw attention. These nobles had a bearing that the town men lacked, and they came their separate ways with a certain pomp and splendor. It added a sense of excitement to the moving of the city.

"I saw the Baron Malabestia with his men and a long sword and a fur-and-leather cape."

"I saw Baron Percy crossing the bridge."

With great men about, great happenings were near, and the townspeople, who needed novelty and excitement to salve them for the loss of their tradition of the land, felt with a tingling in their blood the wonderful promise of a passion, an action, a what they did not yet know.

Guard me for my struggle—I, who will bring salvation. It is the voice of God I hear, who was alone, as I am alone. Christ—Christ—where are you? The sun is black, the moon the color of blood! Why have you turned from me? I am in a sea of darkness. I hear Your command at last: "You will go to the heights to My altar and consecrate yourself against the enemies of man." I cannot go—I seem to be in chains. I am a slave, flogged and covered with blood. I must wait.

"Where is Henry Marshall, De Kuckney? Here we sit like stones in the roadside waiting for Judgment Day." And Malabestia took his dagger and polished it on the edge of his cloak. Percy came in and brought Malabestia's shield and hung it beside his own as a mark of honor.

"I do not know, but I have not seen him since we arrived. He must be gone to some noble's place where the mead-horn is full."

"Let us hope," said Malabestia, "that nothing urges him back with undue haste," and he laughed.

"He could not stand against us," Percy said. "He hates the damned Jews as much as we."

"Ah," said Malabestia turning to Old Percy, "but there will be one man less to remember who was here when King Richard returns and wonders whatever happened to his coin-coneys. I do not like to have things known of me when I cannot find out as much of him as I would like, or which way his little wind blows, but he looks ambitious and so, probably, he will find himself somewhere else in another year or two. Our sweetly born Archbishop is safely out of our way, and as for the Sheriff, poor little man, with no militia, and the keys to the jail fallen down the well and no armor . . ." and they began to laugh until they shook, picturing John Marshall with his authority: parchment; his mace: the morning mist; his militia: air.

"Enough of that, Percy— I will give you Joscenus's house first. Let those whom you favor go in with you. Let me take the house of that Benedict. I like that crying widow. Those plump little winglets of hers—a nice bite out of a savory fat chicken."

"I have never seen their women except walking quickly here and there."

"I had the delight of searching her person somewhat at tax-collecting time—a little here, a little there, as we King's Justices say . . ." And he laughed again.

"We must, on all accounts, get there before the mob. They appreciate nothing but wick-ends anyway."

"I have seen them on campaign," Young Percy said, "and they were like hounds, pissing on what they couldn't eat."

"How do we know when it will happen?" Lord Robert asked, wondering why he asked, since he knew he could do nothing either for or against the happening.

"We are here," Malabestia answered, stretching in his chair. "The *when* will take care of itself."

"While you scour the table, keep an eye on the soup lest it boil over!"

"Run to the Community Hall and borrow a bench to seat our guests!"

In the cramped thatched huts of Northstreet, room was being made for extra sharers of the festival, and even in houses where talk had been strong against admitting more exiles to their crowded shelter, place was made for those already in the city in an effort put forth toward charity and hospitality on this holiday. But Baruch's stone mansion stood vacant except for the family and Bett; somehow the anguish and despair of the refugees and their tenuous and grudged security in this city had begun to struggle even in themselves. They were afraid of the ostentatious fort-house of the York man who had been a victim like themselves.

Rana's heart sickened as she went about her preparations. Baruch had been wealthy and there was always an elaborate table; they had never passed a holiday that was not crowded with guests and travelers. She remembered the first year that the exiles had come from France—so much had happened since that they seemed old residents by now—there had been a whole year of feasting and dinners. Did no one remember that the coward had also been generous?

She went about her work, saddening as the day began to wane. She was coming around the house to get a last load of water from the well that the Jews used almost solely now, and she saw three children standing before the door. They were standing in the manner of all children, holding hands, too frightened to knock, too frightened to go away. They were motionless and speechless; two boys and a little girl. She put down her buckets. "Good afternoon." They made no answer. "Are you all alone in the world?" They looked at her with their wide eyes and still were silent. It was obvious. In a rush of need she wanted to run forward and embrace them, but she was prudent, too. "It is not easy to be alone. Please wait then, where you are."

She left her buckets and turned and went in through the back entrance from the cooking house and then to the front and opened the front door. They were still standing there, motionless. "Good afternoon," she said again. "Tonight is the Passover Feast and you know that it is written: 'Not to have guests at a feast is a terrible poverty.' Please come in and share our festival with us."

They made neither word nor gesture, but entered the house, and when Rana walked for her water, she stumbled once because of the tears that were in her eyes. It was no longer of moment or matter to her that they were not Jews.

From vaulted darkness to vaulted darkness his voice rang:
"Lord, I have come. I have come to lift Thy cause and carry it

to the end." The Church had been forbidden service by its traveling Archbishop, and it was completely dark. Even the sunlight seemed lost among the galleries. Brother Lewis prostrated himself upon the flags before the invisible altar. He found himself repeating the simple prayer by which the Brothers of Welbeck left the world for sleep, and whether by the deeply trodden habit of the old House, not yet shaken, even in these times, in this mission, or because there had been no sleep for him for three days— or was it four? at Amen, lying arms at cruciform on the floor of the Cathedral, Brother Lewis fell asleep. . . .

When he awoke it was from one dream to another.

"I have confessed my sins, being priest and penitent. I have gone through Mass, being hearer and helper. Sealing my vision is all that remains and armed in the consubstantial Body, glory-sword, I will be ready for the sign, for the ending of the world, for the dragon at the core of the earth, for the six beasts and the six changes. I have a Host—it must be consecrated. They have taken the wine—the red wine—the red water of the Spirit, the sea of red, the Red sea, the sea of blood—the blood of sacrifice— I must have wine-blood to consecrate this Host—the blood of salvation. The blood of doom, the Body and Blood. 'This is My Blood . . .' "

With his knife, Brother Lewis opened the beating, ready vein in his arm. Lacking a chalice, he spilled the welling blood onto the bare stone of the Altar. In some pocket or other, he found a bit of dry bread. Completing his Mass, he consecrated, with all the priestly gestures, elaborately, the blood-dipped bread, and offered his body and his blood to the eternal war with Satan and the Enemy of Man. In an anguish of impatience, he finished the ceremony and strode back and forth, back and forth, waiting.

Dusk fell and a silence came on like a waiting time separating the noise of the day's work from the evening revels in the taverns and houses after the curfew time. The Watches, alive to the creeping in of hate and the fear that almost seemed to lower upon the city, walked their courses, aware to the slightest sound of a different rhythm in the twilight. At one of the cookhouses off Northstreet, the steam from a boiling kettle gathered drops of water on a wisp of straw that hung from a roof. Two drops merged; then three. At the waiting fourth drop, the shining smooth straw bent slightly, and the drop, grown large and fat fell heavily into a puddle in the street. A rat woke from its hole and noised in the filth of the sewage pit. The guards stiffened.

Their hands went quickly to the keen blades of swords and the quick points of daggers. A second drop readied. A cat screamed from an alley and the watches tightened their hands upon their weapons until they ached.

Down Northstreet a boy came, lighting his way with a torch. As he turned around the corner of a house, he brushed against the side of it and the sparks burst up into the thatch, smouldering in it for a moment and then the roof took flame. The fire lifted from the roof and a cry went up, "Fire! Fire!" In the empty cathedral, the monk heard the shout go up and he went through the side door which he had broken in. He looked toward the center of the city and there, in the Jews' streets, he saw the flames. He leapt away and ran shouting, and with his arms wide and his cloaks flying: "It is the sign! It is the Holy sign!"

March 17, 1190

THEY had been beginning the Passover Feast. The first blessings were said, the first wine tasted. In the street outside, the life of the city had slowed for the evening. From the tavern at the head of Northstreet, Will the Owl had sent his oldest son for another batch of the small fish from whatever dealer still waited at the market. The customers were impatient, and the boy was in haste and a little drunk. He took a torch that burned at the door in order to light his way back. At the corner of the street that led to Ouse Bridge, he bumped into a passer-by and stumbled to the side of the house.

The thatch was dry and began to smoulder quickly, and then took flame. As the yellow light leapt into the air, the cry at once went up, "Fire! Help here, fire!" A few men began to run. For some first moments, it was all familiar and reasonable like any fire, with the wind figured and help on the way; the ancient pattern of cities and civilization: "As he is, I am." Some stopped and looked at the burning house, and went to beat on the door to rouse the ones inside, thinking: I too would want to be saved. Then, all at once, there was a stopping, a silence. Perhaps they had realized that this was a Jewish house; perhaps it was the time of waiting, idle time while the ladders and buckets were being brought—time to think, to stop thinking. In the silence of their waiting, the fire roared and crackled. The feasters inside were suddenly aware of it and the door was flung open. They came to the doorway shouting and calling and stopped abruptly, faced by the silent crowd; and they went silent also, terrified of breathing a single word against this delicate weather vane. And the fire spread on the roof, eating and crackling, and to the next also. Still they all waited, held, almost, like souls in limbo. And then the turning came. From the far end of the street, where Allhallows Church stood darkening into the night, a stark, white figure flew with its arms out like a cross, screaming, "The sign! The sign!" and then "Glory!", and then the ancient cry of crusade: "God wills it!"

One of the feasters knew then, one who had been in the clutch of it before, knew that the horror had turned upon them, and with a motion that was a last instinct, he lifted his hands to shield his face, and the crowd roared out in a great gush of anger and ran to the burning house and pulled out the protesting Jews and tore them apart with their hands. A new fever, a wildness, a joy seized the passers-by, and the hate that had waited just outside the walls of York for so long, rushed in and was taken up and began to surge through the city.

At the Percy mansion the sound of shouting reached the idle nobles, and they rose, listening to what they heard, and needing no other knowledge. They grabbed their weapons, the great, heavy swords that they had brought with them and Malabestia laughed and said, "So soon! By the Cross, they are wonderfully prompt!"

They ran from the house, across Foss Bridge, past the synagogue, where already some eager looters had begun to mill about the doors. Percy went to them and took command and the rabble, with all their years under this lord or that, walled themselves behind his leadership and rejoiced in the safety of following. They were not frightened any longer—here were their leaders, their deliverers. Over the Ouse Bridge the others ran, to Northstreet, already crowded with lowing, stamping, undecided people. The fire, unchecked, raged on, house by house. Jews, who had opened their doors to the coming-in of their Messiah on this feast night, saw that Hell had come instead to their hearths and doorways—even here, to the safe city, the wise city. Some of them began to run from their houses into the alleys to safety. The crowd, starving for a leader, still stirred and moaned, and suddenly the leaders were there. Malabestia and his men broke through the mill, and waving their swords before them cried, "God wills it! God wills it!" Into the houses the mob streamed.

Malabestia, his squire and the two knights were thinking as well as hating; they fought through the noise and press to the two stone houses that faced each other at the end of the side street. The baron motioned Josce's house to the eager knights with him, while he and his squire turned to the great door of Baruch. The knights gathered back and hurled themselves against the heavy door, which was not bolted and gave easily to them, swinging wide.

Josce's festival table, beautifully laid with more than twenty places, stood glowing before them, the soup still steaming in the bowls. On the fire a goose hissed on its untended spit. There were no people. The knights ran inside, cursing. Somehow the human prey had heard or felt or sensed what was to come, and had risen and fled, taking nothing, but careful, even then, to leave, glowing and serene, the echo of a holiday, the sign of the feast in their house—the triumph of their faith.

De Tampton grabbed a set of candlesticks while some of the crowd pressed in behind them. Together they began to ransack the house for jewels, overturning the Passover table and the holiday foods in their eagerness. They did not find as much as they had pictured finding, and the escape of their victims, with that last gesture that seemed a defiance to which they had no answer, enraged the looters to a great pitch of anger. They tore and spoiled and destroyed, and when there was no more to do, they ran screaming into the streets, seeking to recover the victims who had been lost to them.

Across the street in the house of Baruch, Malabestia and his squires had not been thwarted so. No Christian had known that the Jews did not bolt their doors on this holiday, and they also were surprised when the Baron kicked at the door imperiously and it swung wide. Inside was a family sitting at their festival table, too confused to fight or escape. Malabestia realized that, with the crowd outside soon to get out of hand, there was not time to torture these Jews for the secrets of their hiding places. The three little guests sat at the table with big, frightened eyes, and the girl began to whimper.

Malabestia went forward to get his hands about Rana and tear off her coif and veil for that long fall of hair, and as he stepped away, Richard de Kuckney, the squire, caught sight of Abram who had shamed him before all of York in a fight, the memory of which still burned in him. For this had he sharpened his beautiful sword. Now would the ridicule be over. Abram had risen, kept from his mother by the table, and he stumbled to reach her before Malabestia did. She saw De Kuckney raise his sword for Abram and she forgot the Baron and the world and all the feminine graces which had been given her to live by, and she lifted the heavy trencher from the table and flung it at the squire's head.

While he was off balance with the glancing blow, and with hot food blinding him, Rana screamed, "Safety!" as Abram came toward her, and as he touched her, she hurled him away toward the open door with all the force she had, and cried again, "Safety!"

Abram, finding himself already at a run, and the way clear for a moment, shot from the house and into the confusion of the street. Rana's heart leapt with joy, and she turned toward the Baron a moment later with a brilliant smile on her face. Before what faced her, she lost it, finding herself back in the horror, among strangers and with the sound of carnage in the street outside. She saw ugly death moving toward her with lewd hands and a cold smile, and she shuddered and cried out, "You must not kill me—not now!"

"And why not?" he said, still smiling. He did not have time even to do what he had imagined to that plump chicken.

As he came close she blurted, "My herbs are uncut and my cloth is lying in the dye!" She was trying to explain why it was all so desperately important, the herbs and the cloth and living. She was not dressed for death, not ready, and the house was not set to rights, and . . . But the weapon came down with terrible force, and Rana, as she had been, disappeared in a gush of blood. The children were hewn apart as an afterthought. Rana's forgetting of their faith had decided it for all time.

When Father Odo had heard the shouting for the fire, and that it was so near, he ran as quickly as he could to the church door and opened it, and opened the big side door that led to the cellars where the fire equipment was kept. He had learned that it was wisest to wait until the ladder, pike and bucket men arrived; much time was saved when he directed them and there were fewer fights. He always went with them to give help or last rites to those who needed it, and so he limped quickly back again to get his things and then came and waited with his light for the men.

As the minutes passed, he grew impatient and then a little frightened. Holding his light high, he went out onto the porch of the church. Down the street was the fire, having taken several of the houses now and brushing great strokes of flame into the night. Around the houses and in the street was a press of people, but he could not see what they were doing or why they were not fighting the fire whose flames, unchecked, would soon touch to their own houses. Full of wonder, he went up into the triforium gallery. There was a small door leading to the vault under the roof. Openings had been left there through which one could see the houses and streets nearby. When he crept under the roof supports and looked out, he beheld, unbelieving, a kind of mad convulsion that had taken all the people. He was looking through a peephole that seemed to open on Hell—there—in his very streets.

With wild haste, fed by the shouting and the fires in the houses, the looting went on. Men, as they went by the tables, pushed food into their mouths, or drank, gorging from house to house. As roof after roof blew into flames, the rioters cheered and danced, hacking to death anyone who came from the burning places. In the unburned part of the street, the knights and barons went alone, as if by an understanding honored even in madness: nobles first, commons after. When the interest of ordinary rape began to pale, novel exercises in the ways of death turned pillage to a sport. Lords, loaded down with trinkets and with fine jewels, half-burned silk and worthless pieces grabbed up unthinking, stayed to watch impalements, hangings, guttings, while they ate, and vomited with eating, drank, and staggered with drinking. The Community Hall was being broken into and sacked and so was the synagogue. The courtyard gate had been shut and barred, and the heavy inner doors locked at the last moment. There were the sweaty rioters, swinging themselves against the outer door, gaining the courtyard and then pushing for the door to the sanctuary.

Blinking with disbelief, Father Odo sat back against a stone brace and suddenly he gasped with the perception that broke behind his own eyes. It had been he—he—who had preached salvation through battle, and the end of compromise with evil. He raised his hand ineffectually, saying, "No—no—I meant not this. . . ." He lifted himself heavily, and climbed down the tiny stairwell and limped to the door, muttering and half weeping with anguish, "No—not this way—it is wrong! It is wrong!" And he went out into the street, limping badly, to try to stop the monster of hate that he felt he had fathered.

When Abram broke out of the doorway of his house, he found that surprise and audacity were his only weapons. They served him well. In the chaos of the street he ducked and ran, pushing his way through the knots of screaming people, and not until he had passed by did they realize that he was a Jew escaping them. The fire was spreading the whole length of Northstreet and down side alleys to the river. Since the wind had turned a little to the east, there was hardly any danger to the houses on the western side of the Ouse, and so the people milled about, waiting to move through the stone houses for their turn at them, waiting for the fires to drive more human quarry to them, cheering, singing, now actors, now spectators, in this small crusade of theirs. Only when Abram reached the lower part of Northstreet, where a fork presented three choices to him, making him stop for a moment, did a group of them cry after him and then give chase. Flustered, he took the closest turning, a diagonal way that led back through a cluster of alleys and the backs of hovels and shops. He could hear them coming as he ducked behind a pile of litter to catch his breath. They knew the city as well as he did; he was sure that he must find a hiding place immediately because their efforts were angering them and if they caught him, there would be no mercy. He broke from cover and turned down another passage from which the wakened rats squeaked and thudded before him. The sound was so loud in his ears he was sure they had heard it. They were still half playing, cursing and clattering after him, but if they quieted to catch his sound he would be lost. He made another mistake, nearing Northstreet again in his doubling in and out to escape them. A blind close—a wall— Oh, no! God!
"Hey! Pst!"
He looked about him. A rat squalled and then there was a curse and a clatter. They were quite near.
"Hey! Pst!"
"Who is it?" he whispered, more frightened of this than of his enemies—the promise of safety, then what kind of betrayal?
"Come on in here!" the whisper said, insistently, impatiently. From a wall to the side of the dark close he saw a hand motioning him and part of a face half hidden in a dark doorway. They were

coming—they would make the turn into this close at any moment. He gritted his teeth and went for the doorway. The hand pulled him in and the door shut soundlessly behind them. The room was pitch-black. The hand pulled him, stumbling, back from the door while the bolt slid home by inches.

"Stay here!" the voice rasped in his ear. The hand left him and he heard steps. A door opened and light came with it and the man motioned him toward it. Still gasping for breath, Abram went in and turned to his rescuer. It was the tavernkeeper, Will the Owl. As soon as Abram saw the little man, he remembered what the close was. Will's tavern faced on Northstreet and the door and dark place through which they had come was a back storeroom. In the middle room where they now stood, Will often bedded guests for the night. He motioned Abram to be still and then he parted the heavy hanging which separated the room from the tavern. When he had seen that no one was there, he opened the storeroom door and lifted the plank in the floor which opened on to his cellars. They went down together, Abram holding a light and Will pulling the plank halfway back after him. Abram noticed Will the Owl's scrawny, ricket-twisted legs as he stood on the shaking ladder; the man really looked like an owl, with his grizzled face and staring eyes. His wife cuckolded him for ribbons and brass farthings and he was the laughing stock of half the town. Why was he a savior? Why he, of all people? Abram watched him come clambering down. He looked as he always did and walked as if he was doing now no more than he had always done, as if this night was no different from any other.

Abram spoke in a low voice to him, and the words came still a little breathlessly. "How do you come to save me?"

He remembered that Northstreet was not a Jewish street, though most of the Jews in York lived there; in their pride they never patronized Will's tavern nor greeted him or his children in the street. They had faced the problem of Will the Owl and his drunken guests by pretending that neither of them existed. When Baruch had met Christian borrowers there on some few occasions, he had treated the tavernkeeper with contempt and arrogance.

There was a shelf on the wall for a lamp, and Will put the wicklight there. Then he came back and whispered, "Mark you, I am not knowing who will be coming tonight, up there, or down here. I bring some food and mead when I can. Have you wounds?"

"Please," Abram said, "why did you save me?"

The scrawny man was going up the ladder. "Those men do wrong," he said. He stopped and turned slightly. "It is not good to give suffering to any man." And he turned again and went about his work.

As the slaughter progressed on Northstreet and victims began to become scarce, Malabestia noticed that neither the chief Rabbi nor Joscenus had been taken. He remembered that there had been some little time between the outbreak of the fire and the arrival of himself and his white-gowned madman who still raged and stormed up and down the burning street, quoting Revelations and dipping his hands in the blood of the dead. The Baron's booty was being tucked away for him by Richard and the knights; what remained was for the slow sifting of grimy-handed townspeople. He went across the Ouse Bridge to where the Jews' synagogue stood. Percy and his men had battered the inner door open at last and had gone in, half in terror of the strange, dark God whose riches were kept there. They lifted torches high, and with the dispelling of the shadows of that other world, caught the gleam of silver and of gold. Silver and gold were not magical, and these men who would never, in looting, touch a golden crucifix because the symbol was greater than the riches which formed it, had no such scruples with these foreign trappings. Candlesticks and snuffers and goblets were seized and taken, and then, mounting the platform, Percy tore away what he thought was but a hanging on the wall. Behind this hanging, jewel topped, belled and glittering, radiant, stood The Scrolls of the Law. As he gasped, a voice rang out, full of command from somewhere above them.

"Do not profane those scrolls with your filthy hands!"

The young looters were stunned into silence for a moment. A Spirit, perhaps, a power, conjured by these strange worshipers? One of the men, half unthinking, held his torch higher and caught the shadow of the balcony. "Look!" and he pointed to the others. It was their tangible world again, and with the crowd baying outside, the two knights ran up the narrow stairs to where the quarry lay, terrified, on the floor of the balcony. There were five people, one of whom had seemed to the looters to be the voice of the God. The joke of it amused the young man so that he felt well-disposed toward the pitiful group. He had not understood why the Baron Malabestia had been so intent on having every one of the Jews killed. He was still looking down at them when Percy came up the stairs behind him. "Come on—kill them and be done with it!" he said impatiently, hearing the crowd in the courtyard.

Rabbi Elias looked up at them, trying to bite the fear out of his lip: "Must we be slain for your sacrifice—for your justification?"

The question slowed the young man, but only for a moment. Before *Shema Yisroel*, the last statement of faith, could even begin on the lips that would not stop quivering, Elias was dead. With a moan, Denicosa threw herself across his body, sobbing, "Oh, my bridegroom, my bridegroom!"

Impatient to begin dipping into that great hoard of treasure, the two dispatched Denicosa quickly, and the three others, who had run from death at Norwich only to die at York. The rabble in the courtyard were growing impatient. If the nobles did not act quickly, secondhand glory would not be enough for the salvation-hungry poor. The knights ran down the stairs to the sanctuary and darted for the Ark. Pulling the adornments from The Scrolls, they left the Parchments of the Law, Lily of Jerusalem, which had been treasured so lovingly and read into the soul of every Jewish man in York, unrolled and spoiled on the now filthy floor. Now, there was no one to tell these men that their own forms, codes, beliefs and even the very words they had to frame them, were the heritage of the fathers of these that they had slain; that "Amen" and "Alleluia" were their very words, that Jehovah was their very God.

Malabestia came in like an inspector assessing some piece of work. He went up into the balcony and looked at the five dead. Not here. Joscenus was not there, nor the widow's son, nor the Rabbi-Bishop. For a Jew to escape would be a misfortune, but an important Jew—one like that Josce, with hundreds of marks of transactions in his head—would make this whole affair a stupid blunder and might cost the Baron his life. Where had they found succor?

He stalked away impatiently, while the mob, freed at last, surged into the synagogue to pick the leavings of the place, and to defile with vomit and filth, that which had always been closed to them. Once in the street, he collared a boy out of the turning and running, and shouted into his ear, and the boy left on his errand. In five minutes, a dozen boys were gathered about the baron who was so liberal with his coppers. He explained to them slowly, as if it were a lesson in counting, what he wanted and how he would pay if they could find through what holes in the night those devil Jews had escaped. The boys scattered like flung grain.

In the street, the whirling spectacle went on. The White Brother was roaring the fiery curses of the end of the world; Father Odo, a pathetic, limping creature, went pleading from man to man, begging them to stop. The crowds were dancing and looting and singing and getting dizzy with drink. The Father was a priest after all, and so they did not hurt him, but shouldered him aside like a madman, or baited him a little between the spectacles toward which they crowded like starving animals at the sight of food. Above them the fire dove and rose on the rooftops and in the heat and brightness of the false day of fire, they were like parts of a vision by a poet of the liturgy who evoked the day of the Last Trumpet.

TWICE the heavy board scraped aside over Abram's head, and a shivering, terrified body half stumbled down to the safety of the cellar. One was an old man, who stared at Abram from a bloody face, murmured a prayer, and died; one a young woman, who sat very quietly with her hands in her lap, blank with shock. Soon, Abram's restlessness mounted, until it overwhelmed his fear. Perhaps his mother was still alive somehow, and needed him. Perhaps Bett was hiding in the cooking house. She had been going to serve the food when they had heard the gathering noise before their house. Someone might need him, and here he was, safe in a refuge for women and old men. Over Will's arguments, he prepared to go out again into the streets.

"At least, if you moun do this," Will said, "ye'll take you my hooded cloak. It be of a cut that you will seem a Christian." A good woolen garment—probably the best garment that Will had. Abram threw it over his shoulders and turned his face toward the tavernkeeper so that Will might see how moved he was. If Will recognized anything, it was the danger which Abram faced.

"Be wary—and go and come by the back way. I've set my boys out the front door with a cask to keep the townmen busy."

Abram ducked through the door which Will held open and then shut silently behind him. He wove through the empty, labyrinthine alleys, touching toward the main ways when he could; and back again to Northstreet, peering hard at the dead to see if they might move; turning about the side of a house, waiting and watching. As he looked on at the looting and drinking, he knew that he could do no more where he was, so he struck off in and out of ways to the end of Northstreet, and when the main body of looters moved to the synagogue, farther away, he crossed the Ouse Bridge and went down by the riverbank, wondering if perhaps someone had found a hiding place under the bridge or along the bends in the river. As he clambered down the embankment, he turned and caught a light out of the corner of his eye. It was high above him and to the left. When he looked again, it was gone, but he clapped his hand to his mouth. Of course! It was Clifford's Tower!

He looked up at the great dark bulk of it on Castle Hill. Again, a light showed faintly there for a moment and again was gone. Abram scrambled up the bank, hoping that his eagerness would not betray him. Beside the river, and spreading down from the hill were the town gardens. Abram ran through them and past the little trees that would soon be blossoming and fragrant. This Passover night was death, horror, fire, screaming and madness, agony and cruelty and an apple tree upon whose fragile branch the tiny buds were beginning. He reached the top of the garden and moved quickly on the road which opened from the great enclosure binding Clifford's Tower to the castle. The castle was walled away by itself, but the tower stood sheer and high, and crenelations in the narrowing top made it an excellent place for defense and gave a long view to watchers, over the city and to the forests and moors beyond it. Now that there was no war (or no war that used the name and gave its victims choice of death) the tower was abandoned, and had gone to ruin. Abram had played there as a boy. He reached the door, a small, stoop-shoulder entry through the rod-thick walls. They were on the other side—small, huddled groups, some no more than whimpers in the darkness. To the darkness he addressed himself: "Abram, son of Baruch."

"Thank God! Thank God!" It was Josce.

"Amen. Blessed be He!" It was Yomtob.

Abram was so glad to hear them that he laughed aloud. "There is a woman who was saved—I will bring her . . ." he said. "She will see you and—and she will know you." He humped through the passageway again, and away, and when he returned, he was carrying the staring-eyed young woman from Will the Owl's cellar.

He had risked and suffered; he had been pious and generous and now he was claiming his reward. "Where is Bett?"—to the people clustered about in the dark. Everything seemed to stop, even the groans of the injured. He said again, thinking perhaps that in their confusion they had not heard him, or had forgotten her, "The maiden at our house—Baruch's Bett—where is she?" With the world in ruins about their ears, he could not say 'servant' any more; and where was she—the grave eyes, the work-hardened hands, the soft scholarly voice that came half-surprised itself from the throat of a servant girl?

From somewhere to the side, a gasp came, and then a man's harsh voice. "Have they not done enough, those Christian pigs! What does he say, Abram fil Baruch *Martyr*—does he ask: where is my mother, my cousin, where are my people? For whom does he ask? For a Christian! A Christian!"

There was no use explaining, reminding, trying to prove their case now. Abram knew that she was not there—it was enough; he would have to go and find her. He was about to leave again when Josce's voice spoke out, saying, "I and my family and guests made our way here just at the time of the fire, but there has been soul after soul coming all the time. It is harder to stay and to wait, but it is wiser."

Abram knew that he was right, but his soul ached, wondering for Bett, remembering Rana and how he had run and not stayed with her. Josce had led his family to safety while he . . .

"It is time to seek a better place," Yomtob said. "If Abram wishes, he may stay here below as a guard and to help those in who may find their way here."

There were four stages in the tower: the bottom, in a great colonnaded walk around the inner side with rooms for troops and heavy equipment; the second and third rings were reached by narrow stairs, and their deserted rooms had seen a dozen generations of rats and boys at hide-and-seek. The top ring was the roof and looked out on all sides and down over a smaller breastwork to the inner courtyard below. Josce had gone through all the rooms and to the roof, and it had been his light that Abram had seen. Now they helped the old and injured, pulling and scrambling up the narrow stairways past the first and to the second ring of rooms.

Then Yomtob said, "Rest here and sleep, those who can, and you will have watchers to guard your sleep all night." Afterward he and Josce and some of the others climbed to the roof and were stopped, stunned by the wonderful beauty of the night.

The stars were clear and large in a dark sky, and from its quarter the full moon had risen, setting off the richness of the dark heaven around it and lighting the world only enough so that the watchers from the tower, detached as they were from their lives, their daily ways and worries, saw the whole scene below them and above as if they were strangers to it. It was incomparably lovely to them. The night was mild and scented with the warming earth. The winds were gentle. It was a sweet spring evening; the last gift they would ever be given, unexpected. It had the nature of miracles.

"Why is this night different from all other nights?" They had sat at their tables on this very night and asked the ritual question, and the answer had come to them with fire and blood and madness. Now, singular, separate, so beautiful that it made them weep, the earth and the heaven rehearsed the question to them.

Will the Owl nosed about the streets, hoping for someone else passed by in all the uproar. His wife and children had joined the running and screaming and were swept away, and he was left alone to pursue his slow walk. He came at last upon an unexpected victim, Father Odo, sitting on a stone ledge. Across the bridge and behind the clutch of houses, shops and churches, the roar from the synagogue, bathhouse and communal bake-oven swelled and stilled almost rhythmically. Will did not know what to say to the Father, so he murmured, "Let me take you to your bed. Them there will be tiring soon."

"Oh, no! No!" The priest raised a hand weakly. "I was so dizzied that I had to stop for a moment. I must follow them and keep on following until the last one stops. I must try to urge them away—even one—from doing these things." Even in the merciful moonlight he looked exhausted and beaten. He was about to rise when several boys came at a run around the corner from the ruin of Northstreet and swung to a halt before Will and the priest. Getting their bearings to the sound of the crowd, they were about to dash away. "What do you seek?" Father Odo cried, springing up to catch at them. "He said a silver piece!" "He said a silver piece!" and they were away like arrows over the bridge. The taverner and the priest looked at each other. Money for what? They broke into a run.

The boys were crowding around the Baron, giving him the magical words for their reward. As he loosened his purse, he looked out at the scene before him, and he knew that he would have to spur these people further, that death had to be complete; he must bring them to lay siege to Clifford's Tower. Still in their pious wrath, the mob must be used while they were half sober, still hot for crusade and uncaring about reprisal. Approaching Brother Lewis, whose wild exhortations could still be heard above the roar of the people, the Baron shouted, "I saw him! I saw Satan, carrying his children to safety to begin their evil still again!"

The monk was unaware of him. "I will——"

"I saw them fly across Ouse Bridge," the Baron interrupted. "They gained Clifford's Tower and, hiding there, they begin to chant the spells of destruction against Our Lord and His saints and all His angels!" With that, the Baron seized Brother Lewis by the shoulder and shook him. The Brother stood before him, still listening into another world, and Malabestia raised his arm and cut the monk a smashing blow across the face, and he shouted into his blow, "Satan is in the tower!"

For a moment, the twisted sword of Malabestia's will hesitated, and then, with a cry, he stretched his skeletal arms again and began to intone in a monotonous chant, the passages of hate from Kings, Daniel, and Revelations. As his voice reached them, the people, enthralled, fell silent—listening to his slowly building words, regaining the fervor that had dwindled into revel. Bloody, ascetic, tortured, he looked to them as Christ must have, whom the Jews, the very Jews, dressed in the clothes of the past, had killed. His face was golden in the reflection of their torches. It was as if the One who hung on the crucifix in the Cathedral had come miraculously alive to exhort them to glory. No longer for any hope of pillage, but for the eternal, did the crowd strain to breathe his breath and let his words infuse their souls with new fire. He drew them tight to breaking with his voice, that heavy, cadent chant that rose and rose until their bodies were racked by sound and words no longer had a meaning.

At last, at full fever pitch, Brother Lewis threw his head back so that the face, twisted in pain, seemed to seek out the very

Heaven beyond this night. So must Our Lord have done in His last moment, His moment God and Man in One for the Remission of the Sins of the World.

"To Clifford's Tower, in the Name of God!"

There was a moment of utter silence after the last word, screamed to high Heaven, and they were like bowstrings, released at last from a tautness almost unendurable. With cries for vengeance, with "God wills it! God wills it!", they poured down the Saint John's Church street, across the newly planted gardens and up the hill in a charge, to the base of Clifford's Tower. Almost moved, but not quite moved, alone in the littered street, Richard Malabestia, Baron, sauntered slowly to his next duty.

Yomtob of Joigny looked out into the city from their fortress. He saw the torches of their hunters waving down the streets and heard the cry, "God wills it! God wills it!" and he lifted his head and said softly, "Oh, Thou One, High, Holy and Exalted—what is Your will for us?" Then he went to the breastworks at the center and called down to Abram to barricade the entryway as best he could and come up to safety.

By the time Abram reached the roof the crowd was already surging and milling at the base of the tower. Yomtob took him by the arm around to the dark side of the tower. "Come away from the torches and the noise," he said. "I want to show you an incomparable night."

"What is your God doing to us?" Abram cried to the Rabbi.

"He is giving us everything," the Rabbi said gently to him; "a night of rare beauty, a night of height that has lifted us away from the moment-to-moment causes that circle most of our lives. He has given us a Last Night. Do you know how rare a gift that is? I think that the Holy One grieves most for those who are cut down before they can say good-bye to one another and lift their souls high with the last prayers. 'Poor Jews—my people who so love to have the last word' and so He gave this to us and we must use the gift for those who lie on Northstreet, struck dumb in the middle of the last word." Yomtob breathed in deeply and then exploded into laughter. "I am sorry," he said, spluttering with it. "Excuse me. I was about to say something benign and profound—it is the height, you know, and on an empty stomach —and before I could open my foolish mouth, the Lord saw, and laughed, and afflicted me with the pettiest of petty human gripes: a cramp in the toe!" He took Abram by the arm, still laughing, and said, "Can you not laugh, too? Can you not help but laugh?"

Abram faced him incredulously. "How can you think of it?" He gestured around them at the roof and beyond at the world where fires were still burning. "What is funny about this hell, this horror!?"

"Mankind is so human. Let us at least take the privilege of our tower and see the ridiculous that lies in us between the holy and the evil, and seeing, laugh. If not, why were we scholars?"

"We are no higher than they. The height is an illusion."

"Exactly," said Yomtob. "We are His Purpose, His Instrument." And Yomtob began to chant the ancient Psalm: " 'Out of the depths I cry unto Thee, O Lord . . .' " and the song rose with great beauty into their last night.

THE crowd, all of York, milled and clamored at the base of the tower, and beating them to ever greater heat was the white-robed monk. **32** One by one the nobles left the excitement and returned to the streets of the Jews. Finding nothing of value remaining, they started to seek out Malabestia.

They found him near the Mickle Gate wall, sauntering toward the jail. He was whistling.

"My Lord, my Lord!" Percy cried, catching up with him. "The town has treed the Jews in the tower. They will starve up there and make meals for all the carrion birds in Yorkshire!"

Malabestia turned and looked at them. "Do you not know the least meaning of this affair? A few bits of silver? A little to-and-fro in some Jewess's lap? We must kill these Jews, all of them. The crowd will tire and lose enthusism and go away. They have no purpose in this, really. They will forget when a night of entertainment wears into common morning and their shops call them to work. It is we who have a purpose. We must raise siege to the tower now!"

"But how . . . ?"

"Lacking the keys to his estate here, John Marshall sleeps in the warden's house beside the jail. Where has he been all this time?

It would have been better had he been one of us. He has conscience, I think, but is too frightened and too new to stop what has been started, so he sits and wonders. Siege engines are in the castle yard. We must have his word to break into the yard and get them."

"I could go over the wall with a little help," Richard de Kuckney said, "and open the gates for you from the inside." He was trying to save himself from the shame of having failed again—he could not even kill an unarmed Jew!

"Brave boy," said Malabestia sarcastically. "Marshall would tell the King just who it was who broke in, looted, burned, killed King's people and destroyed the bills of debt that are kept in the cathedral vaults."

"Do we mean to break into the cathedral!?"

"Tell me, Richard dear, to whom would you rather owe? To whom would you give the privilege of tickling you underneath —the King, or the King's Jews?"

"Neither one."

"How apt he is, friends—a scholar of the Church could scarcely give a better answer! Well, the wealth of dead Jews reverts to the King as a hound comes back to the kennel of his master. What if there was no hound—no debt recorded? Who would pay? Who would take?"

"We can raise the siege then, and with the Sheriff's permission," said Percy, "but will he give it?"

"We must force him to give it. We must bloody his hands for this affair, and then convincing him that he is an injured party will not be so difficult. Come, come, time is short!"

John Marshall had been sitting with a watchman off duty, playing chess. He had been alarmed when the call of fire was sounded, but going out into the gathering darkness, had tried not to see the looting or hear the wild exhortations of the fanatic. A religious matter. He forced himself to think so until someone else in authority moved on him with permission to act. Meanwhile, he had no soldiers, not even guards to make King's Persons and possessions safe. He knew, in a vague way, that there had been many who were busy fanning the popular sparks of faith into full fire of action, but he did not know what the single issues were, nor the particular men who could be called real leaders. He liked the Jews no better than did any other nobleman in England, but by the King's authority, he had to preserve what belonged to the

King at any cost. With neither men, arms, nor real concern in the matter, John thought it best to sit quietly beside his empty authority and amuse the night away. Tomorrow he would see what reparations were to be made. It really did not look too serious—the fire would not spread. Some few drunken rowdies would have damages to pay, and maybe the whole thing could be nicely forgotten by the time King Richard came home. He frowned and went back to his game.

As they sat over their pieces, the door to the jail opened and Richard Malabestia walked in heavily with four knights and his squires behind him. There were others standing outside. The watchman rose quickly and left, knowing from the looks he saw on the noble faces that it would be better for him not to remember nor to be remembered.

Acknowledging his rank as High Sheriff, John Marshall remained seated while the others went for stools for themselves. In the silence that followed before talk, as each measured the other, Marshall almost thought he heard the ghost that was his authority, draped piecemeal against the cold, creaking with the anticipation of a compromise. He did not choose to listen to it long.

"My lord Malabestia," he began, "I am sure that you come for some purpose—the hour is late."

"Yes, we have a purpose," Malabestia began smoothly, as if speaking to an old friend. "For many days now, we have wished, these lords and I, to make your better acquaintance and, indeed, to offer our help in making you comfortably settled here. You like good wine, but lack it here. It is said that you lack it. Percy offers you his stores for your pleasure . . . and your table is poorly set, they tell me. Such a pity. Our noble friend here owns lands at Skipton, and I am sure that he will see to your larder."

"I am pleased, my Lords, but with what can I assist you now?"

"You are very apt, Sir Sheriff. It would seem that plots against us, which have been worked by several Jews, are succeeding far beyond the plotters' wishes. Having stolen hordes of baronial silver, gold, jewels and the documents pertaining to those things, the crafty thieves have hidden themselves and their treasure in Clifford's Tower. There they are supplied. The tower has a well of good water and is solidly built. They will be able to maintain themselves for weeks, and certainly have time to destroy the evidence of their fraud. Some of those possessions are on your lists of responsibility—possessions of the King."

"So . . . they are taking refuge in the tower. Is that not archbishop's property?" Poor soul—he did not even know to whom, to what, the buildings belonged.

"No," Malabestia said, hiding his smile, "that tower belongs to the city and thus is Sheriff's business."

"What must be done, then? They must be brought before me so that I might find out just what has been happening here, and what they have taken."

"Of course—that would be the perfect thing, but they will not come out. I know the Jews. They are crude men and cowards with no strength or valor. We will move siege engines—one or two, to the tower's base. Not to use them, of course, but to frighten those craven robbers into submission. When they see that they are lost, they will come down, quaking, to your justice."

"They are King's Persons, and will have to wait for his justice, rather than mine—yet—stealing, you say—and royal property?"

"Our property, yours, the King's."

"Why did they not go to their homes? The stone houses of the two at the end of the street are like small fortresses."

"So many and so valuable were the goods, and so greedy the thieves, that they took the booty to the tower so that there would be no falling out among them later."

"This is Friday, is it not?"

"Yes, what of it?"

"I once heard that Jews number Friday as the morning of their Sabbath, by their laws, and that then they are forbidden to touch treasures or money."

"It might once have been so," Malabestia said impatiently, "but now they strike their blow, thinking, indeed, that we will remember this old law of theirs and not discover them. Sir Sheriff, time is short. Give us leave to move the engines." There was a bite under that voice, which did not escape the Sheriff. He looked at them dubiously. He was afraid. The power of these men filled the shire as their armed, warrior-heavy bodies filled the room. He had never been so alone in his life. As he looked at them, he knew that there was no choice. A decision without strength, real authority or precedent terrified him.

He was helpless. In a gesture of the last pitiful bit of pride, he went to the wall and took down a bunch of keys. They were old and rusty, the Mayor's duplicates; none of them had been used in a decade.

"You will come with us then, and open the door."

It was not really a question, but a command, yet Marshall knew that he did not have to submit so far as that. He was still High Sheriff. "No," he said. "Send a boy back with them." He gave the keys to the Baron, and Malabestia measured him once more, very closely, wondering if he could be forced. They stood very still, waiting, for a long space and at last the Baron's gaze dropped away and the armed men turned and left quickly.

The Sheriff picked up the board and chessmen which had been upset when the men left their seats. He began to replace the pieces slowly. No one could understand these heathen, it was true, but evil as they might be, he had a duty to them, and being king's property they were, in a sense, the only real duty he had. The manner of Malabestia and his men, however, warned him away. The understanding is not always in the words, and the wordless warning had been clear: a delicate secret, their eyes had said; walk into forgetfulness on slippered feet. He must ask nothing. He must do nothing. He put the chessmen away and almost without thinking, opened the door and went into the courtyard of the jail.

It was a beautiful night. The moon was full and there were legions of stars encamped in the sky—armed angels; everyone was armed. The sea wall built to protect the castle and tower from the ravages of the Ouse in flood, obscured Marshall's sight of the base of the tower. Sure enough, there were lights at the top. The city was quiet, but across the river he heard the shouting of a crowd. He thought wonderingly: They did not say that there would be so many going against the Jews. He left the courtyard and took the road to Northstreet, noting the sounds of the crowd at the Tower Hill. He walked close to the still doggedly burning ruin of Northstreet, but he did not enter the street. There would be a better view of the action about the tower from Ouse Bridge.

As he turned into the Bridge Street he caught a glimpse down the length of the Jews' way, and he gasped at what he saw. "Several Jews," the Baron had said. Here the moon showed with its wordless honesty the still smoking heaps of sometime houses, the piles of forgotten pillage, the staring dead—dozens of them! A dupe he was, and he knew it—a dupe for a handful of lives and a sack of pearls, but this was not "several Jews," it was a war, a massacre. He had gone far beyond his depth in assenting to this —this . . . His heart began to pound. I should not have come out, he thought. Had I stayed inside I could have remained unknowing. Here was so clear a wrong that there was no turning away from it, barons or no.

With a feeling of growing dread, Marshall went slowly across the bridge until he could see to the base of Clifford's Tower. The sight filled his eyes and the truth of what Malabestia had meant to do burst on him in all its fearfulness. He stood dumfounded. The entire city was out, screaming and waving torches. The barricade at the small doorway to the tower had been pushed away and fires had been started in the inner courtyard. Billows of choking smoke were being directed up into the tower itself. Around the fringes of the crowd and in and through it, the white monk darted, shouting and waving. The castle gates had been opened and the heavy siege engines were laboring to the tower's base. The crowd was mad with the ecstasy of hating; it was not for judgment, it was for death; not for righteous wrath, but for vengeance; not for a retribution so select that the Sheriff could be cajoled to turn his head; it was murder, total murder, without survivors, without explanations. Marshall knew now that he must act.

He had no soldiers, no men, not even the keys to the armory. There must be a force of men to break up this crowd and stop the slaughter. He paused on the bridge, knowing that he had already made a decision. Now, turning over and over in his mind were thoughts of what was the best way to act upon it. He could take a fast horse and gallop down the Walm Road to the little city of Beverly. There would be a good force enough there, even for his authority, that cobweb strand of his authority. He was almost beginning to move his foot to run, to act, to set himself on a way which would beget motion whose end he was just now trying to unravel. When he saw to the outcome of it, he stopped again. If he went to Beverly, neighboring Hull would hear about the whole affair on that very day, and there were hundreds of boats going down the Humber to its meeting with the Thames and London. London was the seat of influence—the hub of privilege and of recall. If London heard the news—the fresh, uncomposed picture of the happening, John Marshall knew that his career would be destroyed forever. De Glanville, now a minister there might even see that he was held responsible for it all. His reputation would be a snicker in everyone's mouth. A picture passed through his mind of one of the staring corpses lying at the entrance to Northstreet. The dead were but dead. It was up to the living to add or shadow the telling of it; and he had a whole life's work before him. He must straighten the robes of these corpses in the telling, close the eyes, and reframe into peaceful gestures of prayer and quietness the hands that had clutched at life and been torn from it with so much agony. He would not go to Beverly. There must be a city where the news would sift away into the northern wilderness, until its corpse could be decently straightened. It was a full day's ride north to Durham. News told there would tend to go north to the nowhere of Scotland. Coming and going, it was but a day's difference between the two trips. With good speed, only a day would be lost; one day out of all his years of service. He would go out the North Road to Durham.

He continued over the bridge and across the city to the Bootham Gate, going faster and faster as his mind accepted his choice and grew into better reasons for it. Durham had a larger force, and cousin Henry Marshall, York Cathedral's absent Dean was visiting somewhere to the north; it might be wise to get to him also, and enlist his aid. Safety and Law must share the plate with Prudence, after all.

When he came to Bootham stables, he selected the fastest, finest running horse he could. The groom, officiating at a death of Jews, had left the stables open. Even the city gates were unguarded. A light saddle and a hemp bridle (for he was very much in haste) and out the Bootham Gate they clattered, horse and anxious rider, sparking off the stones in the road with the haste of the horse's hoofs.

A man had been watching him as he had turned, shocked, from Northstreet and had come, walking and pausing over the bridge, and at last accepted his own reasoning and broken into a run toward the Bootham Gate and the road north. Lord Robert de Kuckney had been by the river's side, retching his day's meat into the water. The revulsion had swept over him as he had been pushed into the synagogue and had seen the five dead—so reasonlessly dead—and had gagged with the stench of the desecrations of the mob. He had gone to the Ouse bank to be sick alone, and behind him something else had gotten to the looters, so that they had gone roaring away past him toward Castle Hill. He was doubled over with racking pains in his belly, and as they eased, he had leaned against a stone abutment.

At last, he climbed the bank and was about to move on again down the deserted street, when he caught sight of the man on the bridge. Lord Robert had never seen the new Sheriff of the shire, but he knew who the man was at a glance. Suddenly, it seemed to the watcher as if his knowledge had pierced to the very core of this stranger's thought; he saw what Marshall saw in the horror before the tower, knew what he knew of Durham against Beverly, and why the Jews could not be rescued for another two days, and what preferment rested on these niceties of time, distance and reputation. It is a strange thing in man that when he sees incongruities, he laughs, and yet for the typical sometimes, his eyes will fill with tears. Lord Robert had seen his own son hacking away with the ancestral sword at flesh too young or weak to give the blade a moment of resistance. The look of pride upon the young man's face was to be expected, but it made the father writhe as if in his own mortal pain. Now, seeing the Sheriff sorting out his reasons in this moral issue, Lord Robert knew what was going to be done, but when he saw it being done, indeed, he leaned back against the stone post blinded with tears and moaned, "Oh, God, oh, God!—the expedient virtue!" And he felt his gorge rising again.

AS the siege engines were brought close to the base of the tower, and slowly moved into position on their creaking, straining wooden wheels, the pitch of the crowd again grew higher. Little children, carried away by the fervor of their parents, went close to the fire in the inner courtyard to heave brush and wood upon it. Some were licked at by the great tongues of reaching flame and they ran weeping, untended, among the excited revelers.

As the night burned on, the cause seemed to grow greater and more glorious in the minds of the people. At first, the thoughts of booty had shared the mind with righteous anger; then, as they went forth with sticks and implements, to the tower, wealth was forgotten and all that held their minds was the thought of Heaven. Conversion to the True Faith would bring the heretic Jews in sight of salvation and would merit their converters sure places in the golden paradise to come. Now would the simple poor—equals in Christ—assure their glory. As the flames reached higher and higher into the vitals of the tower, the promise of conversion seemed too vague and uncertain a thing to be rewarded by eternal bliss. What if the Jews relapsed—promising for their lives but not for their hearts? Too many half suspected, even perhaps by the measure of their own lives, that belief can only be forced for the knees, the hands, the lips. What if the hearts of these heathen were obdurate? Would there be Heaven then? Everywhere the holy White Brother ran, now on his knees with promises to God, now stretched cruciform against the base of the tower, moaning like Christ upon the Tree, now running to the rioters, screaming above their cheers that the Devil would die, even tonight here, in York. Why not assure a place in Glory by giving death? No lapses into heresy would confront the faithful on Judgment Day. Many Jews lay dead in their burning houses. Let these few go with them to burn their unwasting souls in Hell forever. The mood of the crowd flowed full as the engines were finally placed in position against the wall, and the will of the crowd was death.

By that time, men had run back through the streets to the nearest tavern for some casks to bring to the thirsty Christians working away at their salvation. A few noticed that Will the Owl was not about, but three other taverners came forward eagerly to serve his custom. The man who got a cask up first would make a tidy sum for his night's work. Piously, the taverners decided that they would not charge the drinkers extra, over half a penny for the labor to get the casks up the Castle hill. Tankards might be lost or broken in the excitement—let them drink from their hats or hands or whatever they had with them. The way was lit by flickering torches in the hands of boys, as the first taverner and his helpers staggered with their burdens up the hill to Clifford's Tower. By the time they arrived, breathless and panting with the heavy casks, the scaling ladders had been raised.

A fight had broken out as to who would mount the ladders first. There were thick curses and accusations of cowardice with the heavy, dry voices of rage. Then the men drank shortly, joylessly, in gulps, as if it were part of the work they were going to do. With much shoving and growling, they got themselves into an order of sorts and prepared to mount the ladders.

At last the cry was raised: "God wills it!" and the victors ran to the rungs with the eagerness of zeal and wine hot in their throats. Up and up they went in two lines, losing themselves in the shadow of the tower. Suddenly, one of the great ladders swung wide, away from the tower, and hung swaying in air, balanced for a moment with itself and then fell, crashing to the ground with its occupants screaming as they hung helplessly to the rungs. In a moment the other ladder turned on its axis and fell with the screams of its trapped climbers. With dismay the rioters realized that there had been siege-poles in the floor beneath the turrets—long wooden handles with hooks at their ends, which could reach through holes in the floor beneath the tower's top and push the ladders away until they fell backward of their own weight. The damned Jews were fighting them! The crowd shrieked with fury for its dead and wounded. They had not had the forethought to set their machines at opposite sides of the tower so that there would not be light enough at the dark side to get the poles aligned, displacing the second ladder. Malabestia ground his teeth as he saw the siege repulsed so easily.

The fault with the riot was the rioters. It was true that whatever blame remained at the end of this night would be so diffused and spread so wide that no prosecution could be made nor single fault placed against any one of the leaders of the violence. A mob forgot; it was strong; it was safe, yet the virtues of a mob were countered by its stupidity and the blindness of its passion. These men, shrieking their hatred, were like unthinking children. They did not go to Clifford's Tower with a plan, such as any fledgling warrior would have made for siege. God will provide, and let your scaling ladders fall and splinter, and who will buy the drinks! Malabestia knew also that there could be no satisfaction for these childish believers, seeking only Heaven, in the impersonal fire or catapult. The walls were not their enemies; they wanted only the dying rags of men inside, for to get to the soul one had first to get to the body, and what this rabble wanted was the feel of Jew. Vengeance and sacrifice must be acted upon flesh: live men who could be physically conquered and killed; the fire was only to force surrender. The ardor of the mob made them long for something real over which to have a victory, but if the wall was to be destroyed, the Jews would fall with it and so be lost, eluding again, the eager vengeance of men who vied for Paradise with their hands. This need was no teacher of tactic. Malabestia became more anxious as he watched them. If they would ruin this . . .

The better to do her battle for Heaven, the wife of Will the Owl had taken off her clothes and shoes and was spiritedly and loudly confessing her adultery to anyone who would listen. It was the glory and condition of men that they could fight for

Heaven, but the women had to gain it by confession. The facts, to her sorrow in sacrifice, were already well known, but by a wide jump of the mind, the weight of shame fell on the guiltless Will. Where was he, the cuckold? One of his kinsmen was shamed into striking a blow or two at Will's too loudly erring wife, screaming for God's forgiveness and the honorable loins of husbands. At the other end of the line of milling men and women, a fight had broken out over the possession of a metal-tipped staff. One scaling ladder had been broken against a rock, but the other was being readied again for a new attempt upon the tower.

The dead of the first charge lay unheeded, some where they had fallen. The wounded shouted for comfort above the din. Some of the dead had been dragged out of the lighted circle of the mob and were being stripped and searched over by the hungry children of the poor for coins or crusts, or knives or bits and oddments which could be traded later. They fought and murdered also, over their spoil, a little miniature of the violence of their elders, but none the less passionate; a hatred creeping about in the dark, a death with low curses, sticks and knives and short, hard blows. But because they were starving, they did not take the time to arm themselves with arguments about salvation.

Brother Lewis, as if resting for a moment from the War of God and Satan, looked about and saw that carouse was beginning to take the place of ardor in the mob. Passion for an unseen thing, a spirit, cannot be long sustained, even if it was for one's own spirit, reclothed in light and eating the bread of angels. Already, couples were beginning to wander into the warm, star-crowded darkness, feigning rest. Others were fighting, drinking, swearing, gambling, dancing, joking with lewd eyes and grinning lips; kissing, mincing, pinching, singing, swilling, squalling. Desperately, he looked around for a new brand to thrust before the eyes of this mad beast to bring it to obedience. The scaling ladder had been replaced, this time more cleverly, and a group was dispatched to create a clamor at another point farther around the tower, in order to draw attention away from the ascending fighters. They would begin their noise early so as to drown out the sound of the scraping of the ladder as they placed it securely, and of its groaning as the men mounted it. The halfhearted clamor started and the ladder went up, but few were looking now at the progress of the siege. They were forgetting their cause, abandoning the world to doom. Brother Lewis knew that this must not be.

Pushing the astounded people away, he stood before the ladder, his fleshless arms stretched high over his head.

"O Lord!" he screamed into the din about the tower, "O crucified Lord! Behold Your servants, Your saints, who pledge themselves to aid You!" The chaos quieted a bit as the high, hard voice went on like a file, rasping against the ears and minds of the listeners. "O Lord, fixed to the cross, a jewel hung out of man's sight —we are going to climb again and lay siege against the enemies of life, of all the saints, of Mary, the Blessed Virgin, and all the angels, and I, I your servant, will lead! I will be first to raise myself and face the Devil!"

And turning, in the new silence that was broken only by the artificial croaking of the decoy force, Brother Lewis prepared to mount the ladder. A shadow of the old fervor returned, as if it was a force not in the people, but in the air, like evening mist, to rise and fall upon the crowd, to thin and disperse or to gather and flow, permeating every person to the bone. In a sudden surge of feeling, men lined up after the wild Brother to mount the ladder to their glory. At last they would have their enemies in their hands; face to face they would see and destroy all the injustices which had kept them so long from peace, holiness, joy, tranquillity, health, wealth, youth—the way life must have been made for man so long ago. The good are never vindicated, but they would be now; the way is never clear before a man, but it would be now; the wrongs that shriek to Heaven to be righted would be righted now. In these cornered heathen there suddenly seemed to rest the symbol of all the evil that man had ever known, and for the blotting out of all of the sins of their pasts, for a fresh morning of beginning, the besiegers cried with reawakened hearts: "God wills it!"

There was a grating sound far above them, but their minds were keyed to their own stronger hungers and they did not account for it. Another hard sound, and then, from the darkness at the top of the tower, a large rock, which had topped a turret came hurtling down, thrown or fallen from the dark battlements above the crowd. It split the top of the mounted ladder, banged once against the wall and broke in two; and at the sound, there was the peculiar caught moment before catastrophe; some men half-turned, some smiling, some in odd, frozen postures, some in speech with expressions held grotesquely on their faces and their voices caught in their throats. The crash of the event broke upon them and the halves of the great rock smashed against the siege engines which collapsed, tearing the great ladder apart.

Brother Lewis and the two men who followed him were crushed to death immediately and violently between the base of the ladder and the sheared-off half of rock.

The people drew back, shocked into silence and wonder. The second engine lay splintered before them; bloodied arms and legs stuck from the ruined base-platform and reached forth at nothing. Confused and vague with the exhaustion of their feeling, frightened at the loss of one of their leaders and the seeming invincibility of Satan's devils in the tower, the crowd swayed back and forth. Once again, suddenly and violently, Richard Malabestia threw himself behind the wheels of the action to save his cause. He saw these blind children falling apart in their confusion and wandering toward impotence. These cattle must not stumble into failure; the mob was his harp, his instrument; so he must play them with his music. Tomorrow they would sleep into forgetfulness. Tonight was action; his action. Throwing himself down on his knees, for he needed a position from which to leap, Malabestia shouted, "We will avenge the fallen martyr!" and then, louder, "Victory for His Saint!"

"Revenge the martyr! Justice! Justice!" and the swayed crowd came to heel at his feet. As he thrust his arm forward in a gesture of attack, the people seized the words in their mouths to feed them for rage and action. They mouthed them and shrieked them back, and they tore at the pieces of the broken machines and ran to haul them to the fire inside the tower. If they could not lay siege, they would burn the devils inside the tower. Now, with action, devotion came flooding back. If it took all night, all the months, forever, they would roast these heretics in hell-fire here on earth. The flames mounted higher and higher. Christ's knight would be avenged! Christ's martyr would be justified! Christ's soldier would be remembered! Christ's Saint would be served!

*"Give ear to my prayer, Oh God;
And hide not Thyself from my supplication.
Attend to me and answer me; I am overcome
  by trouble.
I am distraught by the noise of the enemy;
Because of the oppression of the wicked."*

    Yomtob of Joigny, Rabbi, lowered his head and opened his eyes. He was standing by himself on the platform that ringed the top of the tower. Some of the others had gone to seek in the rooms inside for friends or weapons or for the feeling of safety. From the fire which the mob had built below them, smoke billowed through the second level of openings from the tower stairway. Even here with the sweet winds of spring blowing from dark moors, the heat was becoming oppressive. Something in Yomtob wanted to weep—to stop thinking and only to mourn. Out there, beyond the press of hating men, a new springtime waited with its young vines and purple blossoms. Beyond the death and desecration of Northstreet, there were Jews sitting at their holiday, lifting full goblets happily and toasting love and freedom and the triumph of a little people who had been beautiful in the hand of God. Choking and staggering, a figure stumbled from the smoky stair-hole and came toward him. It was Josce. Yomtob sat down so that Josce could also take his ease respectfully, but he was too sick and breathless to acknowledge the courtesy, and Yomtob thought sadly: As the end comes nearer, both victor and victim become less human, and what they have built in a thousand years of law and courtesy, falls from their shoulders, unfamiliar, to the ground.
    "Most of the rooms are empty," Josce panted. "Meir fil Moses has gone mad. We had to tie him down with rope. His little son and daughter died in the smoke that goes from room to room."
    "Tell the people to come up here," said Yomtob. "Since the turret boulder destroyed the other siege ladder, I have not heard a sound to suggest that they plan to scale again or to use a catapult, but the fire has increased. Tell the people that they are safe up here."
    "That is difficult to do, Rabbi. I fought through the smoke,

but I nearly fainted many times. Blasts of air lift the smoke sometimes so that the way is almost clear, but then it can settle down
with its poisoned blanket so that the blinded people die where
they stand."

"We must try to help them, then. Those rooms below are
dangerous."

As they spoke, more people issued from the stairs, bent over
with retching and moaning from the fumes. Josce took sashes
and belts from the weakened men and fastened them together,
tying one end to a hook in the floor. Then he tugged the makeshift guide rope and disappeared into the tower. In a few moments,
Anna and the children emerged, burnt and frightened, then
Jacob fil Vives and some of the others. When Josce appeared
again, blackened and reeking of fire, he went straight to Yomtob
and motioned the Rabbi aside. More were struggling up to the
platform.

"Are these all the ones left alive?" Yomtob asked incredulously, looking about them at the ragged shapes in the moonlight. Thirty or more bent figures rested on the platform, sobbing with fatigue.

"No," said Josce. "The refugees from Norwich and several
others who came just recently from the South are sitting on the
floor of one of the armories. They say that they are tired and will
not move any more for their lives. I have had weariness in my
life, Rabbi, but none like that which sits on their faces like some
awful leper's mark. Somehow, for all their uncaring, the smoke
goes past them, almost as if it, too, were afraid of them, so unnatural is their stillness."

"Is there no one else?"

"Something that I hated to speak of at such a time—I loved
that boy Abram; he was like a son to me. Now he lies muttering in the straw and wringing his hands for that serving-wench.
I said, 'We must gather the old and sick and take them out of
danger,' and all he did was to look at the wall, saying, 'I wonder
where she is' and something like, 'Your part will be straight after
this night for everything, everything is changed . . .' and then
laughing at what he had said. The sight of it angered me to shaking. Behold: outside the Christians bay and shriek for us. Fire
is all about and death in every whiff of smoke, and there he lies,
shattering the dignity of our death, shaking our courage and demeaning our last night with thoughts of some woman! Some
woman whom one does not marry!"

"Good Josce, patience. . . . They would be amazed, I think, all the young, if they heard you call the thing which they call life a shattering and a demeaning. I cannot help remembering that Abram would have been married to her long ago, but for us—but for all of us. I suppose that he feels now that death is close enough to overshadow custom."

"It is sinful, Rabbi, and unseemly. We must bid him amend himself."

"Yes, it is unseemly, and yet somehow, it gives me comfort, Josce. If the loins of the young still teem with life so urgently that they will clasp and hold to their dreams of life even in death's antechamber, then there will be some—there must be some—who have the burning energy to go on when we shall be souls only. We must look after those others down there, and save them if we can. Send some others for them; you have done enough. You must be very tired; we are all too tired."

"Rabbi . . ." said Josce quietly, "about the four from Norwich—they have come a long way to die. Their souls have already died. Let us leave them where they sit. It is a privilege in this time to die to one's own inner rhythm."

Yomtob looked up at the quiet sky. "Yes—I suppose you are right. It is a privilege which I begin to desire for myself."

It was very quiet where she was, and she, too, was quiet. The little fenced cemetery called Jewbury lay outside the city walls far to the east. Beyond it, the Foss River widened, broke and came together again before it went on past the wharves, and beyond that, the miles of moors slept under the moon. Bett sometimes rose and walked about among the marker stones, listening to her mind recite the names of the slumberers. The cemetery had been allowed by a Henry who was now himself housed in the ground. It was only a decade old and Bett knew everyone who rested there. "Good evening to you, Master. . . . Good evening to you, Lady and twin younglings." They had all come there to see her married, and she was even now readying herself in her bridal clothes. The moon is kind to her own chosen ones, and the ragged and bloody dress which Bett wore shimmered in that light. The bridal veil and the virgin's coronet were also gloriously bright, and when she was arrayed, she called to him, "Dear love, dear love—" and then she slowly removed her crown and veil and the bridal dress, until she stood naked in the near-cold but she did not shiver. She closed her eyes for a long time, smil-

261

ing and stretching her arms out westward, to the city and the fires. And then of the rag of cloth that had been a bridal veil, the coif of a married woman and the dress again hanging loose from her body: "Dear love, dear love.

> "The bride is white, the mother, red,
> The bride-sheet lines the birthing bed,
> The blossoms fall . . ."

She lived the moment-months of swelling pregnancy and the triumph of birth on the soft ground, and she bound her breasts for weaning and saw her sons away to the school. A sound came from the road and she stood up, clutching her weaver's knife to protect her children.

"Who is there?" Lord Robert said. "Do not be afraid."

The ragged form in the cemetery did not move. He thought: She is safer there than anywhere else tonight. When dawn comes, I will hide her in St. Elene's or in that chapel outside the wall. "Stay where you are, lady," he called to her. "I will come again. God protect you, lady."

"Shalom." The veiled widow answered him in the ancient word of parting—"Peace."

Abram lay in the darkness of a little room beneath the turreted roof of Clifford's Tower. He felt spent and dried up and he was amazed that people still recognized him, that his features were unchanged. To Josce's bustlings he responded with grunts and apathy. Josce had risen at the first flutter of something coming against them this night in the streets. He had saved his whole household and all his many guests. Abram was a master of his house also, and he had fled and left his mother and his love and the little childish guests behind to die. "Foolish children," he said to the wall. "Everyone in the town could have told you: stay away from that house. In that house of shamed men there will be no protection from a danger." The horror of it rose in him again and he bit his fist with the despair of his thoughts.

The fire was burning hotter and harder all the time in the courtyard. The wooden palings and balustrades of the first level had already caught fire, and sparks were menacing the second. Poisonous throttling vapors were beginning to flow from room to room, lifting and lowering to smother those who waited there. The heat was building beneath them, so that they felt themselves upon a giant skillet, and at last, he knew that he must join the others at the top where there was air to breathe.

He left the room and edged about the balustraded walk, noticing that part of the railing was smouldering from a spark that had lodged there. The heat, rising from the terrible fire beneath, was beginning to become unbearable, and the breath-choking fumes dizzied him to fainting. At last he reached the room with the stairway to the roof and pulled himself up, coughing and gasping. His head beat with pain and when he reached the top and came upon the open night, the fresh air filled him like an intoxicating drink of liquor and he fell down senseless. . . .

When he opened his eyes again, he saw only shadows, and when his head began to clear he heard their voices over him, back and forth, flowing and receding like tides that countered and cross-countered one another in a channel:

"We have come under the view of God—who can stand His gaze?"

"We have sinned—we are sick with generations of evil. God have mercy on us."

"If it were only myself, I would not care, but these children are innocent!"

"Had we not been chosen, we would not be dying!"

"Praise God for His mighty acts. His will be done."

"Did I conceive, carry, and lie in labor for this—to this end?"

He struggled to get up, confused as to where he was. He had not the strength to fight against the streaks of fear which caught at him. He came fully awake in Josce's arms. Josce had realized that his anger at Abram had been anger at something much greater and more tragic than last longings of a young man, and he was no longer shocked at Abram's grief. He held him gently while Anna rubbed his ankles and Yomtob his wrists. Before Abram knew why, he found himself conscious and weeping. And Josce said softly to him, "How miserable a thing it is to have so little time for our farewells. We can say none of the true and fitting things, send none of the gifts of ceremony with our dead."

Far to the east, a thin blade of light appeared, as if the dawn was prying up the darkness that held them prisoner. The clamor at the tower's base had not diminished, nor had the fire slackened, and the heat was building beneath them. In some parts of the platform it was not possible to walk, for the soles of the feet were burned even through shoes. Yomtob looked out at the rind of light and then for a long time at the thirty or so clustered at the outside rim of the tower. At last he said, "My brothers— we have come to the time when we must speak of dying. We will not speak of those who have already died, but of ourselves: the ones who are going to die."

Anna, who had been strong until now, hid her face and began to tremble.

"Our Josce said to me before that death which comes with dignity, in one's own inner rhythm, is a great gift and a privilege. Now, in this time of an impatient slaughter by enemies, we look forward to deaths without that gift. We have waited out the night, but they are still clamoring for our blood. They will hack us limb from limb or let us burn, or give us death by torture, even to sate the fearful appetite that is in them now. Unfortunately, I must leave them my body, but my soul—my soul I plan to give to God before it sees any more of the ugliness of their pious hatred. I have the ritual slaughterer's knife here in my sash. It is clean; kept pure by our Laws, lent mercy by our prayers, made quick by our kindness. I will take death by this knife. Those who wish it, also I will kill. I shall kill quickly and with prayer."

No one stirred for a moment as the words reached into them and twisted for decision in their minds.

Then Josce said, "I thank you, Rabbi. I, and my wife, if she wishes, and my children, if they wish. Let also the two maidens with us outwit the death of enemies."

"Do not die to outwit them. Are you dying to destroy their triumph?" Yomtob asked, wishing for them all at this moment, sainthood, somehow, and a death that might be perfect as no single moment in life had ever been.

"I hate them, Rabbi," Josce said. "I cannot help it. They are murderers and I hate them."

Yomtob saw that perfection, even now, was not to be, and so he smiled a little and said, "I will be proud to follow you into death, my friend, but let us not think of them at all; let us die beautifully. If we cannot reason profoundly any longer, let us at least feel deeply and give our deaths the final dignity of being free from stain and from pettiness. We may not be leaving, we may be arriving . . ."

Josce laughed gently. "Rabbi, you are bidding us be angels before we have stopped being men."

"As you wish it, then."

"Let us at least pray," said another. The ranks of the watchers broke again, and four more came and stood near Yomtob and Josce. From the platform where she lay in a broken body, a woman called to be included. Yomtob raised his hands before his mouth as if almost to funnel his words into the ear of God:

"One forever and eternal, One first and perfect, we are poor in thanks: enrich us. We are frightened in mortality: strengthen us. We are brimming with wrong: inform us. We have lived mindless of the miraculous gift of life: let us remember it. We have been as cruel as children, but not as loving; as fierce as animals, but not as grateful; as mindless as the rain, but not as generous; as barren as the snow, but not as beautiful. We lack all virtue, and yet we are yours. Behold, the knife is informed of its condition by the Will of God, One Name, and we, mortal flesh and subject to our condition by Your will. We will thank You in the voices which You have given us. To have been man was a brilliant destiny, and we thank You for it; now the universe within the body cries for release. Hear us from Your universe and receive us."

Yomtob raised his arms and began slowly in Hebrew, the ancient words of praise given by the sons of the dead to their God. The words had been tried and worn by hundreds upon hundreds of tongues over many generations, and many, many deaths. When the prayer ended and the words only remembered, they looked around, earth's men once more, and wondered, laced again by panic, who was to be first for the knife, informed so sharply, so sharply, of its condition.

An old man spoke: "Rabbi, let us die as nature intended: the old and then the young, the men and then the women, the widows and then the orphans."

"It is so in life," said Josce, "but God gives a gift in nature which we do not have here, and that is time. How brutal it would be to kill the parents in front of the children. We know the reasons for death and we can bear the sight more bravely than they."

"Rabbi"—the womanly Anna had never addressed Yomtob in public before—"let me die knowing for certain that my little lambs are safe in death before me. Then I will not fear to enter, nor hesitate to leave. We will hold their little bodies as they could never hold ours, for comfort."

"It is not fit that our children see us bloodied," said another "and knowing less than we, be frightened and run from this into a more brutal death."

"It shall be so," said Yomtob.

The mothers turned away. The children, some sobbing, some rigid and still, were brought one by one to Yomtob, and Josce and the men, speaking the gentle words of endearment, held them. As the Rabbi raised his knife and sought for that beating carrier of life in the little neck, he remembered as if in a vision, Abraham and his sacrifice of Isaac.

Alas, there will come no angel, no miracle to stay the knife and set a lesser sacrifice upon the altar. The blade cleaved the flesh and found the beating pulse and the child fell. . . . A second. . . . A third. . . .

Josce was holding his little daughter in his arms. He put his face into the soft hair and felt the smooth forehead. "Wait for me," he said. "I will come soon." And then he gave the girl to Yomtob's knife. . . . Another and another and another. The small bodies lay about Yomtob's feet. Josce and two others went and moved them aside and covered them.

"Here is another," said a man.

It was Dieulesault, the third son of Josce. He turned himself from the hands of the older men. "Let me be," he said. "Do not touch me. I have attained my manhood. Two weeks ago, I came to the Ark and read from the Law. In mourning for the others, you have forgotten, but I am as much a man as any other. Let me go to my death like a man and not the afterthought of a group of children!"

At once the vintner opened his mouth to argue, but Anna, brazen for her son's last satisfaction, said, "Let him be taken with them, with the men. If need be, I will sacrifice my place to him." The vintner turned away.

An old man moved to Yomtob's side, saying, "Let the aged go now, for we have run harder and waited longer, feared more and hoped less than those who follow us in time."

Then Yomtob said, "We are the hosts, we men of York, and you are our guests. Let those who wish, come to me now. Come first those who are our visitors, and then, we as hosts, seeing you out of our doors, will follow. Let husbands and wives henceforth be divorced fom one another if they wish it, and each one separately decide to stay or go, and let no shame or anger come from any decision, for we must not let any feelings but those of love end this little night."

Then four came forth that were from Oxford, and a couple together from Lynn, two from Bury, four from Cambridge, three, all the long sad way from London, and they went one by one to

Yomtob and were lifted away by Josce and Cresse of Doncaster. At last they had all been taken a world away in their flight from hate. The handful of food, the parcel packed for the provinces, the last looking backward, tear-blinded, were no longer part of the voyage, for the journey had changed dimensions.

The people of York who were left, looked at one another.

Josce said, "Let us go quickly, we last ones. The dawn is raising sails, the time of safety is short and our beloved Yomtob is very tired."

Some still stood aside, unwilling to die, or afraid, or hoping beyond all reason that the angry mob below would tire or die by miracle, or relent, or have a sudden burst of shame and split their hearts wide for the small measure of mercy.

Among the silent ones stood Abram. In the half-light Yomtob caught his eye, or so it seemed to him, and feeling a need to defend himself in his choice of life, Abram stepped forward and said, "Rabbi, wine drunk by saints must still be made by vintners. Let us be your sextons. The last can cover the next-to-last, but someone must cover the last."

"Let it be as you yourself feel it, only we beg you to remember us as long as you can, and to say over our bodies the prayers for the dead." And Yomtob turned and embraced Cresse and killed him, and then Samuel, and Isaac, and then Dieulesault fil Josce, who stood very straight, so recently a man that his pride was still in a single piece, unbroken by weakness or circumstance.

Anna embraced Josce and said, "Do you remember the day we put in the glass windows? Do you remember the day our first son was born? Do you remember the day we argued and how we made up?" and still holding his hand, she submitted to Yomtob as if he were the Angel of Death. With all her might she turned her mind to the things of which she had spoken, but at the last instant, will for life overcame her, and she began to cry out for life, to be spared, please! please!, but as she opened her mouth, life merged with death and she fell without a murmur.

Josce moved beside her. "Rabbi . . ."

"Good-bye, my friend," said Yomtob. "Love the Law. Love God. Forgive me."

"Does it seem to you that we have outlived the world?" said Josce.

"Yes. I am impatient for my experience."

They embraced and bade each other good-bye. As Yomtob, the eyes of his knife, felt for the place that it would sever quickly and without pain, to let out life, Josce thought: What a pity: here is a new experience, and I will not be able to discuss it with anyone. How many experiences have I not had . . . and now never will have. . . . And at that second he felt the knife. . . . My God, how vulnerable is man! It is so easy, so very easy to die. . . . He was dead before he could realize that his ease was only Yomtob's skill.

Yomtob of Joigny died in a rush of prayer, and the distant sound of an answering chant. When the knife found its place, perhaps the whole glimmering ceremony of the Ark and the Law would come to catch up his voice, his eyes, his love as it sang its slow procession into time past.

March 17, 1190

THE morning moved to York, and some turned in their sleep on the unfamiliar ground and came to themselves in the damp cold of their clothes, grappling for the memory of what had brought them to these strange wakings and with the reality of drink-soured mouths and agues and fouled garments. When light came to Clifford's Tower, the handful who still lived recited the Morning Prayer and the Liturgy for the Dead with their nightmare still about them. Below them in the court the fire was dying, despite the vows of the avenging rioters to keep it raging until doomsday, but smoke still wavered through the openings around the second level of the tower and rose through the center of the roof platform. Weary with feeding its insatiable hunger, some of the spent crowd on the ground stood up, dusted themselves off and went home, stopping by the houses on Northstreet for anything that might be left in the looted and still smoking ruins. Rumor had it that a certain Margit who lived near Mickle Gate had found a jeweled buckle; and there were tales also of ivory combs and silver spoons, but all that present sifting could turn up were a few handfuls of metal bolts, common knives and a hinge or two. Their fervor gone, their limbs weary, their clothing damp and bunched, tired groups of the besiegers of Heaven went to their beds.

But many stayed, watching the tower for a sign of life. Even to these, the day brought its own slow change, for the almost omnipotent sons of Satan, of a night that was past, seemed now to be no more and no less than human—enemies perhaps, and sources of salvation also, but not all evil or powerful beyond the condition of men. When it was fully light, someone had the idea to find out if they were still alive.

"Ho, Jews! How many are you there?"

No answer came.

"Jews!" again went up. The tiring group were glad for something to do.

As they waited a faint voice came down to them, "We are twelve left and one is dying."

A question came again, idly, and the answer went from the tower, more like a question of its own.

Save your strength, Abram thought, as he looked at the back of the man bent over the turrets to speak. He lowered himself through the stair-well and went down into the body of the tower to see if perhaps someone, sleeping or wounded, had fallen in some corner and was spared by the smoke. Most of the bodies had been brought up to the tower platform to be among their kinsmen and hosts, but the four men from Norwich and their eleven women and children still sat together in a little room off the stairway in utter quiet, with their hands composed and their faces lined with the great weariness of which Josce had spoken. Abram left them there, and from room to room went on with his search. He found no one alive, but in one alcove, much like the one in which he himself had lain weeping, he found a little neighbor, a six-month bride, lying in the arms of her husband, only sixteen years old. This death, as if in miniature, made so sweetly and so small, like a scene in a book, was too much for Abram to stand, so he ran away from it and back to the roof stairway.

For a while he leaned against the wall and moaned. The wall to the side of the stairway was lighter in color than the others and its stones seemed smoother, and when he recovered himself, he looked at the wall and he saw in his mind that the wall had a picture. He knew that he must be half mad by now, with sleeplessness, hunger and death, and so he submitted to his madness, flinging his arm wide and saying aloud to the invisible world, "It is this page which was promised me—my gift to the Codex Eboracum. At last I draw my picture for the Code of York; a moment of this life, this time, this world."

He went to the end of the walkway where a wooden beam had fallen and was half burnt. He took handfuls of the charred end of the beam and went back to the wall. He drew by the early light of dawn in great strokes, his vision, with figures almost as large as they were in life. He was not skillful at it, but the picture so burned in his imagination that he knew he had to give it form before him. This night past was to have been the eve of the Passover when they sang the joyful songs; riddling songs and songs of wit and gaiety. At the top of the wall he wrote his text: "Who knows three and who knows four?"—words of the song which they had not had time to sing—"Three are the Fathers. Four are the Mothers."

Abram drew them, but they were not the Four Mothers and Three Fathers of the song; they were Rana, Anna and the young girl whom he had seen lying in her bridegroom's arms, and there was also Bett there, in the veil of his own bride. He drew them, lying dead together, and over their bodies a cloud of ugly birds of prey flapped their wings, and over the heads of the birds hung the halos that belonged to the pious of the churches. The Three Fathers were not Abraham, Isaac and Jacob, as it was to have been in the unfinished song, but Josce, Yomtob and the young groom, dead also, with knives half through their throats, reaching each one arm to the Mothers and one to Heaven, and over them Abram drew the morning star. The world that had been, a collection of little worlds really, with safe laws and ancient precedents, was gone. The world of the Codex was gone and that of the Torah also. The synagogue was despoiled and the Christian shrines of justice deserted. In Hebrew and Latin letters whose shapes writhed with his anguish, Abram drew the subtext beneath the picture which he had seen: "The righteous shall shine as the sun." A bitter joke. A Jewish joke.

There were cries from the platform and he left his wall, not looking back at it because the vision of what he had wanted to draw was so much more perfect than what he had drawn. All his love for them beautified their faces in his vision, all his sorrow for them strengthened their forms in death, all his anger for them twisted in the forms of their killers. As he emerged on to the platform he saw that two men were still leaning between the turrets, shouting to the Christians below.

"What can we do?" one of them asked, as he turned and looked at Abram. The man's face was full of weariness and confusion.

"What do they want?" Abram asked.

"Baptism and then death."

"So?" And Abram gave his bitter smile. "The Religion of Love has put its choice to us with its accustomed bluntness."

"If we are baptized, they say, they will make our deaths quick and with dignity. If not—who knows what excesses they will need now to excite them?"

Abram remembered his father, that other convert, who was baptized and then helped to death. He felt a lump of rage bursting within him. In an anger red behind his eyes and tight to the pit of his throat and his stomach, he leaned over the wall between the turrets and shouted down to them, almost falling in his fury:

"What more will satisfy you, blood drinkers? Have you not slain enough?" He could never tell them; all his rage could never be made speech. "Do you want your victims? Take them! Take them!" and he ran to where the dead lay, and pulling the cover from the corpses, grappled with a cold body with the new strength of his fury. He lifted it and staggered with it to the wall and heaved the bloody, unresisting weight once alive, once a Jew, over the edge with all the force he could manage. As the body fell, there was an "ooh!" from the crowd below. Shock and wonder sounded in their voices as if they were as much amazed at the desperation and anger of the living as at the ugliness and horror of the dead. Another fell and another and another. Abram in rage and a man named Benjamin, hoping for pity, began to haul the dead to the edge, lift them up and throw them over the wall, the children and the women first. As Abram threw them far and hard as he could, the years of anger seemed to carry him to tremendous might and he shouted with each one, "Here he is . . . here she is . . . your prey, your victim!"

Then came the ones who had gone by Yomtob's knife. They were covered with blood and horrible in death beyond anything that Abram had ever seen, and there were so many—surely all this death would be enough to fill their maw. Two or three others came to help them, frightened of Abram, in his rage, or frightened of the dead, or hoping to arouse some spark of pity or some sense of satiety in the creatures below. But *that* one, *that* one was different, and they raised their hands in protest to Abram, but he would not hear. He lifted the empty body, husk of Yomtob of Joigny, and sent it over the wall; then he turned to

271

them but he spoke to the dead leader. "The soul has gone from you, wise teacher—therefore should your body float, light as a leaf, to settle on the ground." It seemed to them that they heard the sound of his bone-shattering fall to an earth of enemies.

When there were no more dead to give, Abram, Benjamin and a refugee from Lynn leaned over the wall and looked down at the crowd. They were still, shocked and sickened by the sight of all that death, and all that blood. The mother and her children, the bridegroom and his bride, the student and his schoolfellows, all flung wide, indiscriminately, in odd postures as they fell. Some of the crowd went pale, turned, and went home without speaking. Others stood fascinated. The silence lasted for long moments while the twelve on the platform looked back and forth at each other and the small hope, stilled so many times, fluttered again a little inside each one. It was not strong enough to build into prayer, so that the Jews just stood or sat and waited. At last they heard a cry from the ground. Abram went again to the ledge.

"Ho, Jews!" The man at the bottom of the tower cupped his hands to address them. He was a bootmaker, and had a shop near the Foss. Abram knew him.

"Speak!" Abram shouted, and he wondered if he, too, in some other day, in some other life, could watch the slaughter of people he knew and had served and liked once.

The man took a breath and began: "You have suffered. Come down and we will give you baptism and you shall live."

"What if we will not be baptized, what then?"

"You will die in the tower. Come down."

Abram stepped back and turned around and gave the people the man's words. They could not speak. He returned to the ledge to give them time for their decision.

"What about the fire?" he shouted. "We cannot come down, for fire and smoke still keep us from the courtyard."

"We will see that the fire be put out."

He turned to them, and one, imperceptibly almost, nodded yes, and then another.

"Put out the fire and we will come," Abram shouted. At least it would give them some time.

"I have had all I can bear," said the man from Lynn. "I will go down and take their Cross and then I will leave this place as far behind me as I can."

One of the women spoke: "Will we be forgiven for abjuring?"

And Abram thought: The Law will forgive you, yes, and

maybe your dead children and maybe your dead fathers, but not the people; never the people. Poor questioner—you could have asked me long before this morning: "What will be said and thought of me?" You could have asked my mother and my cousins and my friends, but now it is too late, and I will not speak, lest you scream with your shame and your guilt; lest you remember how loudly "you would have died first."

They heard the sounds of the fire being stamped out in the court.

A man was deciding. "I will go," he said at last, forcefully. "Life is better than death." But he looked about to see if the rest disapproved.

"I will go also," said another old man.

"After all . . ." said the women.

And so it was decided, and the rest would follow. They did not realize why they needed this unity, one decision, but Abram said to himself, "What a strange thing it is! . . . Here we are, choosing the difference between life and death, and yet the deepest concern seems to be that we might be ashamed in one another's presence."

And thinking of this he laughed a little and said, "Let them chant the Latin over us until they are cross-eyed. They will have to work like oxen in July to make anything of us but Jews."

The taunt eased them and dissolved their shame. Abram saw it and went to the ledge and cried, "We will come down. We will be baptized."

A cheer went up from the ground. Salvation at last. Christ will cherish the ones who have waited through the night and have brought the outlaw and the stubborn, the wronghearted to His throne. Their messages to the trapped "converts" became more courteous then: the fire was almost out, and if the heretics were careful they could venture down the stairways and around the outside of the courtyard and out the door to meet their new brothers in Christ. Slowly, the twelve descended the stairs from the platform into the tower. At the bottom of the first flight the stronger took new holds on the weaker ones and prepared to go by the narrow hallway rounding the inside of the tower. Abram held back.

"Come," said Benjamin, "come."

"I will follow," Abram answered, turning for the wall on which he had drawn. "The heretic must say good-bye to his heresy."

On the ground, a way was being cleared for the arrival of the Jews. Some men even sang, as burning wood was cleared from the fire and smothered with handfuls of earth. Malabestia, watching from a resting place near the castle, rose and came near with Richard, and the other nobles followed.

"Keep your hands on your swords, and when I give the word, fall on them. We must not leave a single one alive to remember this. The way it seems to turn for us now, I think that we can make up a tale about their stealing relics and fighting until we had no choice but to kill them— Perhaps the crowd also. Crowds get out of hand." With a sudden turn, he strode away and joined the group that was clearing the fire.

"Your enemies are clever, my friends. . . . They have fooled you," he said to the small knot of people.

"How so, my Lord?" one asked, but he had left them already and was standing by another group of onlookers.

"Can you not see that this is what they hope for?" he observed, locking his hands together. "They are sure to make the baptism a mockery and bring you to the Devil for your pains." And then he left and joined another few, and another. Then he circled back to the group at the fire.

"The Devil is making fools of you today, my friends. His people could not stand baptism; it would kill them and he will not let them die. He plans to rescue them perhaps, at the last moment, and leave you marked for life by your folly."

And again, when they had turned to answer him, he was with another group, smiling and lifting up and down on the balls of his feet, completely a spectator.

The Jews came slowly from the colonnades around the inside of the courtyard and went carefully past the scattered fire and out the entrance from which the broken door had been taken and burned. As they went through the doorway, they looked, cautiously, to right and left, in the way that animals look sometimes when their noses in the wind catch something dangerous or strange. They were now level with the ones who hated them; eye to eye after a night of separate height. They looked from one person to another, waiting for the first word to be spoken. The Baron Malabestia, young Percy, Richard de Kuckney and the other squire stepped close, moving about the Jews in a tight circle; and then, suddenly and without a word, Malabestia and his men crowded in, raised their weapons and hacked the standing

Jews to pieces. It was too quick for prayer, but not too quick for fear. (There was a gesture from Benjamin—one that said, "Wait —I have not yet stopped hoping," but the gesture was gone in a flash of the hard sword and Benjamin, then, was gone also.)

The killing was short and practical, and there was nothing either of spoil or salvation in it. The watchers merely stood and looked and when it was done they turned dumbly and went to their homes. Malabestia's words would be there later to justify them; some would even remember the final slaughter as a last, heroic victory in which they were sharers of the glorious courage of those who had been able to take their bravery to Jerusalem. The promises, such as are made to naughty children to get them from dangerous perches, the promises which they had made to their victims would be forgotten before the tired rioters had made peace with their beds.

The nobles remained, standing about, looking at the remnants of the city's night out. There were some torn caps, a woman's skirt caught on a bush, some pikes and odd knives, the broken scaling machines and the sixty or so dead bodies. As they prepared to turn away they saw Robert de Kuckney coming up toward them from the gardens by the Ouse. When he saw the wreckage of the place and the dead, in piles on the ground, he turned his head away and swayed with sickness.

"By the Saviour!" Malabestia said, clapping him on the arm with a hearty show of good humor which was a kind of madness here among the corpses, "Look here, I believe our Lord Robert is squeamish!"

"I am not answerable to you!" Lord Robert flashed back, pulling away from the Baron. For a moment it looked as if he might go to his dagger, but he was very tired. He was the son of a shamed father, the kinsman of a mad monk and had been beaten beyond honor or courage.

He looked at the Baron and said quietly, "Explain it to me again—how there is no other way but by the death of all of them; how no one must be left to point us out. Let me warn you, Sir Baron, out of my own knowledge: everyone loves a hero, and while you are a hero, you will have a hundred witnesses to stand and take your part. But you must still beware. Someone will see the action in a different light, or will find a sudden need for what you have destroyed. You will have new enemies: a change in policy, a vengeful husband, a beaten squire, and just as suddenly you will be a hated one and an outcast. No one likes a murderer—I know better than any man here. Sir Baron, wait and see, like water, running out of your hands, your advantages. Suddenly no one will remember the assent they gave, the sword that they thrust home, the will to which they once adhered. Welcome to ruin, Sir Baron."

Malabestia would have liked to kill that coward facing him, of whom nothing could be explained, nothing understood. He knew, however, that he could not kill De Kuckney without starting an endless rope of revenge and feud among the nobility, complicated and bound as they were by blood and marriage. He knew that De Kuckney might give him away unless he made the House have equal benefit in the death of these Jews. Perhaps a sop to the bungling son . . . he might sponsor a knighting, perhaps. Thinking so, he clapped De Kuckney on the shoulder: "Come on, now, with us, and we will rip up the rolls that bear your debts with our own hands. You will be free—as free as all of us!"

Lord Robert knew that he could not stand against Malabestia. The end of the bondage of his house stood in the open way of the Malabestia's gesture. He let the Baron lead him. As he turned from the spot, he saw his son standing by himself and looking so pale and miserable that he thought at first the boy was ill or had been wounded. He was about to raise a hand in greeting when his son muttered a curse and dropped his eyes.

"Let us go for a drink first," young Percy said. "I am as dry as —as Northstreet!"

"We must go and see John Marshall," Malabestia answered. "The revel can wait, but he must be in this with us. I wonder if he is still at the jail. Come."

"You will have to go farther than across the river," Lord Robert said, hating himself for all the protection that he gave so easily. "John Marshall is in Durham."

"Durham!" Malabestia swung around and clenched De Kuckney's shoulder.

"I believe he set out for militia."

"By the . . . !" and Malabestia spat out his curse through his teeth. "Come on, then, quickly. We must be gone before they come!" and they started through the streets to the cathedral. They would have to leave the city before Marshall returned. When they got to the cathedral, they found the open door quickly and went in. Forgetting the Cross and the death of the One who hung above the altar, for whom cathedrals had been built, they clattered across the nave and down the narrow stairs to the gallery where the chests of rolls were kept. Lifting the heavy chest, Malabestia and Percy on one side and the two squires on the other, they heaved the groaning weight up to the height of their knees and let it crash heavily on the floor. The chest split apart at its joints.

"The nut is broken," said young Kuckney, "now to the kernel." And Lord Robert recognized the imitation of Malabestia's dry tone in his son's voice and gesture. It sat on the young man like a jeweled bodice of a court lady on a girl too young for breasts. He had been sensitive and a boy of feeling once. Now he was a victim, like the Jews. The boy had spent too many years with shame.

As they reached into the broken box and swept up the lists of names and debts, Lord Robert shivered. All of the hands that had written were now lifeless: Baruch of York, Josce of York, Cresse of Doncaster, Samson of York . . . the names were signed twice; once in Latin and once in Hebrew. Now the names had no people standing behind them. Malabestia and young Richard scooped up the parchment rolls of debt into their cloaks.

"Let us go and burn these," the Baron said. "I do not want to be seen."

In the end they went out behind the cathedral where the wall was well preserved, and there they burned the records of all debts. As the parchment caught, Lord Robert de Kuckney could not help feeling a sense of ease, a kind wash of relief. Money and lands drained away, the House impoverished and disgraced. The fear and shame were all burning away with the lovely characters of the Jewish writing.

"I once envied that writing," Richard de Kuckney said scornfully. "I was young and knew nothing of strength or honor. I can write my name. It is well enough."

Lord Robert moved closer to his son. He wanted to say, "Forgive me for leaving you in service to so cruel a man for so long that you took on his cruelty as if it were your own. Forgive me my poverty, that I could not redeem you and give you a knighthood early, when you were young and full of beauty."

Instead he said, "Soon you will be a knight, my son." And they turned away from each other. They watched the parchment burn. No evidence must remain.

The clatter of horses sounded from the North Road, drawing reign at Bootham. It was not John Marshall and his men, more than a day's ride away, because of his prudence, but Malabestia and the others were reminded that inquiry would be on them soon. They must melt away and disappear from the city of York. . . . Servants would swear that they had never left their estates. Only Malabestia, who was too well remembered by Marshall and the others, was in any real danger. His horse was ready, his pillage packed and waiting at the townhouse.

He looked at his squires for a moment and then he said, "Go back to your fathers' houses," and he strode off.

Richard de Kuckney called after him, "My Lord! My Lord!" but he did not turn.

"He will need me in Scotland. There I will be able to serve him. There I will please him!" He was still a boy, still clamoring for sacrifice and exile, still hoping for that which he had been promised—respect.

"He has his friends there," Lord Robert said sadly. "He is safe. He has everything he needs."

They looked at one another and there was now no word which they could share; which held the same meaning for both of them. The only law that truly governed the lives of these petty princelings was grounded in the understanding of family and clan, and with its loss, the web of their civilization shook yet weaker in the changing wind of the times.

In the afternoon, three Brothers, White monks, walked through the streets of York, having left their forbidden horses hidden in a grove beyond the outskirts of the city. Men stared at them as they walked, and a few came close, even reverentially crossing themselves or curtseying. The city was unnaturally still. When one woman came near and genuflected to the Brothers, Norbert said gently, "God's blessing follow you, woman." And she answered, "I prayed to him this morning and already my son is improved. He will be a saint within a year—a martyr saint!" and she crossed herself again.

Martyr? Simon was too confused to ask anything more, but the urbane Norbert said gently, "And where is our Brother now?" She pointed toward the castle and the old tower which they had passed at a distance and not given special notice. She did not know at all why nothing had been done, she said. A holy saint should not be left with *them* as vulture-picking.

Them? The Brothers went quickly to the hill and to the base of the tower. The sight was incredible. Simon began to shiver uncontrollably. They were no longer more than reminiscences of human beings, pale, ragged, random shapes, blue-lipped with wide, great, staring eyes. Above them, hanging from the crenelations of the tower, the vultures waited for the men to leave, so that they might rejoin their feast. A little to one side, already a little picked over by the carrion birds was the body of Brother Lewis, their companion in Christ. Wordlessly, the three of them stripped off their cloaks and covered the body of their Brother and what others they could. Simon's eyes were staring through the obscene tangle for Abram's body—at least to cover it—to bury it. But he did not find his friend, though they searched among the dead, and then through the reeking streets of Jews and coughed their way through the Community Hall and the desecrated synagogue. No Abram was there, and yet there were so many Abrams —torn ruins of bodies for whom it was no longer even possible to say: "This was a man," or "This was a woman." As they went, even the dry urbanity of Brother Norbert fell apart, so that when he beheld in the ruins of the synagogue, the last loving gesture of an old wife, he clutched his head and cried out, "Stop it! why are men so evil?" and then "Why to her?" Then he strode out of the place.

"Where are you going, Brother?" the lay monk called after him.

"To see a priest!" And they were obliged to run in order to keep up with a new Brother Norbert, a man who had taken fire.

They found Father Odo at Allhallows, on his knees in penitential prayer.

"Well," said Brother Norbert, "what are you going to do?"

The stunned man looked up at them. He was old now—too old to leap to a forbidden horse and bound away somewhere— and where? Was it not too late for help? He raised his clasped hands to his lips. The leg, which he had driven to serve him all the night, had collapsed beneath him. It was destroyed for all but searing shots of pain that would make him pray for death.

"We can no longer save anyone," he said softly, "but we can still save the truth. Do not ask for reprisals, ask for witnesses. Do not seek vengeance, seek the ear and conscience of this kingdom. I am a ludicrous, useless, miserable old man, but go to Bridlington. A Brother is sitting in a quiet cell there, writing a history of the world, and you will be his latest chapter. He is called William of Newbury, an Augustinian, and a wise and honest man." He looked at Brother Norbert and at the sorrowing Brother Simon. "Perhaps it seems a madness to you—it calls for no swift, desperate action; it is—intellectual——" He saw that he had embarrassed them, White Monks, working monks, whose Rule of labor, prayer and exhortation had been years of nourishment for a vengeful madman at Clifford's Tower. "Bring me your Brother's body. Alas, I can not walk to help you, and if you decide to have this horror chronicled, set down for the recrimination of men's children, get you your witnesses and you may seek out Will the Owl, who is a taverner here."

He was faint with exhaustion and pain. They took him to his little room. Brother Simon and the lay Brother set out to do what was needed, and Brother Norbert stayed behind as nurse and priest at Allhallows.

From the church, the ruined Northstreet led, and the two walked it again, hoping to hear a sound somewhere that might betoken life.

The two stone houses still stood firm in the smoking street, although they gaped through their windows and doors. Their glass, that singular mark of wealth and rank had been destroyed in bursts of resentment so sharp that its shards were ground to powder beneath many many stamping feet. In one, there was nothing but a looted shambles; in the other, bodies of a woman and children, naked with successive pickings-over by ever poorer spoilers. In the back room, where Simon went to be sure that no one hid, the same wreckage and confusion lay. Only a few of the looters had had the courage to venture there—it was so far into a heathen place—that there were still rags and sticks lying about. Absently, Simon picked up this thing and that, turning it over as if it might testify. A stool, two legs splintered. Handfuls of charred parchment. They had tried to burn the heathen Bible. A garment. He was holding it and suddenly began to tremble as the thing became real to him, bearing too true and hard a witness. He had a thunder in his head. It was Bett's red jacket—a torn and dirty ruin that he held. . . . She had been so vain of it. He realized also then that he must be in Abram's house. He sat down on the packed earth floor and when Brother Joseph came near, he looked up weeping and said, "Not twisted and perverse beings—not devils and monsters, but only Abram, my friend, and little cousin Bett." And he wept and beat his fists against the floor because he was so helpless.

They went, grim-faced, about their day. They moved their Brother's body from the tower and officiated at Allhallows and asked questions and listened discreetly with a sense of not truly being there. When night fell, they went to Will's tavern and when he was sure that they could be trusted, he led them down into his cellar, saying in his stiff way, "After all of them was a-gone home I went there. Many was dead in the rooms, but there was three seeming dead was only sleeping. One went away. Two is here." They went down the ladder and moved toward the huddled forms in the straw and there they looked into the faces of those victims who were now the witnesses against a proud and arrogant group of knights.

Under the cover of the darkness, six men rode east from the city toward the Augustinian monastery at Bridlington. The chronicler would take their words and preserve them for the King to read when he returned, or at least, for generations of monks and men to muse on in the midst of a book of the splendors of kings. From Allhallows Church, Father Odo, blinking back his pain, prayed them away and thought of his own guilt with the guilt of York. At Clifford's Tower, the unsleeping carrion birds cried and quarreled over their spoil. Surely no battle of beasts ever yielded so sumptuous a meal; it was the men who were great and powerful. Surely it was the men who were generous and lavish and they were bounteous providers!

March 19, 1190

THE fog was thick, and it held the moisture in it so that the trees were shiny with wetness and the stones in the road sweated. Two feet from the eye the world ended in greyness, as if God had left off creation beyond that rock, that stump, that ditch. But it was March and the fog was not too cold. He was lying in the ditch by the side of the road. Above his head was a bush and from its early leaves a drop of water fell every now and then. How many hours had he been asleep? He got up, almost groaning aloud with the pain of his cramped joints stiffened by the cold and dampness of the earth. He heard a sound, and without thinking, blindly, he threw himself into the ditch again, his heart beating behind his eyes and in his throat. The sound came again. He had to listen for a long time, thinking as he was of death and of hunters who were perhaps out beating the reeds for him, before he realized that the sound was only the sound of a bullfrog at the edge of the embankment. He found the frog and looked at it until his heart was steady, and then he lifted himself again and stumbled into the road. Suddenly he saw through the mist the growing of another shape, bulking into his range. He was held for a moment in the grip of an ancient memory or something he had felt or dreamed. . . . There had come from France, exiles, on such a day and on such a road, and we met them like this, coming upon them almost by falling together. . . . Before he had time to think of what he would do now, in this meeting, he and the shape lurched into one another and both fell to the ground like wounded animals trying to crawl away from each other. From the fog a voice sounded, "O God—God spare me!"

"Who is it?" Abram cried, knowing that child's voice.

"Is it Abram?" came from the mist; and as hard as they had tried to crawl away from each other into the uneasy safety of the fog, they began to search, grappling with the ground and calling each other's name until they bumped their weary bodies again and fell into each other's arms—Abram and his second cousin Samuel, the son of a dead man.

"Oh, my cousin! Oh, my cousin!"

When they were strong enough to rise, they faced each other silently for a long time. Neither wanted to speak of the nightmare, for they did not know if it had yet passed, or if it would not overweigh their words, the safe, trite, shallow boxes of common happenings. For Abram, memory and present motion seemed to mirror one another so that he could not capture either image. He saw himself exiled, walking to the right and his image to the left, and which walk was he living? Suddenly he realized that the eight years between the heavy, foggy day of Yomtob's coming and this day of his own moving onward was a change not of exile but only of exiles—that it was he and not Baruch, dressed splendidly for Yomtob's coming so long ago, who was history. He was of a grain with Egypt, Babylon, Rome, Jerusalem, Troyes, Blois, London . . . York. He had learned from all his questionings and from the brief light of Baruch's glory and shame that it was not the exile which was holy, but only the gift—the great gift of living in the strength to question and to choose. He looked down at the boy.

"How did you escape?" Abram said at last.

"When they came, I was sitting with my parents at the table and I just fell, I think. I stayed under the table for a while and then, when the men were there, I crawled out past them and around a corner and I hid under a dead body and when no one was looking I ran out and hid by the river and then in the morning I went to the Tower and saw. . . . And then I ran away and on and on until I fell down and slept. I want to go to London. Perhaps our mothers will find us there."

Abram could not hurt the boy. Perhaps he had not seen what surely must have happened to them. Perhaps his child's mind had been careful for its little body and had placed forgetfulness between it and the nightmare. He himself had been spared no moment of the horror, and its vision and sound rose in him again and again. He knew that he must speak of it sometime; in London, perhaps he would tell of the dying, the dead, three separate waves of them, spread helplessly to the arguing birds, Yomtob and Rana and Josce and a lost Bett somewhere. In London he would tell it and be able to sleep once more among those of his people who lay in no deeper quietness than sleep.

"How did you escape?" the boy asked.

"It was just good fortune," Abram said, and looked away.

He knew that it had been indecision that had saved him; the same doubt and hesitation which had been with him all of his life. What a pitiful way to remain alive. He had been in the tower and had paused before his scribble on the wall, seeing it in the shafts of sunlight which streamed through the stair-well and the center opening. In the dawn the statement of his bitterness had seemed strong and virile; later its crudity overbalanced everything else to him. When the others went down to their destiny, Abram stayed, drawing in the few more lines with the charred wood. He wondered as he drew if he should be a hypocrite or a dead man— if he should take up the Cross as Baruch had done, or be honest as he wished to be and die martyr, and be that way a hypocrite as well. When he was finished with his picture, he had gone to a window in one of the rooms to look down, and he had seen the killers going away and the new pile of dead on the ground a little farther off from the others and by themselves. He had turned away dumbly and lain down on the stone floor and fallen into a stuporous sleep.

When darkness came, he made his escape, lying in ruts and ditches and creeping past the Watches and swimming in the river until he was out of the city. He had slept again in the ditch by the road, his stomach aching with hunger. He had been given life, but he had no sense of the triumph which so many seemed to feel, that they had been clever or brave and so escaped the fate of all the rest.

But his cousin looked at him with wonder. "You must be cured of your doubting now," the boy said, eager for proof of God now that the world rose before him like a high headland. "You did not abjure—and God saved you."

"A strange choice for a 'righteous remnant,' " Abram said, as he took his cousin's boyish hand and they began to walk again.

He said quietly, "Rabbi Yomtob asked us to remember him. 'I shall build an altar of the broken fragments of my heart. . . .' Remember that prayer he wrote? Elias told me once that Yomtob had called himself a living bell, sounding to people to save themselves; to live and glorify the gift of life. In the tower he was laughing at his humanness; he was extolling the beauty of the night, and I did not understand how or why he did this. It was a message for me—for me because he hoped somehow that I would live. Now I shall be that bell, sounding: Life, Life. I will not exalt death but life, and I shall call God the giver of life, and I will only hate those who hate life."

He looked down at the filthy and exhausted boy. "Let us go and find food and shelter. Let us live and grow and marry and beget children, and if the world is only this fog, then we must father the world again."

"And if we father them," the boy said, growing cheerful at the prospect of being yet alive, "they will not be stupid or vain or evil, will they?"

Abram bit his hand to keep from crying and they began their journey.

About the Author

IT was at American University in Washington, D.C., that Joanne Greenberg first developed an interest in medieval art, music, and Latin poetry, and conceived the idea for THE KING'S PERSONS. Now the mother of two young sons, she lives with her husband in Golden, Colorado, where, to her medieval interests, she has added "land reclamation (a must for all Coloradans)."